Examp

MATHEMATICS

for CSE/O/CS

BOOK 1

Ewart Smith MSc

Head of Mathematics Department
Tredegar Comprehensive School

Stanley Thornes (Publishers) Ltd

First published in 1982 by:
Stanley Thornes (Publishers) Ltd.
Old Station Drive
Leckhampton
CHELTENHAM GL53 0DN
England

Reprinted 1982
Reprinted 1983
Reprinted 1984 with minor corrections
Reprinted 1986

British Library Cataloguing in Publication Data

Smith, Ewart
    Examples in mathematics.
    1. Mathematics—1961–
    I. Title
    510.   QA39.2

    ISBN 0-85950-350-X

A separate Answers Booklet is available from the Publisher on request

Typeset by
Tech-Set, Gateshead, Tyne & Wear
Printed and bound in Great Britain at
The Bath Press, Avon

Preface

This is the first of a two-volume series entitled Examples in Mathematics which offers a wide collection of graded exercises.

Book 1, in particular, provides a reservoir of examples for fourth- and fifth-year pupils studying for CSE examinations in Mathematics and for those O-level pupils who require much practice in basics.

The book is divided into two parts: the first part provides examples on individual topics and is suitable for the fourth year; the second part consists of twenty-five revision papers and may be used in the fifth year.

Book 2 is also intended for O-level and Combined Syllabus examinations. The exercises are more difficult, and there are a number of worked examples.

Both books are a companion to *Examples in Arithmetic* for CSE/O/CS. (All books are available from the publishers.)

My thanks are due to my former colleague Mr Tom Thomas for checking the answers and making several useful suggestions.

Ewart Smith
1982

Contents

Part 1: Exercises

Parallel Lines, Angles and Triangles 1

In each of the following find the angles marked with letters:

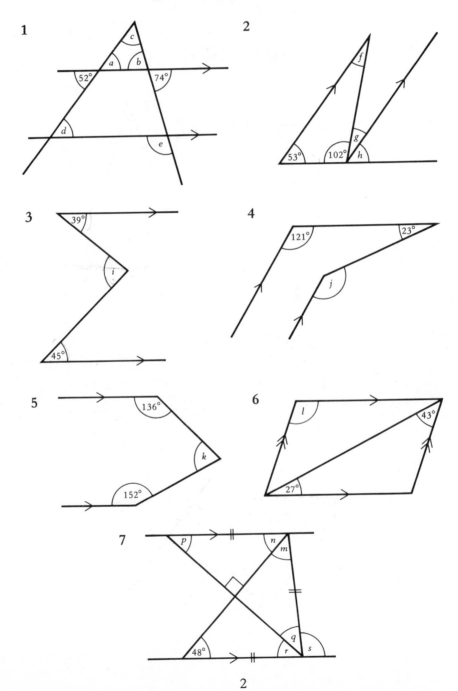

1

2

3

4

5

6

7

8

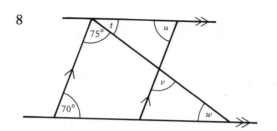

9

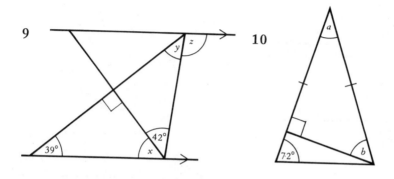

10

11

12

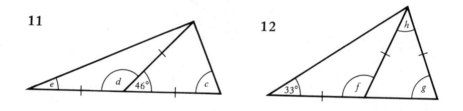

13

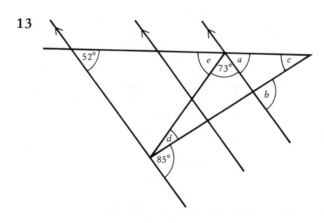

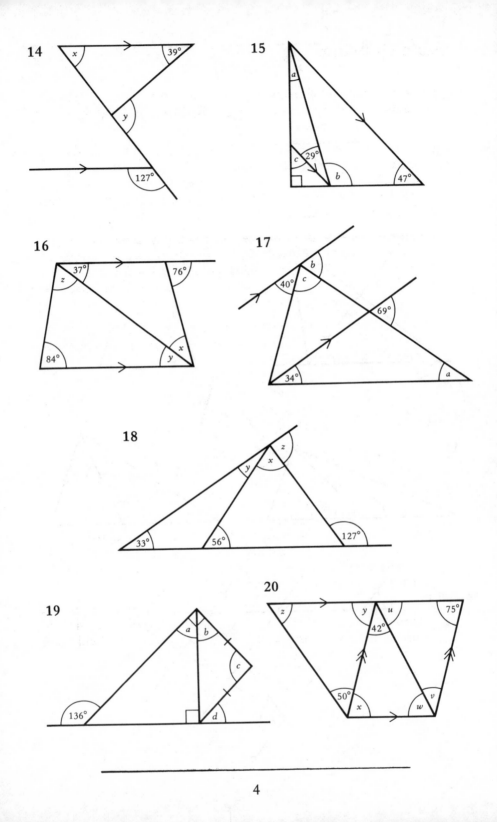

14

x

39°

y

127°

15

a

c 29°

b

47°

16

37°

z

76°

84°

x

y

17

b

40° c

69°

34°

a

18

z

y x

33°

56°

127°

19

a b

c

d

136°

20

z

y u

75°

42°

50°

x

v

w

4

Scale Drawings

1   A football field measures 100 m by 80 m. Using 1 cm ≡ 10 m draw a scale diagram and use it to find the distance between opposite corners.

2   A car travels for 5 kilometres along a straight road towards a crossroads. Here it turns right and travels for 4 kilometres in a perpendicular direction before stopping. Draw a scale diagram of the journey using 2 cm ≡ 1 km. How far is the car in a straight line from its starting point?

3   From a ship (S) the distance and bearing of a lighthouse (L) is 500 m in a direction N33°E, and the distance and bearing of a trawler (T) is 750 m in a direction S57°E. Taking 2 cm ≡ 100 m make a scale drawing and use it to find the distance and bearing of the lighthouse from the trawler.

4   Using 1 cm ≡ 1 m draw the triangle ABC to scale given that AB = 14 m, ∠ABC = 72° and ∠BAC = 50°. Use this diagram to find the lengths of AC and BC.

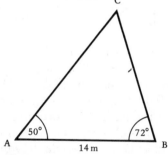

5   From a point 160 m from the base of a church tower the angles of elevation of the base and top of the spire are 32° and 46° respectively. Make a scale drawing using 1 cm ≡ 10 m and use it to find the height of the spire.

6   Standing at one corner A of a triangular field the other two corners B and C are 132 m in a direction N40°W and 94 m in a direction N55°E respectively. Draw a plan of the field taking 1 cm ≡ 10 m and use it to find:
(a) the distance BC,   (b) the bearing of C from B.

7   Viewed from the top of a cliff 45 metres high the angles of depression of two boats directly out to sea are 42° and 29°. Using 1 cm ≡ 5 m make a scale drawing and use it to find:
(a) the distance of each boat from the base of the cliff,
(b) the distance between the boats.

8   An aeroplane takes off from an airfield and follows the following route: 50 km N37°E, 40 km S25°E, 150 km S37°E. Draw a scale diagram taking 1 cm ≡ 10 km, and use it to find the bearing it must set to return to its starting point, and the time it will take if it flies at 500 km/h.

9   A cross-country course starts at the clubhouse, takes a south easterly path for 4.5 km, changes direction to N38°E for 7.5 km before running due N for 3 km. The direction then changes yet again to N70°W for 10 km. Taking 1 cm ≡ 1 km make a plan of the route. Hence find the distance and bearing of the clubhouse from the point where a runner finally turns for home.

10

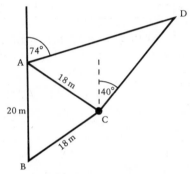

A and B show the positions of the wickets, which are 20 m apart, on a cricket pitch. The batsman at A strikes the ball towards D where AD makes an angle of 74° with the line of the wickets BA. A fielder standing at C, which is 18 m from each wicket runs along the path CD in order to cut off the shot – CD making an angle of 40° with the direction BA. If the fielder intercepts the ball at D make a scale drawing and from it find:

(a) the distance the fielder runs before he retrieves the ball,

(b) the distance travelled by the ball along the ground from bat to hand. (Use 1 cm ≡ 2 m.)

Polygons   3

1   Find (a) the exterior angle, (b) the interior angle, of a regular polygon with:

(i) five sides,   (ii) six sides,   (iii) eight sides,

(iv) nine sides,   (v) ten sides,   (vi) twelve sides,

(vii) twenty-four sides.

2   Fill in the blanks in the following table which gives the connection between the interior angle, the exterior angle and the number of sides for various regular polygons.

Number of sides	Exterior angle	Interior angle
. . .	45°	. . .
. . .	. . .	150°
18	. . .	. . .
20	. . .	. . .
. . .	15°	. . .
. . .	. . .	156°

3   Is it possible to have a regular polygon with an exterior angle of:
    (a) 20°,   (b) 30°,   (c) 40°,   (d) 50°?

4   A pentagon has angles $x°$, $(x+20)°$, $(x+52)°$, $(x-9)°$ and $(x+12)°$. Find x.

5   An octagon has four equal angles each of size $x°$, two angles of size $(x+30)°$, one of size $(x+120)°$ and one of size $(x+12)°$. Find x.

6   ABCDE is a regular pentagon. Calculate the angles of triangle ABD.

7   ABCDEF is a regular hexagon. Calculate the angles of triangle ABE.

8   The exterior angles of a seven-sided polygon are $(x-25)°$, $(x-15)°$, $(x-10)°$, $x°$, $x+10°$, $(x+20)°$ and $(x+30)°$. Find x and hence find the interior angles of the polygon.

9   If ABCDE is a regular pentagon show that the straight lines EB and EC trisect the interior angle of the pentagon AED.

10 ABCDEF is a regular hexagon. Find the obtuse angle between the lines AD and BE.

11 A regular pentagon ABCDE and an equilateral triangle ABF lie on opposite sides of AB. Calculate the angles of triangle ADF.

12 In an octagon each angle except one is 10° greater than the angle next to it in a clockwise direction. Find the size of:
    (a) the smallest angle,   (b) the largest angle.

Multiplication and Division $\qquad$ **4**

Multiply:

1 $x + 3$ by $x + 5$

2 $x - 6$ by $x - 3$

3 $2x + 1$ by $x + 6$

4 $3x + 3$ by $x + 3$

5 $4x + 7$ by $x - 5$

6 $5x + 2$ by $x - 4$

7 $7x - 5$ by $x + 6$

8 $3x + 6$ by $x - 3$

9 $4x - 3$ by $x - 6$

10 $9x - 7$ by $x - 4$

11 $4x - 7$ by $3x - 2$

12 $7x + 5$ by $6x + 3$

13 $8x - 5$ by $3x + 7$

14 $10x - 1$ by $2x - 3$

15 $x^2 + x + 1$ by $x + 1$

16 $2x^2 + x + 3$ by $x + 2$

17 $5x^2 + 3x + 2$ by $2x + 1$

18 $3x^2 + 7x + 8$ by $3x + 5$

19 $5x^2 + 5x + 3$ by $7x + 3$

20 $3x^2 + 7x + 6$ by $3x - 5$

21 $9x^2 - 5x + 6$ by $3x + 8$

22 $4x^2 - 7x + 4$ by $5x - 3$

23 $7x^2 - 9x - 3$ by $4x + 7$

24 $2x^2 - 4x - 1$ by $7x - 2$

25 $4x^2 - 9x - 5$ by $3x - 7$

26 $6x^2 - 5$ by $3x + 7$

27 $4x^2 + 3x - 4$ by $6x - 7$

28 $2x^2 + 3x + 4$ by $2 - 3x$

29 $7x^2 - 3x + 5$ by $5 - 3x$

30 $x^2 + 2x + 1$ by $x^2 + 4$

31 $2x^2 + 4x + 7$ by $x^2 + 4x + 1$

32 $9x^2 - 5x$ by $3x^2 + 9x + 7$

33 $8 - x^2$ by $3x^2 + 7x$

34 $9 - 3x^2$ by $x^2 - 4x + 3$

35 $x^2 - y^2$ by $x^2 + y^2$

36 $x^2 + xy + y^2$ by $x^2 - y^2$

37 $a^2 + 2a + 1$ by $3a - 7$

38 $2a^2 - 4$ by $a^2 - 7a + 6$

39 $a^2 + 7a + 4$ by $a^2 + 5a + 4$

40 $b^2 - 6b + 3$ by $b^3 - 4b + 7$

41 $3 - 2c + 3c^2$ by $5c^2 - 4c + 3$

42 $5x^2 - 9x$ by $3 - 7x^2$

43 $4 - 9x + 5x^2$ by $7x - x^2$

44 $a^2 + 2ab + b^2$ by $a + b$

45 $a^2 - 2ab + b^2$ by $a - b$

46 $x^2 + xy + y^2$ by $x - y$

47 $x^2 - xy + y^2$ by $x + y$

48 $2x^2 + 3xy + y^2$ by $3x^2 - xy + 2y^2$

49 $5a^2 + 3ab - b^2$ by $3a^2 - 4b^2$

50 $x^2 + y^2 + z^2 - xy + yz + zx$ by $x + y - z$

Divide:

51   $x^2 + 7x + 10$ by $x + 2$ 52 $x^2 + 16x + 63$ by $x + 7$

53   $x^2 + 3x - 28$ by $x - 4$ 54 $x^2 - 16x + 63$ by $x - 9$

55   $2x^2 + 7x + 6$ by $2x + 3$ 56 $9x^2 + 47x + 10$ by $9x + 2$

57   $6x^2 + 19x + 15$ by $3x + 5$ 58 $15x^2 + 19x - 10$ by $5x - 2$

59   $4a^2 - 18a + 20$ by $2a - 5$ 60 $14b^2 - 39b + 10$ by $7b - 2$

61   $35 - 81y + 36y^2$ by $5 - 3y$ 62 $12 + 29x - 55x^2$ by $4 - 5x$

63   $a^2 + 11a + 18$ by $a + 2$ 64 $5b^2 + 3b - 14$ by $b + 2$

65   $5x^2 + 23x + 12$ by $4 + x$ 66 $2x^2 - 17x + 30$ by $6 - x$

67   $9a^2 - 6a - 8$ by $3a - 4$ 68 $35 - 58a + 24a^2$ by $5 - 4a$

69   $15x^2 - 26x - 21$ by $5x + 3$ 70 $84x^2 - 71x + 15$ by $7x - 3$

71   $x^3 + 2x^2 + 2x + 1$ by $x + 1$ 72 $x^3 + 3x^2 + 3x + 1$ by $x + 1$

73   $x^3 - 6x^2 + 12x - 8$ by $x - 2$ 74 $2x^3 + 7x^2 + 7x + 2$ by $2x + 1$

75   $x^3 - 27$ by $x - 3$ 76 $x^3 + 8$ by $x + 2$

77   $x^3 - x^2 + x - 6$ by $x - 2$ 78 $x^3 - x^2 - 10x - 8$ by $x + 2$

79   $6x^3 + 22x^2 + 15x + 2$ by $3x + 2$

80   $15x^3 - 34x^2 + 35x - 12$ by $5x - 3$

81   $10x^3 + 33x^2 + 6x - 35$ by $2x + 5$

82   $45 - 23x + 17x^2 - 6x^3$ by $5 - 2x$

83   $12 - x - 2x^2 - 3x^3$ by $4 - 3x$

84   $7x^3 - 20x^2 + 11x + 2$ by $7x + 1$

85   $12x^3 + 45x^2 + 19x - 6$ by $4x + 3$

86   $5x^3 + 4x^2 + 4x - 1$ by $5x - 1$

87   $4x^3 - x^2 + x + 3$ by $4x + 3$

88   $14x^3 - 4x^2 - 35x + 10$ by $7x - 2$

89   $12 - 25x + 16x^2 - 3x^3$ by $4 - 3x$

90   $5 - 11x + 16x^2 - 12x^3$ by $5 - 6x$

91   $2 - 10x + 11x^2 - 12x^3$ by $1 - 4x$

92   $x^4 - 5x^3 + 3x^2 - 5x + 2$ by $x^2 + 1$

93   $2x^4 - 3x^3 + 3x^2 + 3x - 5$ by $x^2 - 1$

94    $3x^4 + 4x^3 - 4x^2 - 5x$ by $x^2 + x$

95    $6x^4 - 11x^3 + 17x^2 - 21x$ by $2x^2 - 3x$

96    $x^4 + x^3 + 2x^2 + x + 1$ by $x^2 + 1$

97    $2a^4 + 3a^3 + 10a^2 + 9a + 12$ by $a^2 + 3$

98    $x^4 + 2x^3 + x^2 - 1$ by $x^2 + x + 1$

99    $6a^4 + a^3 + 11a^2 + a + 6$ by $2a^2 + a + 2$

100   $10x^4 + 13x^3 - 12x^2 - 5x + 2$ by $2x^2 + 3x - 1$

Addition and Subtraction of Fractions   5

Simplify:

1   $\dfrac{a}{2} + \dfrac{a}{3} + \dfrac{a}{4}$

2   $\dfrac{2x}{3} + \dfrac{3x}{4}$

3   $\dfrac{3x}{5} + \dfrac{7x}{10} + \dfrac{4x}{15}$

4   $\dfrac{a}{2} - \dfrac{a}{3} + \dfrac{a}{6}$

5   $\dfrac{3x}{4} - \dfrac{2x}{3} + \dfrac{x}{2}$

6   $\dfrac{5a}{6} + \dfrac{2a}{3} - \dfrac{7a}{12}$

7   $\dfrac{x+3}{4} + \dfrac{x+1}{2}$

8   $\dfrac{y+6}{3} + \dfrac{3y+1}{2}$

9   $\dfrac{5a+2}{6} - \dfrac{a+4}{5}$

10   $\dfrac{4x-3}{2} - \dfrac{2x+1}{3}$

11   $\dfrac{5y-3}{7} - \dfrac{4y+9}{3}$

12   $\dfrac{3x+2}{4} - \dfrac{x+5}{8}$

13   $\dfrac{9x-5}{3} - \dfrac{4x-3}{6}$

14   $\dfrac{5a-2}{12} - \dfrac{4a-5}{8}$

15   $\dfrac{3a+6}{8} - \dfrac{4-3a}{4}$

16   $\dfrac{6x-5}{10} - \dfrac{9-2x}{5}$

17   $\dfrac{a+b}{3} + \dfrac{2a+b}{4}$

18   $\dfrac{5a+2b}{7} + \dfrac{a+5b}{3}$

19   $\dfrac{4x+3y}{5} + \dfrac{2x+y}{10}$

20   $\dfrac{2x+3y}{4} + \dfrac{5x+2y}{10}$

21   $\dfrac{5a+b}{7} + \dfrac{9a-7b}{3}$

22   $\dfrac{2x-5y}{4} + \dfrac{3x-y}{5}$

23 $\dfrac{4a+b}{5} - \dfrac{3a-4b}{6}$

24 $\dfrac{2x+3y}{5} - \dfrac{3x-2y}{4}$

25 $\dfrac{3a+b}{6} - \dfrac{2a-3b}{5}$

26 $\dfrac{5x-3y}{4} - \dfrac{3x+4y}{7}$

27 $\dfrac{3a-5b}{8} + \dfrac{9a-4b}{12}$

28 $\dfrac{4x+y}{9} - \dfrac{3x-5y}{5}$

29 $\dfrac{4a-2b}{3} - \dfrac{3a-5b}{4}$

30 $\dfrac{5x-y}{6} + \dfrac{2x-7y}{9}$

31 $\dfrac{3}{x} + \dfrac{2}{x}$

32 $\dfrac{5}{ab} + \dfrac{3}{bc}$

33 $\dfrac{3}{2x} + \dfrac{2}{3x}$

34 $\dfrac{2}{x} + \dfrac{3}{x^2}$

35 $\dfrac{2}{x+1} + \dfrac{1}{x+2}$

36 $\dfrac{5}{x+3} + \dfrac{1}{x+4}$

37 $\dfrac{4}{x+2} - \dfrac{3}{x+3}$

38 $\dfrac{9}{x+1} - \dfrac{5}{x+4}$

39 $\dfrac{5}{x-1} + \dfrac{3}{x+2}$

40 $\dfrac{4}{x-2} + \dfrac{5}{x-3}$

41 $\dfrac{3}{x-1} - \dfrac{2}{x+2}$

42 $\dfrac{7}{x+1} - \dfrac{3}{x-2}$

43 $\dfrac{5}{x+5} - \dfrac{2}{x-3}$

44 $\dfrac{2}{2x+1} + \dfrac{1}{x+3}$

45 $\dfrac{4}{2x+3} + \dfrac{5}{x+4}$

46 $\dfrac{3}{5x+2} - \dfrac{2}{2x+3}$

47 $\dfrac{2}{4x-1} - \dfrac{5}{4x+1}$

48 $\dfrac{5}{3x+2} + \dfrac{3}{3x+4}$

49 $\dfrac{4}{a+b} + \dfrac{3}{a-b}$

50 $\dfrac{2a+3}{(a-1)^2} + \dfrac{2}{(a-1)}$

Linear Equations

6

Solve the following equations:

1 $4x = 12$

2 $5x = 25$

3 $3x = 27$

4 $5x = 28$

5	$10x = 0$	**6**	$2x - 10 = 8$
7	$4x - 13 = 3$	**8**	$3x - 9 = 0$
9	$12x = -48$	**10**	$7x = -84$
11	$14x = 21$	**12**	$2x - 5 = 7$
13	$5x + 10 = 5$	**14**	$-4x = 8$
15	$7 - 3x = 1$	**16**	$19 - 5x = 6$
17	$-2x = -10$	**18**	$7x - 3 = -31$
19	$6 - 3x = 6$	**20**	$-3x - 5 = 4$
21	$2x + 5 = x + 9$	**22**	$5x + 4 = 3x + 12$
23	$7x - 3 = 4x + 9$	**24**	$4 - 3x = x$
25	$6 + x = 5x$	**26**	$12x - 17 = 7x + 13$
27	$4x + 1 = 8 - 3x$	**28**	$7x - 8 = 12 - 3x$
29	$13x - 35 = 2x + 53$	**30**	$16x - 27 = 23 - 9x$
31	$5(x - 2) = 30$	**32**	$11(x - 3) = 44$
33	$6(2x - 3) = 30$	**34**	$4(5 - x) = 12$
35	$2(2x - 1) = 3$	**36**	$7(x - 3) = 3$
37	$5(x - 6) = 3(x - 4)$	**38**	$4(5x - 8) = 7(x + 1)$
39	$5(3x + 4) = 2(3x + 1)$	**40**	$6(3x + 2) = 7(3 - x)$
41	$11(2x + 3) = 7(2x - 1)$	**42**	$2(x - 8) = 3(x - 9)$
43	$3(x + 7) = 7(3 - x)$	**44**	$3(8x + 7) = 5(2x + 7)$
45	$\frac{1}{2}x = 6$	**46**	$\frac{x}{3} = 7$
47	$\frac{x}{5} = -4$	**48**	$\frac{x}{3} + 1 = 5$
49	$3 - \frac{x}{2} = 1$	**50**	$\frac{2x}{5} = 3$
51	$\frac{x}{4} - 7 = 13$	**52**	$2 + \frac{x}{3} = \frac{1}{2}$
53	$3 - \frac{x}{4} = \frac{1}{3}$	**54**	$5 - \frac{2x}{3} = 9$
55	$7 + \frac{3x}{4} = 19$	**56**	$4 - \frac{5x}{3} = \frac{26}{9}$

57 $\dfrac{x-2}{3} = 4$

58 $3 + \dfrac{2x}{5} = 2\frac{11}{15}$

59 $\dfrac{x+7}{5} = 6$

60 $\dfrac{x+3}{4} - 1 = 0$

61 $\dfrac{3x-2}{4} = 7$

62 $\dfrac{5x-2}{3} + 2 = 0$

63 $\dfrac{5x+3}{6} = 3$

64 $\dfrac{3-x}{2} + 1 = 0$

65 $\dfrac{x-2}{3} + \dfrac{x-4}{2} = 1\frac{1}{2}$

66 $\dfrac{x-5}{2} - \dfrac{x+2}{6} = \frac{1}{2}$

67 $\dfrac{x+6}{9} - \dfrac{x-4}{4} = 1$

68 $\dfrac{4x+5}{5} + \dfrac{2x+1}{2} = 6$

69 $\dfrac{2x-1}{3} + \dfrac{3x+1}{5} = 10$

70 $\dfrac{3x-2}{4} - \dfrac{x-3}{3} = 3$

71 $\dfrac{2x+1}{3} - \dfrac{5x-1}{6} = \frac{3}{2}$

72 $\dfrac{3x+1}{2} - \dfrac{4x-3}{3} = 3$

73 $\dfrac{3x+1}{3} + \dfrac{6x+1}{5} = 2$

74 $\dfrac{5x+2}{4} - \dfrac{7x-1}{3} = 3$

75 $\dfrac{2x-3}{5} + \dfrac{x+14}{2} = 1$

76 $\dfrac{6x+1}{3} - \dfrac{5x-2}{4} = \frac{5}{4}$

77 $\dfrac{x-2}{4} - \dfrac{x+5}{8} = 2$

78 $\dfrac{3x+1}{5} - \dfrac{7x-3}{7} = \frac{6}{7}$

79 $\dfrac{x+3}{5} - \dfrac{x+1}{2} = \frac{5}{2}$

80 $\dfrac{5x-3}{8} + \dfrac{4x-3}{5} = 9$

81 $\dfrac{5x-3}{6} + x = \frac{13}{18}$

82 $\dfrac{4(x+5)}{7} - 2x = \frac{23}{14}$

83 $\dfrac{4x+7}{3} + 3x = 4\frac{1}{15}$

84 $\dfrac{7(2x+3)}{4} - 4x = 2\frac{3}{4}$

85 $\dfrac{3x+7}{2} + x = 1\frac{5}{8}$

86 $x + \frac{1}{3}(5x+2) = 2$

87 $x - \frac{3}{4}(5-x) = 8\frac{1}{2}$

88 $4x + \dfrac{5(x-4)}{6} = 1\frac{1}{2}$

89 $2x - \frac{3}{7}(2x-5) = 17$

90 $4x - \frac{1}{2}(3x+1) = 5\frac{3}{4}$

13

91 $\dfrac{(x-3)}{12}+\dfrac{3(x-1)}{8}=1\frac{2}{3}$ 　　　**92** $\dfrac{2(4-x)}{9}-\dfrac{2(x+5)}{3}=4\frac{2}{3}$

93 $\dfrac{3(2x+3)}{7}-\dfrac{5(5x+3)}{6}=8\frac{5}{7}$ 　　　**94** $\dfrac{(3x+1)}{5}+\dfrac{3(4-x)}{15}=1\frac{4}{15}$

95 $\dfrac{5x+2}{3}+\dfrac{7x-5}{4}=6\frac{1}{4}$ 　　　**96** $\dfrac{x-3}{7}-\dfrac{5x+1}{5}=2\frac{4}{5}$

97 $\dfrac{3(x-2)}{4}+\dfrac{4(x-7)}{3}=1\frac{2}{3}$ 　　　**98** $\dfrac{5(2x+1)}{3}-\dfrac{2(4x+1)}{5}=11\frac{2}{3}$

99 $\dfrac{7(3-x)}{4}-\dfrac{4(5+x)}{3}=20\frac{1}{6}$ 　　　**100** $\dfrac{5(3x-4)}{2}-\dfrac{2(3-2x)}{5}=22$

Brackets 　　　　　　　　　　　　　　　 7

Remove the brackets and simplify:

1 $3(x+2)+5(2x+1)$ 　　　　　　**2** $4(3x+5)+2(5x+7)$

3 $7(x+5y)+3(2x+5y)$ 　　　　**4** $5(a+2b)+2(3a+5b)$

5 $2(x-3y)+3(2x-3y)$ 　　　　**6** $7(2x-5y)+4(x-3y)$

7 $3(2x-3y)-5(3x+4y)$ 　　　　**8** $4(x-4y)-3(2x-7y)$

9 $9(2m-4n)-2(m-3n)$ 　　　**10** $4(x-8y)-3(3y+x)$

11 $5(3x-5y)-4(4y-3x)$ 　　　**12** $10(2x+7y)-3(5y-2x)$

13 $2(a+b)+3(2a-3b)+7a$ 　　**14** $5(x+2y)-3(y-x)-4x$

15 $2(x+y)+3(y+z)-(z+x)$

16 $5(2a-5b)-6(a+3b)-4(a-7b)$

17 $a(b+c)+b(c+a)+c(a+b)$

18 $a(2b-c)-b(3c-a)-2c(a-2b)$

19 $3(x^2-y^2)+4(2x^2-3y^2)$ 　　　**20** $5(a^2+4b^2)-3(3a^2-6b^2)$

21 $4(a^2+2b^2)+3(3b^2+c^2)+5(c^2+a^2)$

22 $(3a^2-4b^2)-3(2a^2-3b^2)+2(a^2+4b^2)$

23 $x(x^2+xy+y^2)-y(x^2+xy+y^2)$

24 $xy(y+z)+yz(z+x)+zx(x+y)$

Find the products:

25 $(x+2)(x+3)$ 26 $(x+5)(x+4)$

27 $(p+3)(p+2)$ 28 $(a+6)(a+7)$

29 $(2x+3)(x+4)$ 30 $(x+4)(3x+2)$

31 $(2x+5)(3x+4)$ 32 $(5a+3)(3a+7)$

33 $(x-3)(x-5)$ 34 $(x-7)(x-9)$

35 $(2x-3)(3x-5)$ 36 $(4x-5)(3x-4)$

37 $(6x-5)(x+5)$ 38 $(7x-6)(2x+3)$

39 $(x+2)(x-2)$ 40 $(2x-3)(2x+3)$

Simplify:

41 $(x+3)(x+4)+x(x+5)$ 42 $(x+7)(x+2)+5(x+5)$

43 $3(2x+3)+x(5x+4)$ 44 $(x-3)(x+4)+x(2x-3)$

45 $(2x-3)(3x-2)+x(5x+4)$

46 $(x+4)(3x-2)+(2x+7)(x+5)$

47 $(3x+5)(2x-3)+(5x-3)(3x+4)$

48 $(5x-7)(2x-3)-(6x-2)(5x+4)$

49 $x^2+2(2x+1)(3x+3)+12$ 50 $4x^2-3(5x-1)(2x+3)-4$

Algebraic Expressions and Inequalities   8

Write each of the following in algebraic form:

1 Twice the sum of x and y.

2 Half of b subtracted from twice c.

3 The sum of x and y divided by their product.

4 The sum of b and c subtracted from unity.

5 The square of the difference between x and y.

6 The sum of x and y divided by the square of the difference between x and y.

7 The product of a and b divided by the square of c.

8 The square of a number x subtracted from its inverse.

9   The square root of a subtracted from b.

10 The sum of the inverse of x and the inverse of y.

11 The square root of the quotient of x and y.

12 The sum of the square of b and the cube of c.

13 The square of the quotient of y and z.

14 Three-quarters of x subtracted from half of y.

15 The square of y subtracted from x.

16 The square of b added to the square of a.

17 Find the cost in pounds of n articles costing x pence each.

18 Find the cost in pounds of forty oranges costing x pence each together with thirty apples costing y pence each.

19 What distance is covered by a car travelling at x m.p.h. for y hours?

20 Calculate the average cost in pence of m apples costing a pence each and n apples costing b pence each.

21 A car travels m kilometres at x kilometres per hour. How long will this take in minutes?

22 Find the area, in square metres, of a rectangle measuring x metres by y centimetres.

23 What is the volume, in cm³, of a rectangular block measuring a mm by b mm by c mm?

24 A carpet is x metres long and y metres wide. If each square metre costs £z find the cost of the carpet.

25 A 'bus travelling x kilometres consumes one litre of fuel for each y kilometres. How many litres are consumed altogether? How much will this cost if the price of fuel is z pence per litre? (Give your answer in pounds.)

26 In a certain school there are p pupils on the register. If q per cent are absent how many pupils are present?

27 In a traffic jam m cars, each of length n metres, stand bumper to bumper. How far back, in kilometres, does the traffic jam stretch?

28 A bottle containing y litres of lemonade is used to fill glasses each of which has a volume of x cm³. How many such glasses may be filled from a full bottle?

16

29 Petrol costs x pence per gallon and a car travels y miles on each gallon. Find the cost in pounds for a journey of z miles.

30 A book is v cm thick and contains w pages. How thick is one page? (Give your answer in millimetres.)

31 Given that x is a whole number greater than 0 find the largest possible value of x which satisfies each of the following inequalities:

    (a) $x + 3 < 7$ (b) $x + 5 < 10$
    (c) $x - 4 < 8$ (d) $x - 10 < 25$
    (e) $2x + 3 < 7$ (f) $5x + 2 < 37$
    (g) $3x - 1 < 15$ (h) $13x + 2 < 126$
    (i) $15 > 7 + x$ (j) $27 > 4 + 5x$

32 Given that x is a whole number greater than 0 find the smallest possible value of x which satisfies each of the following inequalities:

    (a) $x + 9 > 14$ (b) $x + 12 > 33$
    (c) $x - 2 > 16$ (d) $x - 5 > 9$
    (e) $2x + 3 > 21$ (f) $5x + 4 > 23$
    (g) $3x - 1 > 16$ (h) $4x - 9 > 17$
    (i) $27 < 13 + 2x$ (j) $34 < 8 + 6x$

33 Given that x is a whole number greater than 0 find all x which satisfy each of the following inequalities:

    (a) $2 < x + 3 < 5$ (b) $9 < x + 1 < 16$
    (c) $8 \leqslant x - 2 \leqslant 14$ (d) $9 \leqslant 5x + 2 \leqslant 29$
    (e) $14 \leqslant 3x - 5 < 32$ (f) $5 < 4x + 1 \leqslant 12$
    (g) $19 \leqslant 7x - 2 \leqslant 40$ (h) $16 \leqslant 2x - 10 \leqslant 20$
    (i) $5x - 2 \leqslant 2x + 10$ (j) $3x + 4 \leqslant 2x + 7$

The Straight Line   **9**

Find the gradient and y-intercept for each of the following straight lines:

    1 $y = 3x + 2$ **2** $y = 7x + 5$
    3 $y = 9x - 3$ **4** $y = 5 - 4x$
    5 $y = -3x + 2$ **6** $3y = x + 4$
    7 $5y = 2x - 3$ **8** $x - y + 3 = 0$

9 $3x + y + 9 = 0$ 10 $5x + 2y - 4 = 0$

11 $12x - 3y - 7 = 0$ 12 $9x - 5y + 4 = 0$

13 $3y + 2x - 7 = 0$ 14 $\frac{1}{2}x + y - 4 = 0$

15 $\frac{1}{2}x + \frac{1}{3}y - 1 = 0$ 16 $\frac{3}{4}x - \frac{2}{5}y - \frac{1}{2} = 0$

Find the equation of the straight line satisfying the given data in each of the following:

17 Gradient 2, y-intercept 5.

18 Gradient 5, y-intercept -3.

19 Gradient $\frac{1}{2}$, y-intercept 4.

20 Gradient $\frac{3}{4}$, y-intercept $\frac{1}{2}$.

21 Gradient $-\frac{2}{3}$, y-intercept 2.

22 Gradient $-\frac{3}{5}$, y-intercept -7

23 Gradient $\frac{4}{9}$, y-intercept $-\frac{2}{3}$.

24 Gradient $\frac{5}{7}$, y-intercept $-\frac{1}{4}$.

25 Gradient $\frac{12}{13}$, y-intercept $-\frac{5}{13}$.

Find the equation of the straight line with given gradient and passing through the given point:

26 Gradient 2, point $(3, 4)$.

27 Gradient 4, point $(5, 2)$.

28 Gradient $\frac{1}{2}$, point $(4, 5)$.

29 Gradient $\frac{2}{3}$, point $(6, 1)$.

30 Gradient 5, point $(-4, -2)$.

31 Gradient $\frac{4}{5}$, point $(-7, -3)$.

32 Gradient $-\frac{3}{5}$, point $(-5, 0)$.

33 Gradient $-\frac{7}{9}$. point $(0, -5)$.

34 Gradient $\frac{1}{5}$, point $(-9, 5)$.

35 Gradient $-\frac{6}{11}$, point $(-4, -\frac{1}{2})$.

Find the equation of the straight line which passes through the given pairs of points:

36 $(3, 0)$ and $(0, 5)$.   37 $(4, 0)$ and $(0, 3)$.

38 $(2, 0)$ and $(0, -5)$.   39 $(-3, 0)$ and $(0, 7)$.

40 $(0, -5)$ and $(-4, 0)$.   **41** $(1, 2)$ and $(4, 8)$.

42 $(1, -2)$ and $(4, -8)$.   **43** $(3, 2)$ and $(5, 6)$.

44 $(5, 1)$ and $(-2, 3)$.   **45** $(3, -2)$ and $(-5, -6)$.

46 $(-2, -5)$ and $(-5, 4)$.   **47** $(5, 7)$ and $(3, 2)$.

48 $(-4, -3)$ and $(-9, -2)$ **49** $(\frac{1}{2}, 1)$ and $(-2, 3)$.

50 $(-\frac{1}{3}, \frac{3}{5})$ and $(\frac{2}{5}, -\frac{4}{3})$.

51

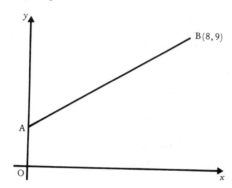

The line AB has gradient $\frac{3}{4}$. A lies on the y-axis and B is the point $(8, 9)$.

(a) Find the coordinates of A.

(b) Give the equation of AB in the form $y = mx + c$.

(c) Calculate the length of AB.

52

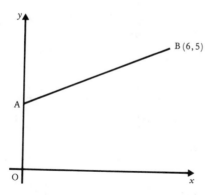

The line AB has gradient $\frac{2}{3}$. A lies on the y-axis and B is the point $(6, 5)$.

(a) Find the coordinates of A.

(b) Give the equation of AB in the form $y = mx + c$.

(c) Calculate the length of AB.

53

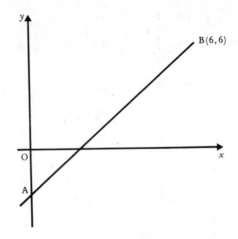

The gradient of AB is $\frac{4}{3}$. A lies on the y-axis and B is the point $(6,6)$.

(a) Find the coordinates of A.

(b) If the equation of AB is $y = mx + c$, write down the values of m and c.

(c) Calculate the distance AB.

54

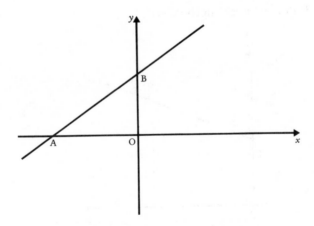

The straight line with equation $4x - 3y + 12 = 0$ intersects the x-axis at A and the y-axis at B.

(a) Find the coordinates of A.

(b) Find the coordinates of B.

(c) Calculate the length of AB.

20

55

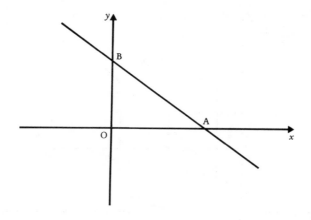

The straight line with equation $5x + 4y - 40 = 0$ cuts the x-axis at A and the y-axis at B.

(a) Find the coordinates of A.

(b) Find the coordinates of B.

(c) If the equation is re-written in the form $y = mx + c$ give the values of m and c.

56

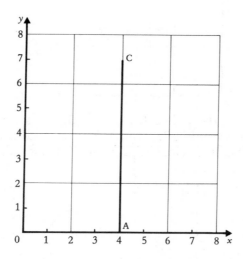

Given the points A(4,0) and C(4,7) plot the point B(1,4). Join AB and BC. Complete the quadrilateral ABCD so that it is symmetrical about AC. Give the coordinates of D and calculate the area of the quadrilateral.

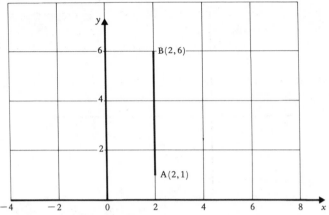

Given the points A(2, 1) and B(2, 6) plot the point C(– 3, 4). Join AC and BC. Complete the quadrilateral ABCD so that it is symmetrical about AB. Give the coordinates of D and calculate the area of the quadrilateral.

58

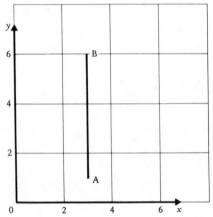

A and B are the points (3, 1) and (3, 6) respectively. Plot the points C(1, 4) and D(2, 1). Join AD, DC and CB. Complete the figure so that it is symmetrical about AB, and calculate its area.

59

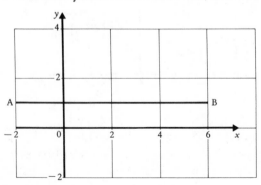

A and B are the points $(-2, 1)$ and $(6, 1)$ respectively. Plot the points $C(2, 4)$ and $D(5, 3)$. Plot the reflections of C and D in the line AB and mark them respectively E and F. Join AC, CD, DB, BF, EF and EA.

Write down the coordinates of E and F, and the area of the completed figure.

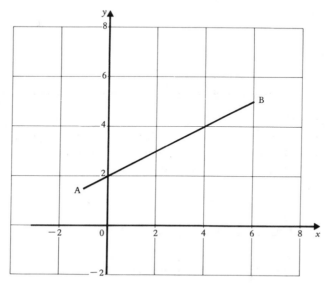

Given the points $A(-1, \frac{3}{2})$ and $B(6, 5)$, plot the points $C(-1, 4)$ and $D(2, 8)$. Join A to C , C to D and D to B. Complete the figure so that it is symmetrical about AB. If E is the reflection of D in the line AB and F is the reflection of C write down the coordinates of E and F. Calculate the area of the completed figure.

Indices   **10**

Simplify the following:

1	$a^2 \times a^3$	2	$a^5 \times a^3$	3	$x^7 \times x^3$
4	$a^5 \div a^2$	5	$x^{12} \div x^7$	6	$\dfrac{x^4}{x^3}$
7	$\dfrac{a^{16}}{a^9}$	8	$\dfrac{a^6}{a^9}$	9	$x^3 \times x^0$
10	$\sqrt{(a^3 \times a^5)}$	11	$\sqrt{(x^7 \times x^5)}$	12	$\dfrac{x^{12}}{x^6}$

23

13 $(a^3)^2$	14 $(a^4)^{-\frac{1}{2}}$	15 $(x^2 \times x^3)^{\frac{1}{2}}$
16 $x^{\frac{1}{2}} \times x$	17 $(a^{\frac{3}{4}})^{\frac{4}{3}}$	18 $(a^{\frac{2}{3}})^6$
19 $a^2 \times a^3 \times a^{-5}$	20 $8^{\frac{1}{3}}$	21 9^0
22 $9^{\frac{3}{2}}$	23 $32^{\frac{3}{5}}$	24 $27^{\frac{5}{3}}$
25 $4^{-\frac{3}{2}}$	26 $100^{-\frac{1}{2}}$	27 $(\frac{1}{4})^2$
28 $(\frac{1}{4})^{\frac{1}{2}}$	29 $(\frac{1}{4})^{-\frac{1}{2}}$	30 $(\frac{9}{4})^{-\frac{1}{2}}$
31 $(\frac{3}{7})^0$	32 $(\frac{1}{125})^{-\frac{1}{3}}$	33 $10^0 \times 9^0$
34 $(25)^{-\frac{3}{2}}$	35 $(49)^{\frac{3}{2}}$	36 $(\frac{1}{100})^{-\frac{1}{2}}$
37 $32^{-\frac{2}{5}}$	38 $12^{\frac{1}{2}} \times 3^{\frac{1}{2}}$	39 $8^{\frac{1}{2}} \times 12^{\frac{1}{2}} \times 6^{\frac{3}{2}}$

40 $\dfrac{24^{\frac{2}{3}} \times 16^{\frac{1}{3}}}{18^{\frac{1}{3}}}$

Simultaneous Linear Equations 11

Solve the given pairs of simultaneous linear equations:

1 $x + y = 8$	2 $2x + y = 5$
$x - y = 2$	$x - y = 4$
3 $5x + y = 8$	4 $3x + y = 11$
$x - y = 4$	$x + y = 3$
5 $x + 3y = 13$	6 $x - 3y = 7$
$x + 2y = 9$	$x + y = 3$
7 $2x + y = 7$	8 $5x - y = 17$
$3x + 2y = 12$	$2x + 3y = 0$
9 $3x + 2y = 3$	10 $5x + 7y = 4$
$2x + 3y = 7$	$x + 2y = 2$
11 $4x - y = 10$	12 $3x + 5y = -14$
$3x + 5y = 19$	$3x - 2y = 14$
13 $7x + 5y = 6$	14 $5x - 3y = 11$
$3x - 4y = 21$	$4x + y = 19$
15 $8x - y = 6$	16 $3x + 4y = 26$
$7x + 5y = 17$	$4x - 3y = 18$
17 $5x + y = 22$	18 $3x - 4y = 30$
$2x - 5y = 25$	$4x + 5y = 9$

19 $6x - 5y = 11$
$4x + 3y = 1$

20 $10x + 3y = -24$
$5x - 4y = -23$

21 $3x + 2y + 9 = 0$
$2x + y + 7 = 0$

22 $5x + 2y = 31$
$x = 3y + 13$

23 $x + 2y = 10$
$3x = 5y - 3$

24 $4x = -5y - 8$
$6x = 2y + 26$

25 $2x + 3y = 2$
$8x - 9y = 1$

26 $4x - 6y = 13$
$x + y = 2$

27 $12x - 3y = 1$
$4x + 6y = 5$

28 $7x - 5y = 16$
$4x + y = -14$

29 $x - 2y = 2$
$3x - y = -2$

30 $2x - 3y = 4$
$2x + 3y = -10$

31 A year ago a mother was four times as old as her daughter. In three years time she will be three times as old as her daughter. Find the present age of the daughter.

32 A year ago a father was four times as old as his son. Three years ago he was five times as old as his son. Find his son's age in two years time.

33 Five apples and three oranges cost £1.35 whereas three apples and five oranges cost £1.45. Find the cost of an orange and the cost of an apple.

34 Two pens and five pencils cost £1.20 whereas three pens and two pencils cost £1.14. Find the cost of each.

35 The cost of printing 5 large photographs and 12 small photographs is £6.64, while the cost of printing 7 large and 10 small is £7.12. Find the cost of one large and one small.

36 A bookseller offers the same book either with a hard cover or with a soft cover. Three copies of the hard cover together with ten copies of the soft cover cost £26.80, whereas five copies of the hard cover and twenty-one copies of the soft cover cost £52.25. Find the cost of each type of book.

37 Two numbers are such that if 11 is added to the first the answer is twice the second, and if 25 is subtracted from the first the answer is half the second. Find the two numbers.

38 Two motorists arrive at a petrol station. The first buys 5 gallons of petrol and 2 pints of oil and pays £11.70. The second buys 8 gallons of petrol and 3 pints of oil and pays £18.60. Find the price of petrol per gallon and oil per pint.

39 In a supermarket 3 jars of lime marmalade together with 5 jars of orange marmalade cost £4.30, while 5 jars of lime and 4 jars of orange cost £5. Find the cost of each type of marmalade per jar.

40 A housewife buys 4 jars of coffee and 3 packets of tea for £9.40 while a second housewife buys 5 jars of coffee and 6 packets of tea for £13.55. If a third housewife buys one jar of each how much will she have to pay?

Factors   12

Factorise:

1   $x^2 + 7x + 12$ 2 $x^2 + 6x + 5$

3   $x^2 + 9x + 14$ 4 $x^2 + 7x + 10$

5   $a^2 + 11a + 28$ 6 $6 + 5b + b^2$

7   $m^2 + 13m + 42$ 8 $n^2 + 12n + 27$

9   $x^2 + x - 12$ 10 $x^2 + 2x - 15$

11 $x^2 + 5x - 14$ 12 $20 - a - a^2$

13 $b^2 - 3b - 28$ 14 $12 + 4m - m^2$

15 $t^2 - 7t - 18$ 16 $x^2 - 8x + 15$

17 $x^2 - 9x + 14$ 18 $30 - 11x + x^2$

19 $a^2 - 9a + 20$ 20 $b^2 - 3b + 2$

21 $c^2 - 15c + 56$ 22 $y^2 - 11y + 28$

23 $2x^2 + 5x + 2$ 24 $3x^2 + 10x + 3$

25 $5x^2 + 27x + 10$ 26 $3b^2 + 13b + 14$

27 $4a^2 + 23a + 15$ 28 $5a^2 + 21a + 4$

29 $2x^2 - 3x - 2$ 30 $3x^2 - 13x - 10$

31 $5x^2 - 14x - 3$ 32 $5a^2 - 6a - 8$

33 $6 + 19a - 7a^2$ 34 $6x^2 + 11x + 4$

35 $10x^2 + 19x + 6$ 36 $28x^2 + 15x + 2$

37 $15a^2 + 22a + 8$ 38 $14b^2 + 19b + 6$

39 $6x^2 - 5x - 4$ 40 $10x^2 - 11x - 6$

41 $21x^2 - 22x - 8$ 42 $20x^2 + 13x - 15$

43	$63x^2 + 10x - 8$	44	$16a^2 + 34a - 15$
45	$14b^2 - 25b - 6$	46	$20x^2 - 23x + 6$
47	$27x^2 - 51x + 20$	48	$56a^2 - 31a + 3$
49	$16y^2 - 16y + 3$	50	$9z^2 - 21z + 10$
51	$x^2 - 16$	52	$x^2 - 49$
53	$x^2 - y^2$	54	$9x^2 - y^2$
55	$a^2 - 4b^2$	56	$9a^2 - 16b^2$
57	$25y^2 - 16z^2$	58	$x^2 - 100y^2$
59	$x^2 - \dfrac{y^2}{4}$	60	$25 - a^2$
61	$9 - x^2$	62	$\dfrac{x^2}{9} - \dfrac{y^2}{16}$
63	$16 - y^2$	64	$2 - 18b^2$
65	$8x^2 - 2$	66	$75a^2 - 3$
67	$4a^2 - 36b^2$	68	$(x + 2)^2 - 9$
69	$(x - 3)^2 - 16$	70	$25 - (x + 1)^2$
71	$49 - (a + 2)^2$	72	$(2x + 1)^2 - (3x + 2)^2$
73	$(4a + 3b)^2 - (2a + b)^2$	74	$2x^2 + 8x$
75	$7x^2 - 14x$	76	$4ax + 12ay$
77	$3a(b + c) - (b + c)$	78	$a(x - y) - b(x - y)$
79	$3x(y + z) - 2(y + z)$	80	$3a(2x + y) - 4b(2x + y)$
81	$2x^2 + 2x - 40$	82	$6a^2 - 9a - 6$
83	$x^3 + 3x^2 - 4x$	84	$a + 2a^2 + a^3$
85	$x^3 - x^2 + x - 1$	86	$x^2 - y^2 - (x + y)$
87	$x^2 - y^2 - 4(x - y)$	88	$ab + 4a + 3b + 12$
89	$xy + 1 - x - y$	90	$a(b - 1) - b^2 + 1$
91	$xy + 3x - 2y - 6$	92	$2ab - 3b + 4a - 6$
93	$10xy + 15x - 2y - 3$	94	$4ab - 4a + 3b - 3$
95	$10 - 5b - 4a + 2ab$	96	$12 - 20y - 5yz + 3z$
97	$a^2(1 + b) - b^2(1 + a)$	98	$9a^2 - b^2 - 15a + 5b$
99	$x^4 - 2x^2 - 8$	100	$6x^4 + 7x^2y^2 + 2y^4$

Quadratic Equations

13

Solve the following equations:

1   $(x-2)(x-8) = 0$ 2 $(x-4)(x-7) = 0$

3   $(x-5)(x-2) = 0$ 4 $(x-4)(x+3) = 0$

5   $(x+8)(x-9) = 0$ 6 $(x+3)(x+10) = 0$

7   $(x+13)(x+4) = 0$ 8 $(2x-1)(x-5) = 0$

9   $(3x-5)(x-3) = 0$ 10 $(2x-3)(x+5) = 0$

11   $(5x-4)(x+3) = 0$ 12 $(2x+3)(x-4) = 0$

13   $(5x+3)(x-9) = 0$ 14 $(7x+5)(3x+5) = 0$

15   $(12x+5)(4x+7) = 0$ 16 $(5x-3)(4x+5) = 0$

17   $(13x-1)(2x+1) = 0$ 18 $(6x+4)(x-7) = 0$

19   $(x-6)(4x+16) = 0$ 20 $(2x+3)(3x-9) = 0$

21   $x(x-4) = 0$ 22 $x(x+7) = 0$

23   $3x(x-5) = 0$ 24 $2x(2x-7) = 0$

25   $3x(5x+8) = 0$ 26 $(x-5)x = 0$

27   $(3x-8)x = 0$ 28 $(5x+9)x = 0$

29   $x^2-4 = 0$ 30 $x^2-9 = 0$

31   $4x^2 = 9$ 32 $25x^2-16 = 0$

33   $4x^2-1 = 0$ 34 $x^2-4x+3 = 0$

35   $x^2-11x+28 = 0$ 36 $x^2-12x+27 = 0$

37   $x^2-11x+30 = 0$ 38 $x^2+x-12 = 0$

39   $x^2+4x-45 = 0$ 40 $x^2+5x+6 = 0$

41   $x^2+12x+35 = 0$ 42 $x^2+5x = 0$

43   $x^2-3x = 0$ 44 $x^2-5x = 24$

45   $x^2-3x = 10$ 46 $x^2+x = 20$

47   $x^2-21 = 4x$ 48 $x^2-63 = 2x$

49   $x^2 = 9(x-2)$ 50 $x^2+20 = 9x$

51   $2x^2-5x+2 = 0$ 52 $2x^2-3x+1 = 0$

53   $3x^2-13x+4 = 0$ 54 $7x^2+13x-2 = 0$

55   $5x^2-23x-10 = 0$ 56 $6x^2-13x+6 = 0$

57	$27x^2 - 15x - 2 = 0$	58	$35x^2 + 52x + 12 = 0$
59	$12x^2 + 31x + 20 = 0$	60	$3x^2 - 5x - 2 = 0$
61	$2x^2 + x - 6 = 0$	62	$5x^2 - 11x + 2 = 0$
63	$32x^2 - 52x - 7 = 0$	64	$25x^2 + 15x + 2 = 0$
65	$8x^2 + 10x - 3 = 0$	66	$5x^2 - 14x = 0$
67	$9x^2 + 5x = 0$	68	$4x^2 + 7x = 0$
69	$4x^2 - 2x = 0$	70	$5x^2 - 10x = 0$
71	$2x^2 - 23x + 63 = 0$	72	$9x^2 + 85x + 36 = 0$
73	$8x^2 + 2x - 1 = 0$	74	$5x^2 - 19x - 4 = 0$
75	$2x^2 - 3x - 14 = 0$	76	$16x = x^2 + 63$
77	$x(x-2) = 15$	78	$x^2 = \dfrac{5x - 2}{3}$
79	$x^2 - 2 = \dfrac{x}{6}$	80	$x + 1 = \dfrac{6}{x}$

81 Two positive numbers differ by 5 and their product is 84. Find them.

82 One number is 4 more than another, and the sum of their squares is 250. Find the two numbers.

83 The sum of the squares of three consecutive positive numbers is 77. Find them.

84 The sum of two numbers is 20 and the difference between their squares 120. Find them.

85 The length of a rectangle is 5 cm more than the width. If the area of the rectangle is 104 cm² find its width.

86 The area of a rectangle is 98 cm² and its length is twice its width. Find the sides.

87 In a right-angled triangle the sides forming the right-angle are such that one is 7 cm more than the other. Find these sides, given that the length of the hypotenuse is 13 cm.

88 A lawn is two metres longer than it is wide. It is surrounded by a path 2 metres wide and the combined area of lawn and path is 168 m². Find the length and breadth of the lawn, and the area of the path.

89 The sum of the squares of two consecutive even numbers is 20 more than the square of the next even number. Find them.

90 The side of one square is 5 cm longer than the side of another square. Find the sum of their areas, given that the difference between their areas is 115 cm².

91 A rectangular lawn, measuring 20 metres by 15 metres, is surrounded by a path of uniform width. If the total area of the path is 114 m² finds its width.

92

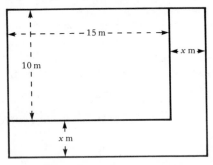

A lawn, measuring 15 metres by 10 metres has a path of uniform width x metres running along one of the long sides and one of the short sides as shown in the diagram. If the area of the path is 84 m² form an equation in x and solve it.

93

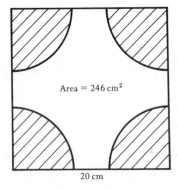

Area = 246 cm²

20 cm

A square sheet of metal of side 20 cm has equal quadrants cut from its corners as shown in the diagram. If the area of the remaining piece is 246 cm² find the radius of the circle from which the quadrants are taken. ($\pi = 22/7$.)

94 A train, travelling at x km.p.h takes t hours to travel 360 kilometres. If the speed is increased by 30 km.p.h. the time for the journey is reduced by one hour. Find the speed of the train.

95 A room is x metres wide, $x + 3$ metres long and $x - 2$ metres high. If the total area of all four walls is 78 m² form an equation in x and solve it. What is the volume of the room?

30

96 A length of wire is cut into two pieces. The first piece is bent to form the four sides of a square, and the second piece is bent to form a circle of diameter equal to the side of the square. If $\pi = 22/7$ and the combined area of square and circle is $87\frac{1}{2}$ cm² find: (a) the side of the square, (b) the length of the original wire.

97 A length of wire 20 cm long is cut into two pieces. The first piece is bent to form the four sides of a square of side x cm, and the second piece is bent to form the four sides of a rectangle whose length is twice its width, and whose area is twice the area of the square. Find the dimensions of each figure.

98 A concentric hole is bored along the axis of a wooden cylinder radius 7 cm, length 10 cm so that the volume of wood remaining is three times the amount removed. Find the radius of the cylindrical part which is removed.

99 A circular lily pond of diameter 12 metres is surrounded by a path of uniform width whose area is equal to the area of the surface of the pond. Calculate the width of the path in metres correct to two decimal places.

100 The parallel sides of a trapezium are of length $x - 2$ cm and $x + 4$ cm. If the distance between these sides is x cm and the area of the trapezium is 72 cm² form an equation in x and solve it to find the lengths of the parallel sides.

Change of Subject $\qquad$ 14

In each of the following formulae change the subject to the letter given in brackets:

1 $D = ST$ (S)

2 $A = lb$ (l)

3 $A = \frac{1}{2}bh$ (b)

4 $F = ma$ (a)

5 $C = 2\pi r$ (r)

6 $F = \mu R$ (μ)

7 $V = wr$ (w)

8 $E = Ri^2$ (R)

9 $P = 2a + 2b$ (b)

10 $2s = a + b + c$ (a)

11 $y = mx$ (m)

12 $I = \dfrac{PRT}{100}$ (R)

13 $A = \dfrac{(a+b)}{2}h$ (a)

14 $A = \dfrac{(a+b)}{2}h$ (h)

15 $V = \pi r^2 h$ (h)

16 $pv = 30$ (p)

17 $y^2 = 4ax$ (a)

18 $v = u + at$ (a)

19 $P = L + 2\pi R$ (R)

20 $V = \frac{1}{3}\pi r^2 h$ (h)

21 $T = \dfrac{2\pi}{w}$ (w)

22 $V^2 = 2gh$ (g)

23 $A = \frac{1}{2}r^2\theta$ (θ)

24 $\dfrac{W}{P} = \dfrac{a}{b}$ (P)

25 $y = mx + c$ (m)

26 $C = 90 - \frac{1}{2}A$ (A)

27 $A = 2(ab + bc + ca)$ (a)

28 $y = \dfrac{2}{\sqrt{x}}$ (x)

29 $A = \pi r^2$ (r)

30 $V = \pi r^2 h$ (r)

31 $\dfrac{1}{u} + \dfrac{1}{v} = \dfrac{1}{f}$ (f)

32 $v^2 = u^2 + 2as$ (a)

33 $V = \frac{4}{3}\pi r^3$ (r)

34 $V = \frac{1}{3}\pi r^2 h$ (r)

35 $a = \sqrt{(b^2 + c^2)}$ (b)

36 $T = 2\pi\sqrt{\dfrac{L}{g}}$ (g)

37 $mg - T = ma$ (m)

38 $b = \sqrt{(l^2 - h^2)}$ (l)

39 $a^2 = b^2 + c^2$ (c)

40 $A = \pi(R^2 - r^2)$ (r)

41 $F = \frac{9}{5}C + 32$ (C)

42 $A = 2\pi R(R + h)$ (h)

43 $S = \left(\dfrac{u+v}{2}\right)t$ (v)

44 $a^2 = x^2 + y^2 + z^2$ (z)

45 $Ax + By + C = 0$ (y)

46 $\dfrac{1}{a} + \dfrac{1}{b} = \dfrac{1}{c}$ (a)

47 $S = \dfrac{a}{1-r}$ (r)

48 $C = \dfrac{nE}{R + nr}$ (r)

49 $E = \frac{1}{2}m(v^2 - u^2)$ (v)

50 $A = P\left(1 + \dfrac{r}{100}\right)$ (r)

Determinants and Matrices

Find the following determinants:

1 $\begin{vmatrix} 4 & 3 \\ 2 & 5 \end{vmatrix}$
2 $\begin{vmatrix} 5 & 9 \\ 2 & 7 \end{vmatrix}$
3 $\begin{vmatrix} -3 & 5 \\ 5 & 4 \end{vmatrix}$

4 $\begin{vmatrix} 14 & 3 \\ 9 & 2 \end{vmatrix}$
5 $\begin{vmatrix} 6 & 12 \\ 3 & 6 \end{vmatrix}$
6 $\begin{vmatrix} -7 & 5 \\ 5 & -4 \end{vmatrix}$

7 $\begin{vmatrix} 113 & 56 \\ 5 & 2 \end{vmatrix}$
8 $\begin{vmatrix} -9 & 15 \\ 7 & -8 \end{vmatrix}$
9 $\begin{vmatrix} 46 & 13 \\ 12 & 13 \end{vmatrix}$

10 $\begin{vmatrix} -15 & -7 \\ 14 & -9 \end{vmatrix}$
11 $\begin{vmatrix} 23 & 0 \\ 15 & -1 \end{vmatrix}$
12 $\begin{vmatrix} -16 & 7 \\ -1 & 0 \end{vmatrix}$

Use the method of determinants to solve the following pairs of linear equations:

13 $x + 3y - 7 = 0$
$4x - 2y - 7 = 0$

14 $x + y - 1 = 0$
$2x - 3y + 8 = 0$

15 $x - 3y = 0$
$4x - 5y - 14 = 0$

16 $11x + 7y + 6 = 0$
$9x + 2y - 10 = 0$

17 $3x + 5y + 14 = 0$
$3x - 2y - 14 = 0$

18 $6x - 2y - 26 = 0$
$4x + 5y + 8 = 0$

19 $4x + 3y - 1 = 0$
$6x - 5y - 11 = 0$

20 $2x + 3y = 3$
$3x + 2y = 7$

21 $6x + 4y = 5$
$3x - 12y + 1 = 0$

22 $x - y = 4$
$7x + 3y = 13$

23 $7x - 9y = -33$
$9x - 7y = -15$

24 $3x + 4y = 6$
$4x = 5y - 23$

25 $2x = 1 - y$
$x = 2y + 8$

26 $x - y - 4 = 0$
$2x = 13 - 3y$

27 $x - 4y + 10 = 0$
$5x + 3y = 19$

28 $3x - 5y + 3 = 0$
$x + 2y = 10$

29 $2x + 4y + 1 = 0$
$5x - 3y - 4 = 0$

30 $3x - 4y = 40$
$2x + 3y = 4$

31 If $A = \begin{pmatrix} 4 & 3 \\ 3 & 2 \end{pmatrix}$ and $B = \begin{pmatrix} 5 & 2 \\ 3 & 2 \end{pmatrix}$ find:

(a) $A + B$,   (b) $2A - B$,   (c) $3A - I$,
(d) AB,   (e) BA,   (f) A^2.

32 If $X\begin{pmatrix} -5 & 4 \\ 2 & 6 \end{pmatrix}$ and $Y=\begin{pmatrix} 7 & -3 \\ 8 & 2 \end{pmatrix}$ find:

(a) $3X+2Y$, (b) $4X-Y$, (c) X^2, (d) XY.

33 If $A\begin{pmatrix} 9 & 4 \\ 7 & 5 \end{pmatrix}$ and $B=\begin{pmatrix} 8 & 3 \\ 5 & 2 \end{pmatrix}$ find:

(a) $A+2B$, (b) $3A+2B$, (c) $3B-A$,
(d) BA, (e) AB, (f) B^2.

34 If $A=\begin{pmatrix} -4 & 7 \\ 5 & -4 \end{pmatrix}$ and $B=\begin{pmatrix} -9 & 5 \\ -2 & 6 \end{pmatrix}$ find:

(a) $4A$, (b) $2B$, (c) $B+2A$,
(d) $B-I$, (e) BA, (f) B^2.

35 If $X=\begin{pmatrix} 12 & -3 \\ 0 & 7 \end{pmatrix}$ and $Y=\begin{pmatrix} -9 & 15 \\ 3 & -4 \end{pmatrix}$ find:

(a) $X+3Y$, (b) $X-Y$, (c) $I-Y$,
(d) XY, (e) X^2, (f) X^3.

36 If $A=\begin{pmatrix} 5 & 6 \\ 6 & 7 \end{pmatrix}$ find A^{-1} and use this value to find AA^{-1} and $A^{-1}A$.

37 If $X=\begin{pmatrix} 9 & 5 \\ 8 & 5 \end{pmatrix}$ find X^{-1} and use this value to find XX^{-1} and $X^{-1}X$.

38 If $M=\begin{pmatrix} -4 & -5 \\ 2 & 3 \end{pmatrix}$ find M^{-1} and hence find the value of MM^{-1} and $M^{-1}M$.

39 If $Y=\begin{pmatrix} 16 & 6 \\ 3 & 3 \end{pmatrix}$ find Y^{-1} and the value of YY^{-1}.

40 If $Z=\begin{pmatrix} 5 & 6 \\ 3 & -4 \end{pmatrix}$ find Z^{-1} and ZZ^{-1}.

41 If $A=\begin{pmatrix} 7 & 2 \\ 5 & 3 \end{pmatrix}$ and $B=\begin{pmatrix} 6 \\ 3 \end{pmatrix}$ find AB.

42 If $X=\begin{pmatrix} -6 & 4 \\ 4 & 5 \end{pmatrix}$ and $Y=\begin{pmatrix} -8 \\ 3 \end{pmatrix}$ find XY.

43 If $C=\begin{pmatrix} 9 & 13 \\ 7 & -4 \end{pmatrix}$ and $D=\begin{pmatrix} 13 \\ -8 \end{pmatrix}$ find CD.

Solve the following using matrix methods:

44 $\begin{pmatrix} 1 & 1 \\ 1 & -1 \end{pmatrix} \begin{pmatrix} x \\ y \end{pmatrix} = \begin{pmatrix} 7 \\ 1 \end{pmatrix}$
45 $\begin{pmatrix} 2 & -1 \\ 3 & 1 \end{pmatrix} \begin{pmatrix} x \\ y \end{pmatrix} = \begin{pmatrix} 8 \\ 17 \end{pmatrix}$

46 $\begin{pmatrix} 5 & 2 \\ 2 & 1 \end{pmatrix} \begin{pmatrix} x \\ y \end{pmatrix} = \begin{pmatrix} -7 \\ -2 \end{pmatrix}$
47 $\begin{pmatrix} 7 & -1 \\ 3 & 1 \end{pmatrix} \begin{pmatrix} x \\ y \end{pmatrix} = \begin{pmatrix} 9 \\ 1 \end{pmatrix}$

48 $\begin{pmatrix} 3 & -5 \\ 4 & -3 \end{pmatrix} \begin{pmatrix} x \\ y \end{pmatrix} = \begin{pmatrix} -1 \\ 6 \end{pmatrix}$
49 $\begin{pmatrix} 4 & 3 \\ 2 & 5 \end{pmatrix} \begin{pmatrix} x \\ y \end{pmatrix} = \begin{pmatrix} 18 \\ 16 \end{pmatrix}$

50 $\begin{pmatrix} 4 & 5 \\ 6 & -2 \end{pmatrix} \begin{pmatrix} x \\ y \end{pmatrix} = \begin{pmatrix} -8 \\ 26 \end{pmatrix}$

Calculations including Squares, Square Roots and Reciprocals   16

Find:

1   5.231 x 27.43   2   721.2 x 3.142

3   67.9 x 34.16   4   127.2 x 35.64

5   17.92 x 2.006   6   4.937 x 32.43

7   27.94 x 18.21   8   527.1 x 4.724

9   53.21 x 8.924   10   82.69 x 33.75

11   4.32 x 16.3 x 59.2   12   7.97 x 26.1 x 3.26

13   52.14 x 3.921 x 7.93   14   93.98 x 13.21 x 5.97

15   $\dfrac{93.41}{15.32}$ 16 $\dfrac{302.7}{47.93}$

17   $\dfrac{527.3}{176.9}$ 18 $\dfrac{36.43}{9.814}$

19   $\dfrac{2049}{78.53}$ 20 $\dfrac{1275}{394.2}$

21   $\dfrac{42.7 \times 53.9}{78.5}$ 22 $\dfrac{13.92 \times 72.14}{105}$

23   $\dfrac{72.16 \times 93.75}{427.9}$ 24 $\dfrac{8.724 \times 49.26}{23.72}$

25   $\dfrac{593.\overset{.}{6} \times 4.249}{200.9}$
26   $\dfrac{63.79 \times 23.14}{98.22}$

27	$\dfrac{22.6 \times 14.9}{9.36 \times 16.7}$	28	$\dfrac{47.9 \times 3.14}{5.92 \times 19.76}$
29	$\dfrac{8.436 \times 521.4}{227.4 \times 1.732}$	30	$\dfrac{5.693 \times 426.2}{19.72 \times 63.12}$
31	17.04×0.763	32	41.2×0.937
33	0.297×53.9	34	0.561×27.32
35	0.7261×21.2	36	72.3×0.517
37	426.2×0.372	38	516.4×0.726
39	317.4×0.923	40	0.0937×44.71
41	0.092×29.53	42	71.62×0.0237
43	472.5×0.00536	44	0.007536×9.217
45	0.931×0.264	46	0.173×0.429
47	0.5261×0.3333	48	0.8917×0.4664
49	0.0072×0.826	50	0.5494×0.0372
51	0.3159×0.00937	52	0.0624×0.0148
53	0.4624×0.03163	54	0.02149×0.01623
55	$\dfrac{0.927}{0.531}$	56	$\dfrac{0.726}{0.436}$
57	$\dfrac{0.2614}{0.1731}$	58	$\dfrac{0.9264}{0.3453}$
59	$\dfrac{0.7173}{0.6241}$	60	$\dfrac{0.8267}{0.3454}$
61	$\dfrac{0.426}{21.4}$	62	$\dfrac{0.927}{19.17}$
63	$\dfrac{0.9271}{54.21}$	64	$\dfrac{0.7264}{127.3}$
65	$\dfrac{0.2249}{17.42}$	66	$\dfrac{0.3443}{63.72}$
67	$\dfrac{9.49}{13.42}$	68	$\dfrac{16.4}{42.7}$
69	$\dfrac{127.4}{529.2}$	70	$\dfrac{6.364}{49.21}$
71	$\dfrac{163.2}{249.2}$	72	$\dfrac{19.89}{74.26}$

$73 \quad \dfrac{362.1}{5006}$

$74 \quad \dfrac{43.92}{267.1}$

$75 \quad \dfrac{0.49 \times 27.23}{17.92}$

$76 \quad \dfrac{0.7261 \times 13.9}{9.984}$

$77 \quad \dfrac{0.4231 \times 27.93}{34.52}$

$78 \quad \dfrac{0.9193 \times 55.62}{293.2}$

$79 \quad \dfrac{731.4 \times 5.92}{0.3377}$

$80 \quad \dfrac{29.17 \times 4.315}{54.11}$

$81 \quad \dfrac{17.92 \times 62.3}{51.92 \times 103.4}$

$82 \quad \dfrac{43.27 \times 7.149}{63.52 \times 9.372}$

$83 \quad \dfrac{9.26 \times 0.435}{59.8 \times 3.64}$

$84 \quad \dfrac{32.91 \times 0.2614}{52.94 \times 16.64}$

$85 \quad \dfrac{126.1 \times 0.0424}{0.9216 \times 32.41}$

$86 \quad \dfrac{0.09215 \times 5.263}{49.11 \times 15.34}$

$87 \quad \left(\dfrac{16.21 \times 31.41}{43.2 \times 5.61}\right)^2$

$88 \quad \left(\dfrac{124.6 \times 13.61}{427.2 \times 1.932}\right)^2$

$89 \quad \left(\dfrac{24.92 \times 0.636}{9.21}\right)^2$

$90 \quad \left(\dfrac{62.92 \times 0.4146}{15.62}\right)^2$

$91 \quad \sqrt{\dfrac{527.2 \times 92.6}{727.9}}$

$92 \quad \sqrt{\dfrac{4.367 \times 2.925}{7.142 \times 0.936}}$

$93 \quad \sqrt{\dfrac{54.72 \times 0.926}{16.31 \times 21.49}}$

$94 \quad \sqrt{\dfrac{0.7214 \times 0.5936}{13.62 \times 4.92}}$

$95 \quad \left(\dfrac{31.43 \times 16.92}{45.17 \times 8.214}\right)^3$

$96 \quad \left(\dfrac{0.736 \times 59.21}{25.92 \times 1.364}\right)^3$

$97 \quad \sqrt[3]{\left(\dfrac{73.1 \times 14.23}{24.97}\right)^2}$

$98 \quad \sqrt{\left(\dfrac{450.4 \times 0.172}{5.932 \times 16.70}\right)^3}$

$99 \quad \sqrt[4]{\left(\dfrac{39.52 \times 74.93}{15.47 \times 82.61}\right)^3}$

$100 \quad \sqrt[5]{\left(\dfrac{59.36 \times 41.24}{924.5 \times 16.31}\right)^3}$

$101 \quad 5.147^2$

$102 \quad 9.834^2$

$103 \quad 19.36^2$

$104 \quad 45.7^2$

$105 \quad 0.7584^2$

$106 \quad 0.2372^2$

$107 \quad 0.067^2$

$108 \quad 0.0078^2$

$109 \quad 0.04936^2$

$110 \quad 0.1493^2$

$111 \quad 3.142^2$

$112 \quad 169^2$

113 0.9246^2	114 0.0946^2	115 0.009463^2
116 $\sqrt{56.93}$	117 $\sqrt{127.4}$	118 $\sqrt{407}$
119 $\sqrt{5643}$	120 $\sqrt{1078}$	121 $\sqrt{32.75}$
122 $\sqrt{0.759}$	123 $\sqrt{0.8362}$	124 $\sqrt{0.1539}$
125 $\sqrt{0.5566}$	126 $\sqrt{0.07432}$	127 $\sqrt{0.0064}$
128 $\sqrt{0.007947}$	129 $\sqrt{0.5893}$	130 $\sqrt{0.0008}$

131 $\dfrac{1}{19}$ 132 $\dfrac{1}{27}$ 133 $\dfrac{1}{364}$

134 $\dfrac{1}{54.9}$ 135 $\dfrac{1}{73.3}$ 136 $\dfrac{1}{2393}$

137 $\dfrac{1}{6582}$ 138 $\dfrac{1}{6332}$ 139 $\dfrac{1}{9342}$

140 $\dfrac{1}{449.3}$ 141 $\dfrac{1}{582.5}$ 142 $\dfrac{1}{123.4}$

143 $\dfrac{1}{0.76}$ 144 $\dfrac{1}{0.847}$ 145 $\dfrac{1}{0.939}$

146 $\dfrac{1}{0.4663}$ 147 $\dfrac{1}{0.2773}$ 148 $\dfrac{1}{0.9942}$

149 $\dfrac{1}{0.0352}$ 150 $\dfrac{1}{0.00983}$ 151 $3.852^2 + \sqrt{76.4}$

152 $6.594^2 + \sqrt{93.49}$ 153 $0.763^2 + \sqrt{0.689}$

154 $\sqrt{456.9} + 33.75^2$ 155 $\sqrt{0.6583} + 0.564^2$

156 $56.93^2 + \sqrt{4573}$ 157 $1.769^2 + \sqrt{4.455}$

158 $5.749^2 + \dfrac{1}{0.3824}$ 159 $27.33^2 + \dfrac{1}{0.07335}$

160 $1.732^2 + \dfrac{1}{3.762}$ 161 $0.6673^2 + \dfrac{1}{76.33}$

162 $\dfrac{1}{274.5} + 0.3664^2$ 163 $\dfrac{1}{50.24} + 0.792^2$

164 $\sqrt{84.66} + \dfrac{1}{0.7463}$ 165 $\sqrt{3.762} + \dfrac{1}{0.9933}$

166 $\sqrt{572.3} + \dfrac{1}{0.06443}$ 167 $\sqrt{0.9573} + \dfrac{1}{42.72}$

168 $\sqrt{0.007\,335}+\dfrac{1}{0.05887}$ 169 $\sqrt{0.2365}+\dfrac{1}{6.338}$

170 $\sqrt{53.77}+\dfrac{1}{0.4773}$ 171 $\dfrac{1}{\sqrt{73.26}}$ 172 $\dfrac{1}{\sqrt{3.614}}$

173 $\dfrac{1}{\sqrt{592.6}}$ 174 $\left(\dfrac{1}{2.143}\right)^2$ 175 $\left(\dfrac{1}{0.7263}\right)^2$

176 Given that $\log 4 = 0.6021$ find without using logarithm or antilogarithm tables:
(a) $\log 400$, (b) $\log 0.04$, (c) $\log 16$,
(d) $\log 64$, (e) antilog $\bar{1}.6021$.

177 Given that $\log 0.7 = \bar{1}.8451$ find without using logarithm or antilogarithm tables:
(a) $\log 7$, (b) $\log 49$, (c) $\log(49 \div 0.7)$,
(d) antilog 2.8451.

178 Given that $\log 25 = 1.3979$ find without using logarithm or antilogarithm tables:
(a) $\log 0.25$, (b) $\log 5$, (c) $\log 125$,
(d) antilog $\bar{2}.3979$.

179 Given that $\log 3 = 0.4771$ find without using logarithm or antilogarithm tables:
(a) $\log 300$, (b) $\log 9$, (c) $\log 81$,
(d) $\log(21 \div 0.7)$.

180 Given that $\log 64 = 1.8062$ find without using logarithm or antilogarithm tables:
(a) $\log 6.4$, (b) $\log 8$, (c) $\log 4$, (d) $\log 32$.

Sets **17**

1 Copy the Venn diagram given below four times. Use these diagrams to shade the areas which represent the following subsets:
(a) $A \cup B$, (b) $A \cap B$, (c) A', (d) $(A \cap B)'$.

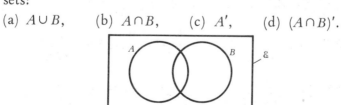

2 Copy the Venn diagram given below four times. Use these diagrams to shade the areas which represent the following sub-sets:

(a) $X \cap Y$,   (b) X',   (c) $(X \cup Y)'$,   (d) $X' \cap Y'$.

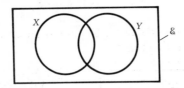

3 Given $\& =$ (Positive whole number $\leqslant 15$)
            $A =$ (multiples of 3)
            $B =$ (multiples of 4)

list the elements of the following sets:

(a) A,   (b) B,   (c) A',   (d) $A \cap B$,   (e) $A \cup B$.

4 Given $\& =$ (positive integers less than 13)
            $A =$ (prime numbers)
            $B =$ (odd numbers)

list the elements of the following sets:

(a) A,   (b) B,   (c) $A \cup B$,   (d) $(A \cup B)'$;
(e) $(A \cup B')'$.

Find also $n(A \cup B)$ and $n(A \cap B)$.

5 Given $\& =$ (positive integers less than 13)
            $X =$ (prime numbers)
            $Y =$ (factors of 12)

list the elements of:

(a) X,   (b) Y,   (c) $X \cup Y$,   (d) $(X \cup Y)'$,
(e) $X' \cap Y$.

6 Given $\& =$ (A E G I N O R S T)
            $A =$ (the letters in the word SAINT)
            $B =$ (the letters in the word STRING)

show these on a suitable Venn diagram.

7 Given $\& =$ (the letters of the alphabet)
            $A =$ (vowels)
            $B =$ (consonants)

write down the sets:

(a) A,   (b) $A \cap B$,   (c) B'.

8   Given $\&$ = (A D E I O P R S T U W)
        X = (the letters in the word SPORT)
        Y = (the letters in the word ADIDAS)
    draw a Venn diagram to illustrate these sets, and use it to find:
    (a) $X \cap Y$,   (b) X',   (c) $(X \cup Y)'$,   (d) $(X' \cup Y)'$.

9   Use set notation to describe the shaded areas in each of the
    following Venn diagrams:

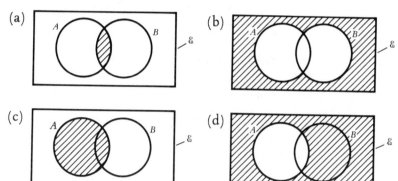

(a)   (b)
(c)   (d)

10

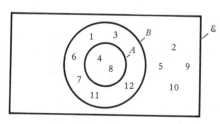

The Venn diagram shows two sets A and B which are subsets
of the universal set $\&$. List the elements of the following sets:
(a) $A \cup B$,   (b) $A \cap B$,   (c) B',   (d) $(A \cup B)'$.
Find $n(A)$ and $n(A \cap B)$.

11

The Venn diagram shows two sets A and B which are subsets of
the universal set $\&$. List the elements of the following sets:
(a) A,   (b) $A \cup B$,   (c) A',   (d) B'.

41

12 $\mathcal{E} = (1, 2, 3, 4, 5, 6, 7, 8, 9, 10)$
$A = (\text{odd numbers})$
$B = (\text{prime numbers})$

(a) List each of the following sets: (i) A, (ii) B, (iii) $A \cap B$, (iv) $(A \cup B)'$.

(b) What is the value of $n(A)$ and $n(A \cup B)'$?

13 The areas shaded in each of the given Venn diagrams are subsets of the universal set. Express these shaded areas in set language.

(a) 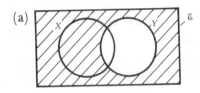 (b)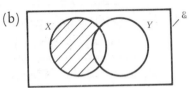

(c)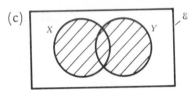

14 Given $\mathcal{E} = (\text{positive integers} < 17)$
$A = (\text{odd numbers})$
$B = (\text{multiples of 3})$

list the following subsets:

(a) A,   (b) B,   (c) $A \cap B$,   (d) $(A \cap B)'$.

15 Given $\mathcal{E} = (\text{positive whole numbers} < 13)$
$X = (\text{factors of 21 other than 1 and itself})$
$Y = (\text{odd numbers})$

list the subsets:

(a) X,   (b) Y,   (c) Y',   (d) $X \cup Y$,   (e) $(X \cup Y)'$,
(f) $X' \cup Y$.

16 Given $\mathcal{E} = (x : 3 \leqslant x \leqslant 12)$ where x is integer
$A = (\text{multiples of 3})$
$B = (\text{even numbers})$

list the sets:

(a) A,   (b) B,   (c) $A' \cap B'$,   (d) $(A \cup B)'$.

17 $\mathcal{E} = (x : 0 < x \leqslant 15)$ where x is integer
$P = (\text{prime numbers})$
$Q = (\text{even numbers})$

(a) List the following: (i) $\mathcal{E}$, (ii) P', (iii) Q', (iv) $P \cap Q$.

(b) Find $n(P \cup Q)$ and $n(P')$.

18 $\& = (n: 2 \leqslant n \leqslant 14)$ where n is integer)
     $A = $ (odd numbers)
     $B = $ (even numbers)
     $C = $ (prime numbers)

List each of these sets and draw a Venn diagram to illustrate this information.

Give, in set language, an empty set.

19   (a)   The diagram represents the sets A, B and C.
     $A = $ {all the whole numbers}
     $B = $ {all the even numbers}
     $C = $ {all the whole numbers which will divide exactly by 3}

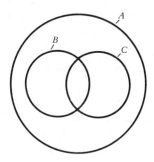

    Copy this diagram.

    Then write the numbers 2, 3, 4, 5, 6, 7, 8, 9 in the correct regions on the diagram.

   (b)   The diagram represents sets X, Y and Z.

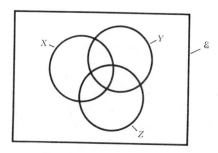

    Copy this diagram TWICE.

    Label the diagrams you have drawn (1) and (2).

    On diagram (1) shade the region representing the set $X \cup Y$.

    On diagram (2) shade the region representing the set $(X \cup Y) \cap Z$.

20 The pupils in a class were asked which of the subjects Art, Woodwork and Metalwork they took. The results were as follows:

> 5 took Art only
> 4 took Art and Woodwork only
> 8 took Woodwork only
> 3 took Woodwork and Metalwork only

(a) Draw a diagram to illustrate these sets, label it, and show the above information on it.

Now use the following results to fill in more information on your diagram and to answer the questions:

> Altogether 17 pupils took Woodwork

(b) How many took Art, Woodwork and Metalwork?

> Altogether 13 pupils took Art
> Altogether 9 pupils took Metalwork

(c) (i) How many took Art and Metalwork only?
   (ii) How many took Metalwork only?

21 (a) The Universal set $U = \{1, 2, 3, 4, 5, 6, 7, 8, 9,\}$,
    $A = \{x : 2 \leqslant x \leqslant 6\}, B = \{x : x > 3\}$ and $C = \{x : x < 8\}$.
    List the sets: (i) A, (ii) A', (iii) $A \cup (B \cap C)$.

(b) The Universal set $U = \{1, 2, 3, 4, 5, 6 \ldots\}$
    (i) What is the name given to the set $\{1, 4, 9, 16 \ldots\}$?
    (ii) What is the name given to the set $\{3, 6, 9, 12 \ldots\}$?
    (iii) List the first five elements of the set of prime numbers.

22 The Venn diagram below shows the numbers of pupils in a class of 35 who study one or other of the sciences Biology (B), Physics (P), Chemistry (C) (or none of these).

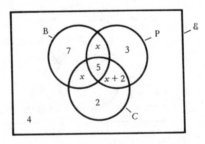

(a) How many pupils do not study a science?
(b) How many pupils study just one of these sciences?
(c) Write down IN TERMS OF x the number of pupils who are studying one or more of these sciences. Hence, or otherwise, find the value of x.

23 In a class of 30 boys, 16 like cricket (C), 13 like tennis (T) and 7 like neither.

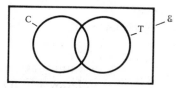

(a) In the Venn diagram fill in the correct numbers in the regions.

(b) Use your diagram to find how many boys:
    (i) like both cricket and tennis,
    (ii) like EITHER cricket OR tennis but not both,
    (iii) do not like tennis.

24 The universal set $\& = \{1, 2, 3, 4, 5, 6, 7, 8, 9, 10\}$, $A = \{2, 4, 6, 8\}$, $B = \{1, 3, 5, 7\}$, $C = \{3, 6, 9\}$.

(a) List the elements in the set $(A \cup B) \cap C$.

(b) Write down the value of $n(A \cup C)$.

(c) List the elements in the complement of $A \cup B \cup C$.

25

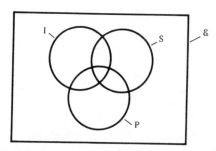

There are eight people A, B, C, D, E, F, G and H, all of whom can speak at least one of the languages Italian (I), Portuguese (P) and Spanish (S).

    A and B speak all three
    Only A, B and F can speak both Italian and Portuguese
    G and H speak Spanish only
    C and E speak Italian
    C speaks two languages
    No one except A and B speaks Portuguese and Spanish
    Only four people speak Portuguese

Copy the Venn diagram and put the letters A, B, C, D, E, F, G and H in their correct regions.

26 The number of elements in a universal set $\mathcal{E}$ is 28. A and B are subsets of $\mathcal{E}$, $n(A) = 18$, $n(B) = 16$ and $n(A \cap B) = 9$. By drawing a Venn diagram find:
(a) $n(A \cup B)$,   (b) $n(A \cup B)'$.

27 The number of elements in a universal set $\mathcal{E}$ is 35. $n(X) = 21$, $n(Y) = 11$ and $n(X \cap Y) = 6$. Draw a Venn diagram and find:
(a) $n(X \cup Y)$,   (b) $n(X \cup Y)'$.

28 Given

$$X = \{A, C, E, G, J, L\}$$
$$Y = \{B, E, G, H, K\}$$
$$Z = \{C, G, H, L\}$$

write down the elements in:
(a) $Y \cup Z$,   (b) $X \cap Y$,   (c) $X \cap Y \cap Z$.

29

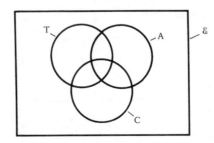

A questionnaire on 'Holiday Transport' given to sixty people produced the following facts: 40 had used a car (C), 28 had used an aeroplane (A), 16 had used a train (T), 18 had used both a car and an aeroplane, 5 had used both a car and a train, 4 had used only a train, 20 had used only a car and 6 had not been on holiday. Copy the Venn diagram and mark x as the number questioned who had used all three forms of transport. Calculate:

(a) the value of x,

(b) the number who went on holiday but did not use a car,

(c) the number who used more than one form of transport.

30 Forty staff take a school meal which includes the offer of fresh fruit. 18 take an apple, 12 take an orange, 11 take a pear, 9 take an orange but not an apple, 7 take an orange only, 8 take a pear only and no one takes all three fruits. Copy the Venn diagram and find how many:

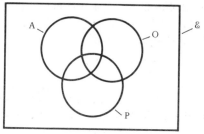

(a) take an apple and a pear,

(b) do not take an orange,

(c) select two fruits,

(d) do not take any fruit.

Graphs

18

1 In each of the following find the equation of the straight line shown:

(a)
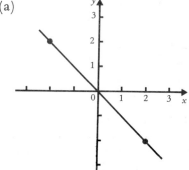

(b)
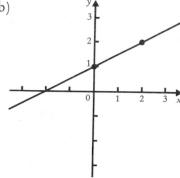

(c)
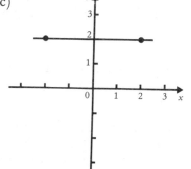

(d)
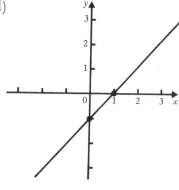

(*continued overleaf*)

(e)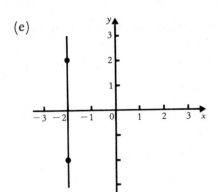

(f)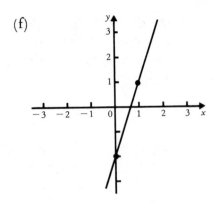

2   Copy and complete the following tables:

x	-1	0	3
$y = 3 - 2x$	5		

x	-3	0	4
$y = \frac{1}{2}(x-4)$	-3.5		

Taking 2 cm as unit on each axis draw the graphs of $y = 3 - 2x$ and $y = \frac{1}{2}(x-4)$. Choose your axes so that x ranges from -3 to $+5$ and y ranges from -5 to $+6$.

Use your graph to solve the simultaneous equations

$$y = 3 - 2x$$
$$y = \frac{1}{2}(x - 4)$$

3   Copy and complete the following tables:

x	-2	0	4
$y = 5 - x$		4	

x	-2	1	3
$y = 2x - 1$	-5		

Draw the graphs of $y = 5 - x$ and $y = 2x - 1$ on the same axes taking 2 cm as unit on both axes. Choose your axes so that x ranges from -3 to $+5$ and y ranges from -6 to $+6$.

Use your graph to solve the simultaneous equations

$$y = 5 - x$$
$$y = 2x - 1$$

4   Copy and complete the following tables:

x	-1	0	3
$y = 2x - 1$	-3		

x	-2	0	5
$y = \frac{1}{2}(x + 2)$	0	1	

On the same axes, taking 2 cm as unit on each axis, draw the graphs of $y = 2x - 1$ and $y = \frac{1}{2}(x + 2)$.

Use your graph to write down the solution of the simultaneous equations

$$2x - y - 1 = 0$$
$$x - 2y + 2 = 0$$

5   Copy and complete the following tables:

x	-3	1	5
$y = -\frac{1}{2}(x + 7)$		-4	

x	-5	0	5
$y = \frac{1}{5}(11x + 5)$		1	12

On the same axes draw the graphs of $y = -\frac{1}{2}(x + 7)$ and $5y = 11x + 5$ using 1 cm as unit on each axis. Choose your axes so that x ranges from -7 to $+7$ and y ranges from -12 to $+12$.

Use your graph to solve the simultaneous equations

$$x + 2y + 7 = 0$$
$$11x - 5y + 5 = 0$$

6   ABC is a triangle in which the equations of the three sides are as follows:

$$\text{AB: } 2y = -(x + 1)$$
$$\text{BC: } 3y = 2x + 9$$
$$\text{AC: } x = 3$$

Complete the following tables and use them to graph the lines $2y = -(x + 1)$ and $3y = 2x + 9$.

x	-3	0	5
$y = -\frac{1}{2}(x + 1)$			-3

x	0	$1\frac{1}{2}$	$4\frac{1}{2}$
$y = \frac{1}{3}(2x + 9)$		4	

Plot these points on the same axes, taking 2 cm as unit on each axis, and hence draw the graphs of the given lines together with that of the line $x = 3$. Use your graph to find the coordinates of A, B and C.

If BD is drawn perpendicular to AC to meet AC at D measure BD and hence find the area of triangle ABC.

7   The three lines AB, BC, CA have equations $3y = 2(x - 6)$, $y = 6 - x$ and $3y = 8(x + 3)$ respectively. Take x values of $-3, 0$ and 9 for AB; $-4, 0$ and 8 for BC; $-6, -3$ and 0 for AC, finding in each case the corresponding y values. Use these values of x and y to draw the graphs of the three lines and from your graph determine the coordinates of A, B and C.

49

8

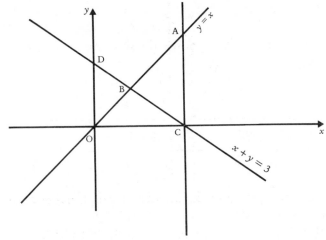

Copy the given diagram on to graph paper using 2 cm as unit on each axis.

(a) Write down the coordinates of A, B, C and D.

(b) Shade the region defined by the inequalities $x + y \geqslant 3$, $y \leqslant x$, $x \leqslant 3$.

(c) Write down the inequalities which define the region within the triangle OBD.

9

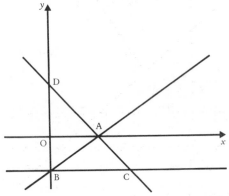

Draw the given diagram on graph paper taking 2 cm as the unit on each axis. AB has equation $x - 2y = 4$, AC has equation $x + y = 4$, and BC is parallel to the x-axis.

(a) Find the coordinates of A, B and C.

(b) Write down the equation of BC.

(c) Shade the region defined by the inequalities $x \geqslant 0$, $x + y \leqslant 4$, $x - 2y \geqslant 4$.

(d) Define the region within triangle ABC using suitable inequalities.

10

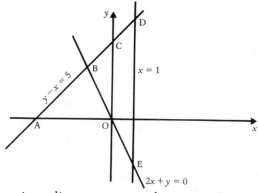

Draw the given diagram accurately on graph paper taking 2 cm as unit on each axis.

(a) Write down the coordinates of A, B, C, D and E.

(b) Find, by calculation, the length of AC correct to three significant figures.

(c) Shade the region which satisfies all the inequalities $2x + y < 0$, $y - x < 5$, $y > 0$.

(d) If $P(x, y)$ is a point *within* the triangle BDE write down the three inequalities connecting x and y.

11

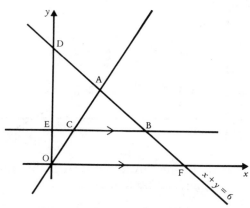

The equation of the line AB is $x + y = 6$.

(a) Find the coordinates of D and F, the two points where this line cuts the axes.

(b) If C is the point $(1, 2)$ and the line AC passes through the origin find the equation of AC and the coordinate of A.

(c) Write down the coordinates of B.

(d) Shade the area defined by $y \leqslant 2x$, $x + y \leqslant 6$, $y \geqslant 2$.

(e) State the four inequalities necessary to define the area within the quadrilateral ACED.

12

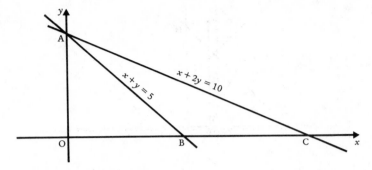

The straight lines AB and AC have equations $x + y = 5$ and $x + 2y = 10$ respectively.

(a) Find the coordinates of A, B and C.

(b) Find the gradient of AB.

(c) Write down the three inequalities which define the region within the triangle ABC.

(d) Calculate the area of triangle ABC.

13

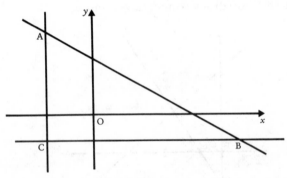

ABC is a triangle formed by three straight lines with equations $x = -2$, $y = -1$ and $x + 2y = 6$.

(a) Complete the following:

The equation of AB is
The equation of BC is
The equation of AC is

(b) Write down the coordinates of A, B and C.

(c) Shade the area which satisfies the inequalities $x + 2y > 6$, $x > 0$, $y > 0$.

(d) Write down the coordinates of all the points within the triangle ABC which have both coordinates as positive whole numbers.

14

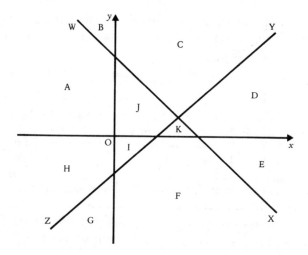

Two straight lines WX and YZ have equations $2x + y = 8$ and $x - y = 3$ respectively. A, B, C, D, E, F, G, H, I, J and K are regions of the graph. Which region is represented by the inequalities:

(a) $x < 0$, $y > 0$, $2x + y < 8$,

(b) $x - y < 3$, $2x + y < 8$, $y < 0$, $x > 0$.

15

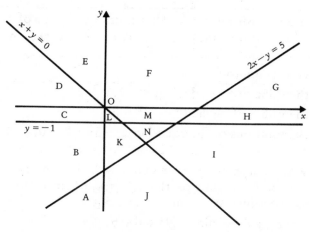

Three straight lines have equations $x + y = 0$, $y = -1$ and $2x - y = 5$ as shown. A, B, C, D, E, F, G, H, I, J, K, L and M show regions of the graph.

(a) Use inequalities to define the region marked M.

(b) Which regions are defined by the inequalities $x > 0$, $x + y < 0$, $2x - y > 5$?

53

16   Draw the graph of $y = x^2$ for values of x from $-3\frac{1}{2}$ to $+3\frac{1}{2}$ taking half-unit intervals. Take 2 cm as unit on each axis.

Use your graph to find:

  (a) $\sqrt{5.4}$,   (b) $\sqrt{9.5}$,   (c) -2.7^2,   (d) 1.7^2.

17   Calculate the missing values in the following table which gives the value of $x^2 - 5x + 4$ for given values of x.

x	0	$\frac{1}{2}$	1	$1\frac{1}{2}$	2	$2\frac{1}{2}$	3	$3\frac{1}{2}$	4	$4\frac{1}{2}$
$x^2 - 5x + 4$	4	$1\frac{3}{4}$		$-1\frac{1}{4}$	-2	$-2\frac{1}{4}$		$-1\frac{1}{4}$	0	$1\frac{3}{4}$

Use these values to plot the graph of $y = x^2 - 5x + 4$ for values of x from 0 to $4\frac{1}{2}$. Take 4 cm as the unit on each axis.

From your graph find:

  (a) the values of x for which $x^2 - 5x + 4 = 1$,

  (b) the value of $x^2 - 5x + 4$ when $x = 3.2$.

18   The table gives values of $5x - x^2$ for given values of x.

x	$-\frac{1}{2}$	0	1	2	3	4	$4\frac{1}{2}$	5	$5\frac{1}{2}$
$5x - x^2$	$-2\frac{3}{4}$	0		6	6		$+2\frac{1}{4}$		$-2\frac{3}{4}$

Fill in the missing values and hence draw the graph of $y = 5x - x^2$ for values of x from $-\frac{1}{2}$ to $5\frac{1}{2}$. Take 2 cm as the unit on each axis.

Use your graph to find:

  (a) the value of $5x - x^2$ when $x = 1.3$,

  (b) the values of x when $5x - x^2 = 3$,

  (c) the solutions of the equation $x^2 - 5x + 2 = 0$.

19   Draw the graphs of $y = x^2$ and $y = 2x + 3$ on the same axes, using 2 cm as the unit on the x-axis and 1 cm as the unit on the y-axis, for values of x from -3 to $+5$.

Use your graphs to find 3.9^2 and $\sqrt{5}$.

Write down the values of x at the points of intersection of the two graphs and find the equation for which these x-values are the roots.

20   Draw the graph of $y = x^2 - 4$ for values of x between -3 and $+3$. Use 2 cm to represent unit on both axes.

21 Draw the graph of $y = 9 - x^2$ for values of x between -3 and $+4$. Use 2 cm to represent one unit on the x-axis and two units on the y-axis.

Find the two values of x which correspond to $y = 6$.

22 Draw the graph of $y = x^2 - 3x - 4$ for values of x from -3 to $+5$. Use 2 cm to represent one unit on the x-axis and two units on the y-axis.

Find the values of x which make y unity.

23 Draw the graph of $y = 2x(x-5)$ for values of x from -1 to $+6$. Take 2 cm as the unit on the x-axis and as two units on the y-axis.

Use your graph to find the minimum value of y.

24 The relationship between the mass (m grams), of a circular metal plate, and the radius (r cm), is given in the table below for different values of r.

r (in cm)	3	4	6	8	9	10	12
m (in grams)	210	370	850	1500	1900	2325	3350

Draw axes for m and r taking 1 cm as unit on the horizontal r-axis and 2 cm $\equiv$ 250 g on the vertical m-axis and plot the points given in the table. Draw a smooth curve to pass through these points and from your graph find:

(a) the mass of a plate with radius 11 cm,

(b) the radius of a plate of mass 700 g.

25 A stone is thrown vertically upwards from the edge of a cliff. The table shows the distance (s metres) the stone is above the point of projection for various times (t seconds) from the time it is thrown.

Time (t) in seconds	0	1	2	3	4	5	6
Distance (s) in metres	0	13	16	9	-8	-35	-72

Using 2 cm = 1 second on the horizontal t-axis and 2 cm = 10 metres on the vertical s-axis draw a graph to represent this data and from it find:

(a) the time taken for the stone to return to its starting point,

(b) how far it is below the top of the cliff after $4\frac{1}{2}$ seconds,

(c) the time taken for the stone to reach the water which is 80 metres below the top of the cliff.

26 A pottery manufactures jugs with varying capacities but always of the same shape. The table gives the capacity (C litres) for given heights (H cm).

Height of jug (H) in centimetres	4	6	8	10	12	14	16	18
Capacity (C) in litres	0.06	0.2	0.5	1	1.7	2.7	4.1	5.8

Draw a graph to represent this data taking 1 cm as unit for H and 4 cm as unit for C.

From your graph find:

(a) the height of a jug which will hold 3 litres,

(b) the capacity of a jug which is 13 cm high.

27 Water is boiled and left to cool. The temperature of the water at different times is given in the following table:

Time in minutes	0	1	2	3	4	5	6	7	8	9
Temperature in °C	100	79	64	52	44	38	33.5	29.5	26.5	24

On graph paper draw axes taking $2 \text{ cm} \equiv 1$ minute on the horizontal axis and $2 \text{ cm} \equiv 10°C$ on the vertical axis. Plot the points given in the table and join them with a smooth curve. Use your graph to find:

(a) the temperature after $1\frac{1}{2}$ minutes,

(b) the time taken to cool to 50°C,

(c) how long the water takes to cool from 70°C to 40°C.

28 The table below gives the recorded temperature in the town of Caipa over a 24-hour period.

Time	Mid-night	2	4	6	8	10	
Temperature in °F	12	11	9.5	10	19	35.5	
Time	Noon	2	4	6	8	10	Mid-night
Temperature in °F	60	78	68	34	22	15	13

Draw axes, using $2\,\text{cm} \equiv 2\,\text{hours}$ on the horizontal (long) axis and $2\,\text{cm} \equiv 10°\text{F}$ on the vertical axis. Plot the points given above and join them with a smooth curve. From your graph estimate:

(a) the temperature at 9 a.m. and 9 p.m.,

(b) the times at which the temperature is 50°F,

(c) the fall in temperature between 5 p.m. and 9 p.m.,

(d) the lowest temperature recorded.

29 Complete the following table which gives the values of $2x^2 + 3x - 5$ for values of x from -4 to $+3$:

x	-4	-3	-2	-1	$-\frac{1}{2}$
$2x^2$	32	18	8	2	$\frac{1}{2}$
$+3x$	-12	-9	-6	-3	$-1\frac{1}{2}$
-5	-5	-5	-5	-5	-5
$2x^2 + 3x - 5$	15	4		-6	-6

x	0	1	2	$2\frac{1}{2}$
$2x^2$	0		8	$12\frac{1}{2}$
$+3x$	0		6	$7\frac{1}{2}$
-5	-5	-5	-5	-5
$2x^2 + 3x - 5$	-5		9	15

Taking 2 cm as unit for x and 1 cm as unit for y draw the graph of $y = 2x^2 + 3x - 5$ joining the points with a continuous smooth curve.

(a) (i) Write down the values of x where your graph crosses the x-axis.

   (ii) Write down the equation for which these x values are the roots.

(b) From your graph estimate the minimum value of $2x^2 + 3x - 5$

(c) From your graph estimate the value of $2x^2 + 3x - 5$ when $x = 1.7$.

30 Complete the following table which gives values of $12-2x-3x^2$ for values of x between -4 and $+4$.

x	-4	-3	-2	-1	0
12	12	12	12	12	12
$-2x$	8	6		2	
$-3x^2$	-48	-27	-12	-3	
$12-2x-3x^2$	-28	-9		11	

x	1	2	3	$3\frac{1}{2}$	4
12	12	12	12	12	12
$-2x$	-2	-4	-6	-7	-8
$-3x^2$	-3		-27	$-36\frac{3}{4}$	-48
$12-2x-3x^2$	7		-19	$-31\frac{1}{4}$	-44

Taking $2\,\text{cm} \equiv 1$ unit on the x-axis and $2\,\text{cm} \equiv 5$ units on the y-axis plot the graph of $y = 12-2x-3x^2$.

Use your graph to:

(a) find the values of x which make $12-2x-3x^2 = 0$,

(b) estimate the maximum value of $12-2x-3x^2$ and the value of x for which this maximum occurs.

Pythagoras' Theorem   19

1 ABC is a right-angled triangle with sides a, b and c the hypotenuse being c. Use the result of Pythagoras to find the missing side in each of the following:

(a) $a = 3\,\text{cm}$, $\quad b = 4\,\text{cm}$, $\qquad c = \qquad$.

(b) $a = 5\,\text{cm}$, $\quad b = 12\,\text{cm}$, $\qquad c = \qquad$.

(c) $a = \qquad$, $\quad b = 24\,\text{cm}$, $\qquad c = 26\,\text{cm}$.

(d) $a = 9\,\text{cm}$, $\quad b = 12\,\text{cm}$, $\qquad c = \qquad$.

(e) $a = \qquad$, $\quad b = 20\,\text{m}$, $\qquad c = 25\,\text{m}$.

(f) $a = 10\,\text{m}$, $\quad b = 24\,\text{m}$, $\qquad c = \qquad$.

(g) $a = \qquad$, $\quad b = 120\,\text{cm}$, $\qquad c = 150\,\text{cm}$.

(h) $a = \qquad$, $\quad b = 1.2\,\text{cm}$, $\qquad c = 1.3\,\text{cm}$.

(i) $a = 2\,\text{cm}$, $\quad b = \qquad$, $\qquad c = 5.2\,\text{cm}$.

(j) $a = 1.8\,\text{m}$, $\quad b = 2.4\,\text{m}$, $\qquad c = \qquad$.

2   XYZ is a right-angled triangle with sides x, y and z, the longest side being z. Use Pythagoras' result to calculate the missing side in each of the following, giving your answers correct to three significant figures.

(a) $x = 5$ cm, $y = 6$ cm, $z =$

(b) $x =$, $y = 8$ m, $z = 9$ m.

(c) $x = 15$ cm, $y = 30$ cm, $z =$.

(d) $x =$, $y = 16$ m, $z = 30$ m.

(e) $x = 18$ m, $y =$, $z = 42$ m.

(f) $x = 7.3$ cm, $y =$, $z = 9.4$ cm.

(g) $x = 12.6$ cm, $y = 8.4$ cm, $z =$.

(h) $x =$, $y = 23.7$ cm, $z = 52.1$ cm.

(i) $x = 0.65$ m, $y = 0.93$ m, $z =$.

(j) $x =$, $y = 0.24$ km, $z = 0.59$ km.

3   Use the theorem of Pythagoras to determine whether the largest angle in the triangles with the given sides is acute, 90° or obtuse.

(a) 8 m,   10 m,   12 m.

(b) 13 cm,   15 cm   24 cm.

(c) 9 m,   14 m,   16 m.

(d) 4.9 cm,   7.3 cm,   9.8 cm.

(e) 2.7 cm,   3.6 cm,   4.5 cm.

(f) 60 m,   72 m,   53 m.

(g) 32 cm,   27 cm,   40 cm.

(h) 10.5 cm,   34.5 cm,   36 cm.

(i) 0.42 km,   0.67 km,   0.98 km.

(j) 52 m,   49 m,   36 m.

4

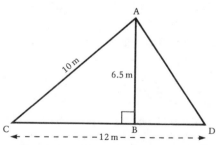

In the given diagram AB represents a vertical flagstaff 6.5 m high with AC and AD restraining wires which are attached to points in the level ground at C and D. If CD = 12 m and AC = 10 m use the result of Pythagoras to calculate: (a) BC, (b) AD, as accurately as your tables permit.

5   In a rectangle one side is 20 cm and the diagonals are 52 cm. Calculate the perimeter.

6   The diagonals of a rhombus are 7 cm and 16.8 cm. Calculate the perimeter.

7   The diagonal of a square is 29.70 cm. Find: (a) a side, (b) the area, of the square.

8   The side of a rhombus is 12 cm, and one diagonal is 20 cm. Find the length of the other diagonal.

9
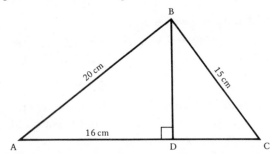

Using the given diagram find: (a) BD, (b) DC.

10 M is the midpoint of the side BC in an equilateral triangle ABC of side 16 cm. Calculate AM.

11 A soccer pitch measures 106 m by 70 m. How far is it between opposite corners?

12 A rugby pitch measures 100 m by 68 m. How far is it between opposite corners?

13 The two vertical masts of a sailing ship have heights 47 m and 32 m. If the distance between their highest points is 25 m find the distance between the masts on the deck of the ship.

14 Find the length of the longest pencil which may be placed in a rectangular box measuring 13 cm by 8 cm by 7 cm.

15 The diagram shows a ladder AB resting on horizontal ground DAE in a narrow street 7 m wide. The foot of the ladder A is 4 m from the base of a vertical wall DB and touches the wall at a point 7 m above the ground. How long is the ladder?

   The ladder is now turned about A so that it rests against a vertical building on the opposite side of the street at a point C. How high is C above the ground?

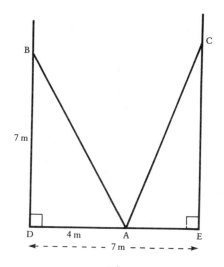

16

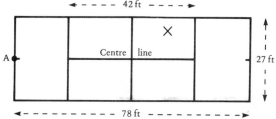

The diagram shows a tennis court measuring 78 feet by 27 feet. A tennis player standing at A attempts to serve into the rectangle marked X. If he strikes the ball at a height of 9 feet above the ground find the longest straight path which the ball may travel if it is to strike the ground within X. If it travels at 180 feet per second how long will it take from the time it leaves the racket until it strikes the ground?

17 The diagram represents the front of a house. Find the height of the ridge above ground level.

Find the length of a ladder which rests on the ground at a distance of 3.5 m from the base of the house and reaches to the ridge.

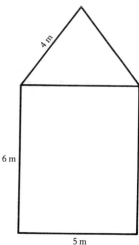

18 From a point A a boy walks 350 metres due north to a point B. At B he turns east and walks 420 metres to C where he turns and walks 760 metres in a southerly direction to a fourth point D. How far is D from the starting point?

19

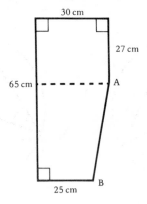

The diagram shows the section through a kitchen wall cupboard, AB representing the sliding glass door. Find AB correct to the nearest millimetre.

20

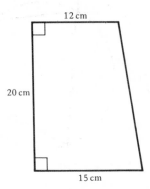

The figure shows the dimensions for a wooden book-end which is to be made by a form of twenty second-year pupils. Find:

(a) its perimeter,

(b) its volume if the wood is uniformly 1.5 cm thick,

(c) the total volume of wood used by the form if each pupil requires two book-ends.

The Circle

In questions 1–14 O is the centre of the circle. Find, without giving reasons, the value of each of the angles marked with a letter.

1

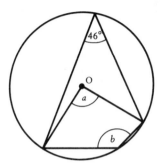

2

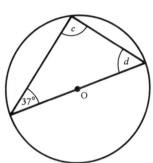

3

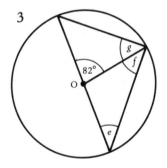

4

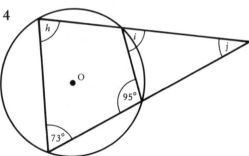

5

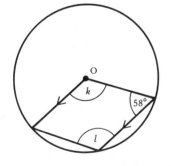

6

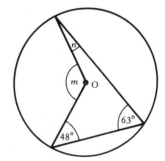

7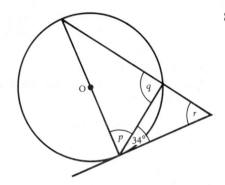

8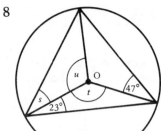

9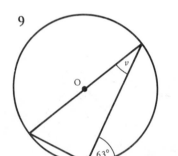

10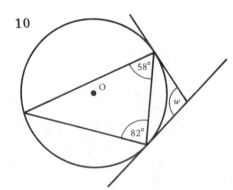

11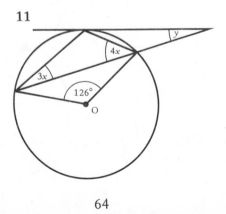

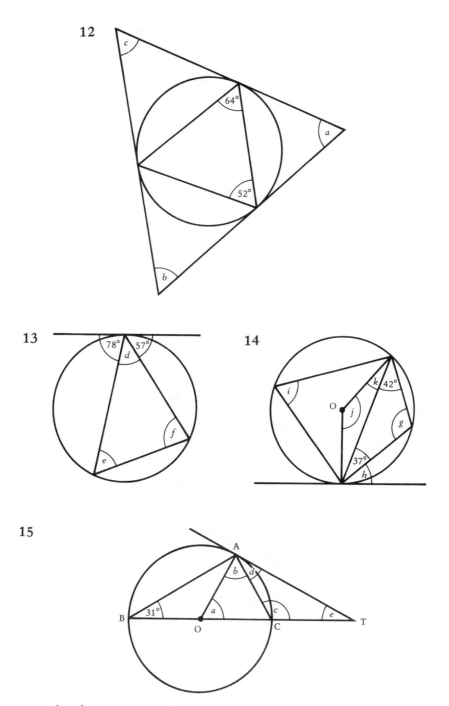

The diameter BC of a circle centre O is produced to meet the tangent at A in T. If ∠ABC = 31° find the angles marked $a, b, c,$ d and e.

16 ABCD is a cyclic quadrilateral with FDE the tangent to the circle at D (∠FDA is acute). The diagonal BD passes through the centre of the circle O. If ∠BDC = 34° and ∠BCA = 40° calculate, giving reasons, ∠DBC, ∠DAC, ∠CAB, ∠ACD, ∠CDE and ∠FDC.

17 ABC is a triangle inscribed in a circle centre O with DCE the tangent at C such that ∠BCE = 64°. If AB = BC find, giving reasons, ∠CAB, ∠ABC and ∠ACD.

18 ABC is a triangle inscribed in a circle such that AB is parallel to the tangent CT at C. If ∠ABC = 57° find ∠BCT and ∠CAB. What can you deduce about triangle ABC?

19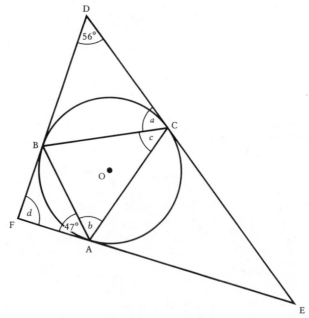

The tangents to a circle centre O, at A, B and C intersect at D, E and F as shown in the diagram. If ∠BDC = 56° and ∠FAB = 47° find the angles marked a, b, c and d.

20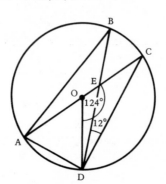

A, B, C and D are four points on a circle centre O. AOC is a diameter which intersects BD in E. ∠COD = 124° and ∠CDB = 12°. Find ∠AOD, ∠ABD, ∠ACD, ∠ADC and ∠BDO.

21

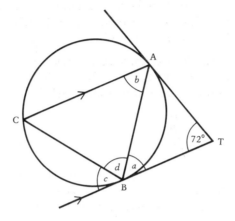

TA, TB are tangents from an external point T to a circle ABC. AC is parallel to TB and ∠ATB = 72°. Find the angles marked a, b, c and d.

22 TA, TB are the tangents from an external point T to a circle such that ∠TAB = 57°. C is a point on the circle such that C and T are on opposite sides of AB, and TB is produced to D. If ∠CBD = 63° find ∠ABT, ∠ATB, ∠ACB and ∠CAB.

23 A tangent TC and a secant TAOB are drawn from an external point T to a circle centre O. CA, CB and OC are joined. If ∠CTB = 34° find ∠AOC, ∠ABC, ∠OAC and ∠ACT. What kind of a triangle is COT?

24 ABCD is a cyclic quadrilateral inscribed in a circle centre O. AB = BC and OA, OC and AC are joined. If ∠BAC = 43° calculate ∠ABC, ∠ADC, ∠AOC and ∠OAC.

25 TA is a tangent and TBC a secant, each drawn from an external point T to a circle centre O. CA is parallel to OB and AB and OC are joined. If ∠COB = 140° calculate ∠CAB, ∠CBO, ∠CBA, ∠TAB and ∠ATC.

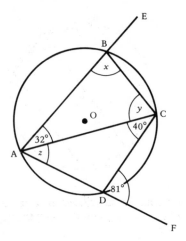

26

ABCD is a cyclic quadrilateral. The sides AB and AD are produced to E and F respectively. If ∠CDF = 81°, ∠ACD = 40°
and ∠BAC = 32° find the angles marked x, y and z.

27

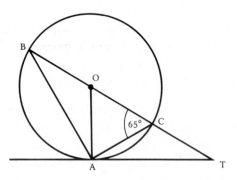

The diameter BC of a circle centre O is produced to meet the
tangent at A in T. If ∠OCA = 65° find ∠CAT, ∠AOC and ∠OAB.

28 ABCD is a cyclic quadrilateral inscribed in a circle centre O with
the diagonals AC and BOD intersecting at X. If ∠DAC = 57°
and ∠ACB = 27° find ∠DOC, ∠ODC, ∠OCB, ∠BAC, ∠ABD and
∠AXB.

29 ABCD is a cyclic quadrilateral with AB parallel to DC and the
diagonals AC and BD intersecting at X. The tangents to the
circle at A and D intersect at T and TD is produced to a point
E. If ∠ATD = 96° and ∠CDE = 34° find ∠DAT, ∠ACD, ∠ABD,
∠CBD, ∠ADC and ∠BCD.

30

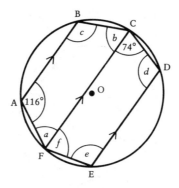

ABCDEF is a hexagon inscribed in a circle. AB, FC and ED are parallel, ∠BAF = 116° and ∠DCF = 74°. Find the angles marked *a*, *b*, *c*, *d*, *e* and *f*.

Constructions

21

1 (a) Draw a straight line AB and mark a point P some distance away from AB. Construct the perpendicular from P to AB.

   (b) Draw two straight lines AB, AC such that ∠BAC is acute. Construct the bisector of ∠BAC.

2 Mark two points A and B, 8 cm apart. Construct the perpendicular bisector of the join of AB.

3 Draw a straight line AB and mark a point C some distance away from AB. Construct the line through C parallel to AB.

4 Construct a triangle PQR with PR = 12 cm, ∠QPR = 60° and ∠QRP = 30°.

5 Construct a triangle ABC with AB = 11.5 cm, BC = 9 cm and CA = 7 cm.

6 Construct a triangle PQR in which PQ = 5.5 cm, QR = 6.3 cm and ∠PQR = 120°. Construct the perpendicular from R to PQ produced. Measure and record its length.

7 Construct a triangle XYZ in which XY = 13 cm, YZ = 11 cm and XZ = 7 cm. Construct the circumcircle to this triangle. Measure and record its radius.

8 Construct a square of side 9.5 cm.

9 Construct a rectangle with adjacent sides 10.5 cm and 6.8 cm. Measure and record the length of a diagonal.

10   Construct a rhombus with diagonals of length 7 cm and 5 cm. Measure and record the length of a side of this rhombus.

11   Draw a circle of radius 5 cm and use it to construct a regular hexagon of side 5 cm.

12   Draw a circle of radius 5.5 cm. Construct a regular octagon whose vertices lie on this circle. Measure and record the length of a side of this octagon.

13   Construct an angle of 75°.

14   Construct an equilateral triangle ABC of side 8 cm, and construct the perpendicular from A to BC. Measure and record its length.

15   Construct a triangle ABC given that AB = 12 cm, BC = 10 cm and $\angle$ABC = 60°. Measure the length of AC. Construct the circumcircle to this triangle. Measure and record the length of its radius.

16   Construct a triangle ABC with AB = 9.5 cm, BC = 7 cm and $\angle$ABC = 30°. By construction find a point D such that ABCD is a parallelogram. Measure and record the lengths of the two diagonals of this parallelogram.

17   Construct a parallelogram ABCD whose diagonals intersect at X given that AC = 10.6 cm, BD = 8.2 cm and $\angle$AXD = 60°. Measure the lengths of the sides of the parallelogram.

18   Construct a rectangle with diagonals of length 11.2 cm containing an angle of 45°. Measure and record the lengths of the sides of the rectangle.

19   Construct a trapezium ABCD given AB = 12.2 cm, BC = 7.3 cm, DC = 8.5 cm and $\angle$ABC = 60°. Measure and record the lengths of AD, AC and BD.

20   Draw a circle of radius 6.8 cm and mark a point P 9.2 cm from its centre. Construct the tangents from P to the circle. Measure and record their lengths.

21   Construct an isosceles triangle ABC with AB = BC = 9.2 cm and $\angle$BAC = 45°. Measure the length of BC.

22   Construct a triangle ABC with AB = 10.5 cm, BC = 8.4 cm and $\angle$ABC = 90°. Construct the circumcircle to this triangle. Measure and record its radius.

23   Construct a triangle PQR in which PR = 8.4 cm, $\angle$QPR = 30° and $\angle$QRP = 45°. Construct the circumcircle to this triangle. Measure and record its radius.

24 Draw AB = 11.2 cm. Using a constructional method find the point C which divides AB in the ratio 3:5. Measure and record the length of AC.

25 Draw XY = 9.7 cm. Using a constructional method find the point Z which divides XY in the ratio 5:2. Measure and record the length of ZY.

26 Construct a triangle PQR in which PQ = 13.7 cm, RQ = 8.8 cm and ∠PQR = 90°. Construct the inscribed circle to this triangle. Measure its radius.

27 Construct a quadrilateral ABCD with AB = 10 cm, BC = 6.5 cm, AC = 10 cm, AD = 8 cm and CD = 4.5 cm. Measure and record the length of DB.

28 Construct a quadrilateral ABCD with AB = 9.2 cm, BC = 7.8 cm, AD = 5.3 cm, ∠ABC = 60° and ∠CAD = 60°. Measure and record the length of CD.

29 Construct a quadrilateral PQRS given PQ = 7.8 cm, PR = 9.4 cm, PS = 7.2 cm, ∠QPR = 30° and ∠SPR = 45°. Measure the length of the diagonal QS.

30 Construct a quadrilateral ABCD with AB = 5 cm, BD = 7 cm, AD = 6.3 cm, ∠DBC = 60° and ∠BDC = 45°. Construct a line through C parallel to BD cutting AB produced at E. Measure and record the length of AE.

Similar Triangles 22

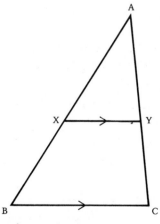

Questions 1–10 refer to the diagram given above.

1   AB = 4 cm, AX = 3 cm, AC = 6 cm. Find AY.

2   AX = 4 cm, AY = 3 cm, AC = 5 cm. Find AB.

3   AX = 2.1 cm, XB = 1.4 cm, AY = 1.8 cm. Find YC.

4   AY = 2.4 cm, YC = 1.8 cm, XB = 2.4 cm. Find AX.

5   AX = 5.5 cm, AB = 13.2 cm, AY = 4.5 cm, XY = 3.5 cm. Find AC and BC.

6   AX = 8 cm, AB = 14 cm, AY = 5 cm, XY = 7 cm. Find AC and BC.

7   BX = 4 cm, AY = 9 cm, AC = 12 cm, BC = 20 cm. Find AX, AB and XY.

8   AC = 4.4 cm, XY = 3 cm, BC = 5.5 cm, AX = 3.5 cm. Find AY, YC and AB.

9   AY = 4 cm, XY = 3 cm, AC = 7 cm and $\angle$AYX = 90°. Find AX, BC and AB.

10 AX = 0.9 m, AB = 1.5 m, XY = 1.5 m and $\angle$BAC = 90°. Find BC, AY and AC.

11

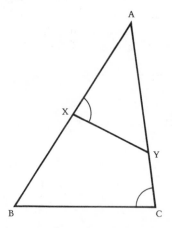

X and Y are points on the sides AB, AC respectively of a triangle ABC such that $\angle$AXY = $\angle$ACB. Calculate:

(a) AX and AY if AB = 35 cm, BC = 25 cm, AC = 30 cm and XY = 15 cm;

(b) AB and AC if BC = 1.8 cm, AY = 1.2 cm, XY = 0.6 cm and AX = 0.9 cm;

(c) AB, AX and the ratio $\dfrac{\triangle \text{ABC}}{\triangle \text{AXY}}$ if BC = 5.6 cm, AC = 8.4 cm AY = 8 cm and XY = 4 cm;

(d) BC, AY and the ratio $\dfrac{\triangle AXY}{\triangle ABC}$ if AB = 15 cm, AC = 10 cm, XY = 8.4 cm and AX = 7 cm.

12

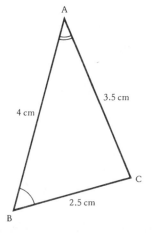

ABC and DEF are similar triangle with ∠ABC = ∠DEF and ∠ACB = ∠DFE. BC = 9 cm, DE = 4 cm, DF = 3 cm and EF = 6 cm.

(a) Complete the statement $\dfrac{AB}{} = \dfrac{AC}{DF} = \dfrac{}{EF}$.

(b) Calculate AB and AC.

(c) Find the ratio of the area of triangle ABC to the area of triangle DEF.

13

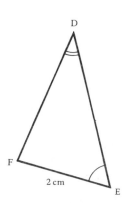

ABC and DEF are two similar triangles with ∠ABC = ∠DEF and ∠BAC = ∠EDF. AB = 4 cm, AC = 3.5 cm, BC = 2.5 cm and FE = 2 cm.

(a) Complete the statement $\dfrac{AB}{DE} = \dfrac{}{} = \dfrac{}{}$.

(b) Find DE and DF.

(c) Find $\dfrac{\triangle ABC}{\triangle DEF}$.

14

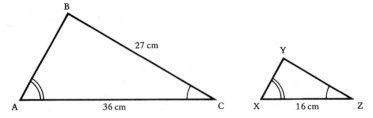

ABC and XYZ represent the cross-sections of two similar wooden wedges. AC = 36 cm, BC = 27 cm, XZ = 16 cm and the area of triangle XYZ is 72 cm².

(a) Calculate YZ.

(b) Find the area of triangle ABC.

(c) If the two wedges are similar what is the ratio of their volumes?

15

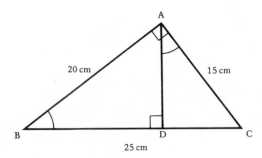

ABC is a right-angled triangle with D the foot of the perpendicular from A to BC and ∠BAC = 90°. AB = 20 cm, AC = 15 cm and BC = 25 cm.

(a) Indicate why triangles ABC and ABD are similar and complete the ratios $\dfrac{AB}{DB} = \dfrac{}{BA} = \dfrac{AC}{}$.

(b) Indicate why triangles ABC and ADC are similar and complete the ratios $\dfrac{AB}{DA} = \dfrac{BC}{} = \dfrac{AC}{}$.

(c) Calculate AD, BD and DC.

(d) Find $\dfrac{\triangle ABD}{\triangle ADC}$.

16

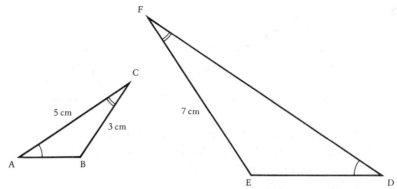

Two similar triangles ABC and DEF have their equal angles marked. AC = 5 cm, BC = 3 cm and EF = 7 cm.

(a) Complete the statement $\dfrac{AC}{BC} = \dfrac{}{FE}$.

(b) Hence calculate FD and find the value of the ratio $\dfrac{AB}{ED}$.

17

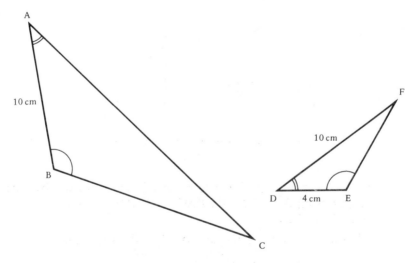

ABC and DEF are two similar triangles with $\angle A = \angle D$ and $\angle B = \angle E$. AB = 10 cm, DE = 4 cm and DF = 10 cm.

(a) Complete the statement $\dfrac{}{AB} = \dfrac{DF}{DE}$.

(b) Calculate AC.

(c) Calculate the ratio $\dfrac{BC}{EF}$.

18

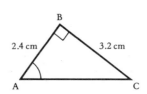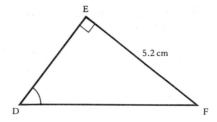

Triangles ABC and DEF are similar with $\angle B = \angle E = 90°, \angle A = \angle D$, AB = 2.4 cm, BC = 3.2 cm and EF = 5.2 cm. Find:

(a) the length of AC,

(b) the lengths of DE and DF,

(c) the ratio of the areas $\dfrac{\triangle ABC}{\triangle DEF}$.

19

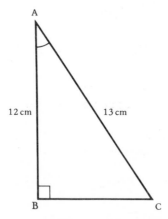

Triangles ABC and DEF are similar with $\angle B = \angle E = 90°, \angle A = \angle D$, AB = 12 cm, AC = 13 cm and EF = 4 cm.

(a) Find BC.

(b) Complete the statement $\dfrac{BC}{EF} = \dfrac{AC}{} = \dfrac{}{DE}$.

(c) Find DE and DF.

(d) Find the ratio of the areas $\dfrac{\triangle ABC}{\triangle DEF}$.

20 ABC is a triangle in which AB = 10 cm and AC = 7.5 cm. X is a point on AB such that AX = 4 cm and Y is a point on AC such that XY is parallel to BC. Calculate:

(a) the length of AY,

(b) the ratio of the areas $\dfrac{\triangle AXY}{\triangle ABC}$,

(c) the ratio of the area of the triangle AXY to the trapezium XYCB,

(d) the ratio of the areas $\dfrac{\triangle \text{AXY}}{\triangle \text{BXY}}$.

Functions and Mappings   23

1   Write down the image set of $\{-1, 0, 1, 2, 3\}$ under the mapping $x \to x^2$.

2   Write down the image set of $\{0, 1, 3, 5, 7\}$ under the mapping $x \to 3x - 5$.

3   Write down the image set of $\{-3, -2, -1, 0, 1, 2, 3\}$ under the mapping $x \to 4 - 3x$.

4   The function f maps x onto $f(x)$ where $f(x) = 7 - 2x$. If A is the set $\{1, 2, 4\}$ onto what set is A mapped by f? Find the value of x if f maps x onto 1.

5   The function f maps x onto $f(x)$ where $f(x) = \dfrac{5}{x + 2}$. If B is the set $\{0, 1, 2\}$ onto what set is B mapped by f? Find the value of x if f maps x onto 1.

6   The function g maps x onto $g(x)$ where $g(x) = 4x + 3$. If C is the set $\{-1, 0, 2\}$ onto what set is C mapped by g? Find the value of x if g maps x onto -9.

7   The function g maps x onto $g(x)$ where $g(x) = 5 - 3x$. Calculate:
(a) $g(3)$, (b) $g(-4)$, (c) the value of x if g maps x onto 14,
(d) the set $f(A)$ onto which g maps $A = \{x : 1 \leqslant x \leqslant 2\}$.

8   The function f maps x onto $f(x)$ where $f(x) = kx - 3$. Find k if f maps 3 onto 3.

9   The function g maps x onto $g(x)$ where $g(x) = 6 + kx$. Find k if g maps 3 onto -3.

10 The function f maps x onto $f(x)$ where $f(x) = 4 - kx$. Find k if f maps 4 onto 8.

11 The function f maps x onto $f(x)$ where $f(x) = 4x - 3$ and the function g maps x onto $g(x)$ where $g(x) = x^2$.
Calculate: (a) $f(3)$, (b) x if $f(x) = 17$, (c) $f[g(x)]$.

12　The function f maps x onto $f(x)$ where $f(x) = 7 - 2x$ and the function g maps x onto $g(x)$ where $g(x) = x^3$.

Calculate: (a) $f(-2)$, (b) x if $f(x) = 5$, (c) $g(-2)$, (d) x if $g(x) = 64$, (e) the value of x if f maps $g(x)$ onto -9.

13　The function f maps x onto $f(x)$ where $f(x) = 3 + 4x$ and the function g maps x onto $g(x)$ where $g(x) = 3x^2$.

Find: (a) $f(4)$, (b) x if $f(x) = 23$, (c) $g(-3)$, (d) $f[g(-3)]$, $g[f(4)]$.

14　The function f maps x onto $f(x)$ where $f(x) = x^2 + 3x + 2$ and the function g maps x onto $g(x)$ where $g(x) = 2 + 3x$.

Calculate: (a) $f(-2)$, (b) $g(-3)$, (c) the values of x if f maps x onto O, (d) what f maps $g(x)$ onto, in terms of x in its simplest form.

15　The function f maps x onto $f(x)$ where $f(x) = 8 + 5x - 2x^2$ and the function g maps x onto $g(x)$ where $g(x) = 5x - 3$.

Find: (a) f(-3), (b) $g(4)$, (c) the values of x if f maps x onto -10, (d) what f maps $g(x)$ onto, in terms of x in its simplest form.

16　The function f maps x onto $f(x)$ where $f(x) = 5 + 4x$.

Find: (a) $f(3)$, (b) the value of x if f maps x onto 53, (c) the set $f(A)$ onto which f maps $A = \{x : 1 \leqslant x \leqslant 3\}$.

17　The function g maps x onto $g(x)$ where $g(x) = 6 - 3x$.

Find: (a) $g(5)$, (b) x if g maps x onto 33, (c) the set $f(B)$ onto which g maps $B = \{x : -1 \leqslant x \leqslant 1\}$.

18　The function g maps x onto $g(x)$ where $g(x) = x^2$ and the function h maps x onto $h(x)$ where $h(x) = 4x + 3$.

Find: (a) $g[h(3)]$,　(b) $h[g(3)]$.

19　The function f maps x onto $f(x)$ where $f(x) = 3x^2$ and the function g maps x onto $g(x)$ where $g(x) = 7 - 2x$.

Find: (a) $g[f(4)]$,　(b) $f[g(4)]$.

20　The function f maps x onto $f(x)$ where $f(x) = \dfrac{7}{3x - 2}$. If A is the set $\{0, 2, 4\}$ onto what set is A mapped by f?

Vectors

1   If A, B and C are the points $(2, -3), (-2, 4)$ and $(3, 2)$ respectively write down the vectors $\overrightarrow{AB}, \overrightarrow{BC}$ and $\overrightarrow{CA}$.

2   If X, Y and Z are the points $(-1, -4), (2, 5)$ and $(6, -3)$ respectively write down the vectors $\overrightarrow{XY}, \overrightarrow{ZY}$ and $\overrightarrow{ZX}$.

3   If A, B and C are the points $(1, 1), (5, 6)$, and $(7, 3)$ respectively write down the vectors $\overrightarrow{CB}, \overrightarrow{AB}$ and $\overrightarrow{AC}$.

4   Which of the vectors given below is: (a) parallel to (b) perpendicular to, the vector $\begin{pmatrix} -3 \\ 2 \end{pmatrix}$?

$$\begin{pmatrix} -3 \\ -2 \end{pmatrix}, \begin{pmatrix} 6 \\ 4 \end{pmatrix}, \begin{pmatrix} -6 \\ 4 \end{pmatrix}, \begin{pmatrix} 12 \\ -8 \end{pmatrix}, \begin{pmatrix} 3 \\ -2 \end{pmatrix}, \begin{pmatrix} 2 \\ 3 \end{pmatrix}, \begin{pmatrix} 2 \\ -3 \end{pmatrix}$$

5   Which of the following vectors is: (a) parallel to (b) perpendicular to, the vector $\begin{pmatrix} 3 \\ -1 \end{pmatrix}$?

$$\begin{pmatrix} 3 \\ 1 \end{pmatrix}, \begin{pmatrix} 1 \\ 3 \end{pmatrix}, \begin{pmatrix} 6 \\ -2 \end{pmatrix}, \begin{pmatrix} 2 \\ -6 \end{pmatrix}, \begin{pmatrix} -1 \\ -3 \end{pmatrix}, \begin{pmatrix} -3 \\ 1 \end{pmatrix}$$

6   A is the point $(-2, -2)$, $\overrightarrow{AB} = \begin{pmatrix} 7 \\ -2 \end{pmatrix}$ and $\overrightarrow{AC} = \begin{pmatrix} 0 \\ 8 \end{pmatrix}$.

   (a) Find the coordinates of B and C.
   (b) Find the gradient of BC and the vector $\overrightarrow{CB}$.

7   ABC is a triangle such that A is the point $(-4, -2)$, $\overrightarrow{AB} = \begin{pmatrix} 6 \\ 6 \end{pmatrix}$ and $\overrightarrow{AC} = \begin{pmatrix} 8 \\ -2 \end{pmatrix}$. Find:

   (a) the coordinates of B and C,
   (b) the vector $\overrightarrow{CB}$,
   (c) the coordinates of M, the midpoint of BC.

8   P, Q, R and S are four points such that P is $(-6, 4)$, R is $(6, 2)$, $\overrightarrow{PQ} = \begin{pmatrix} 8 \\ 2 \end{pmatrix}$ and $\overrightarrow{PS} = \begin{pmatrix} 8 \\ -8 \end{pmatrix}$. Calculate:

   (a) the coordinates of Q and S,
   (b) the vectors $\overrightarrow{QR}$ and $\overrightarrow{RS}$.

   What can you conclude about the quadrilateral PQRS?

9 A, B, C and D are four points such that C is $(-2, -4)$, $\overrightarrow{CD} = \begin{pmatrix} -2 \\ 6 \end{pmatrix}$, $\overrightarrow{CA} = \begin{pmatrix} 4 \\ 8 \end{pmatrix}$ and $\overrightarrow{CB} = \begin{pmatrix} 6 \\ 2 \end{pmatrix}$. Find the coordinates of A, B and D.

10 ABC is an isosceles triangle with $\angle BAC = 90°$, $AB = AC$ and M the midpoint of BC. If A is the point $(2, 3)$, C the point $(6, -4)$ and B the point $(x, -1)$ find:
(a) the vector $\overrightarrow{AC}$,
(b) the value of x,
(c) the vector $\overrightarrow{BC}$.

11 a, b and c are vectors such that
$$a = \begin{pmatrix} 2 \\ 3 \end{pmatrix}, \quad b = \begin{pmatrix} -2 \\ 4 \end{pmatrix} \quad \text{and} \quad c = \begin{pmatrix} 16 \\ 3 \end{pmatrix}$$
Find vectors x and y such that:
(a) $a + x = b$,
(b) $2y - 3b = 2c$.
Find scalars r and s which satisfy $ra + sb = c$.

12 a, b and c are vectors such that:
$$a = \begin{pmatrix} 2 \\ 1 \end{pmatrix}, \quad b = \begin{pmatrix} 3 \\ -2 \end{pmatrix} \quad \text{and} \quad c = \begin{pmatrix} -3 \\ 2 \end{pmatrix}$$
Find:
(a) $a + b + c$,
(b) $2a - b + 3c$,
(c) x if $x + a - b = 3c$.

13 Vectors a, b and c are such that
$$a = \begin{pmatrix} 2 \\ 3 \end{pmatrix}, \quad b = \begin{pmatrix} -1 \\ 2 \end{pmatrix}, \quad c = \begin{pmatrix} 4 \\ -2 \end{pmatrix}$$
Find:
(a) $a + 2b + 3c$,
(b) $3c - b + 2a$,
(c) x if $2x + c = a - 4b$.

14

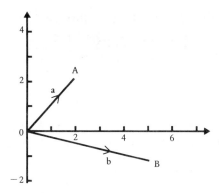

In the diagram $\overrightarrow{OA}$ = a and $\overrightarrow{OB}$ = b.

(a) From the point O draw the vector $\overrightarrow{OC}$ such that $\overrightarrow{OC}$ = a + b.

(b) Find $\overrightarrow{AB}$ in terms of a and b.

(c) Give the components of $\overrightarrow{AB}$.

15 Quadrilateral ABCD is such that B is $(2,5)$, C is $(8,2)$, D is $(2,0)$ and $\overrightarrow{AD} = \begin{pmatrix} 4 \\ -2 \end{pmatrix}$. Calculate:

(a) the vector $\overrightarrow{BC}$,

(b) the coordinates of A,

(c) the geometrical relationship between AD and BC.

16 In a triangle OAB, $\overrightarrow{OA}$ = a and $\overrightarrow{OB}$ = b. E is a point on AB such that AE:EB = 2:1. Find, in terms of a and b:

(a) $\overrightarrow{AB}$, (b) $\overrightarrow{AE}$, (c) $\overrightarrow{OE}$.

17

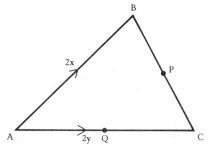

In the triangle ABC, P and Q are the midpoints of BC and AC respectively. AB = 2x and AC = 2y.

(a) (i) Find $\overrightarrow{CB}, \overrightarrow{CP}$ and $\overrightarrow{AP}$ in terms of x and y.

(ii) If G is a point on AP such that AG = $\frac{2}{3}$AP find $\overrightarrow{AG}$ in terms of x and y.

(b) (i) Find BQ in terms of **x** and **y**,

(ii) If H is a point on BQ such that $BH = \frac{2}{3}BQ$ find $\overrightarrow{HB}$ in terms of **x** and **y**. Hence find $\overrightarrow{AH}$ in terms of **x** and **y**. What conclusion may be drawn about the points G and H?

18

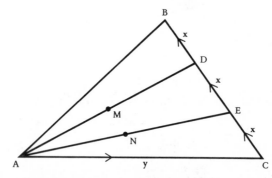

ABC is a triangle with D and E points on BC such that $\overrightarrow{CE} = \overrightarrow{ED} = \overrightarrow{DB} = x$ and AC = **y**.

(a) Find $\overrightarrow{AE}$ and $\overrightarrow{AD}$ in terms of **x** and **y**.

(b) If M and N are the midpoints of AD and AE respectively find $\overrightarrow{AM}$ and $\overrightarrow{AN}$ in terms of **x** and **y**.

(c) Find $\overrightarrow{NM}$ in terms of **x** and **y**.

(d) What conclusion can you draw about NM and CB?

19

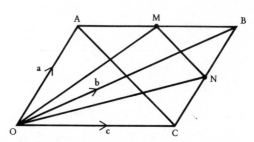

OABC is a parallelogram with M and N the midpoints of AB and BC respectively. $\overrightarrow{OA} = a$, $\overrightarrow{OB} = b$ and $\overrightarrow{OC} = c$.

(a) Find $\overrightarrow{AB}$ and $\overrightarrow{CB}$ in terms of **a** and **c**,

(b) Find $\overrightarrow{OM}$ and $\overrightarrow{ON}$ in terms of **a** and **c**,

(c) Find $\overrightarrow{MN}$ and $\overrightarrow{AC}$ in terms of **a** and **b**,

(d) What can you conclude about MN and AC?

20 From an origin O, three points A, B and C are such that $\overrightarrow{OA}$ = **a**, $\overrightarrow{OB}$ = **b** and $\overrightarrow{OC}$ = **c**. If M is the midpoint of AC and if G is the point on BM such that BG:GM = 2:1 find, in terms of **a**, **b** and **c**

(a) $\overrightarrow{AC}$ and $\overrightarrow{AM}$,   (b) $\overrightarrow{OM}$ and $\overrightarrow{MB}$,   (c) $\overrightarrow{MG}$ and $\overrightarrow{OG}$.

Trigonometry

25

1 Find the tangent of each of the following angles:
30°, 56°, 76°, 34°, 80°, 24°12′, 56°36′, 45°18′, 73°54′,
33°48′, 62°42′, 36°44′, 57°16′, 75°51′, 20°14′, 50°26′, 77°19′,
49°37′, 12°04′, 29°44′.

2 Evaluate each of the following:
30 tan 47°, 20 tan 56°, 12 tan 74°12′, 8 tan 74°18′,
7 tan 27°48′, 5 tan 47°42′, 6 tan 37°44′, 20 tan 56°04′,
5 tan 56°14′, 60 tan 23°19′, 9 tan 66°43′, 11 tan 4°11′.

3

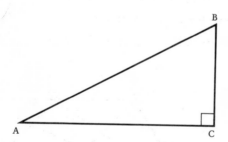

Using the diagram given above find BC in each of the following cases:

(a) ∠A = 42°, AC = 10 cm   (b) ∠A = 56°, AC = 20 cm
(c) ∠A = 60°12′, AC = 8 cm   (d) ∠A = 73°48′, AC = 7 cm
(e) ∠A = 47°33′, AC = 9 cm   (f) ∠A = 55°17′, AC = 6 cm
(g) ∠A = 23°47′, AC = 30 cm   (h) ∠A = 58°52′, AC = 4 cm
(i) ∠A = 15°40′, AC = 5 cm   (j) ∠A = 73°15′, AC = 50 cm

4 Find the log tan of each of the following angles:
56°, 78°, 34°, 65°12′, 37°42′, 62°36′, 56°44′, 7°03′, 61°34′,
16°47′, 82°37′, 54°16′, 63°51′, 49°31′, 22°07′.

5 Find:

(a) 62.4 tan 73°48'   (b) 735 tan 24°43'
(c) 9.34 tan 43°51'   (d) 14.6 tan 37°55'
(e) 24.3 tan 63°08'   (f) 6.93 tan 9°05'
(g) 88.9 tan 13°49'   (h) 4.33 tan 42°42'

6 Evaluate:

(a) $\dfrac{10}{\tan 56°}$ (b) $\dfrac{45}{\tan 47°}$ (c) $\dfrac{71}{\tan 62°}$

(d) $\dfrac{82}{\tan 27°18'}$ (e) $\dfrac{16}{\tan 50°36'}$ (f) $\dfrac{90}{\tan 16°42'}$

(g) $\dfrac{672}{\tan 56°29'}$ (h) $\dfrac{8}{\tan 41°27'}$ (i) $\dfrac{16.2}{\tan 37°44'}$

(j) $\dfrac{27.9}{\tan 68°09'}$

7

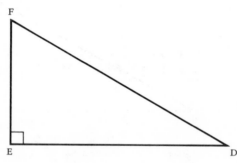

Using the diagram given above find ED in each of the following cases:

(a) ∠D = 72°, EF = 9 cm   (b) ∠D = 81°, EF = 25 cm
(c) ∠D = 52°12', EF = 52 cm   (d) ∠D = 74°48', EF = 19 cm
(e) ∠D = 31°24', EF = 14 cm   (f) ∠D = 50°35', EF = 72 cm
(g) ∠D = 45°39', EF = 53.4 cm (h) ∠D = 25°55', EF = 4.31 cm
(i) ∠D = 15°37', EF = 731 cm   (j) ∠D = 59°16', EF = 75.9 cm

8

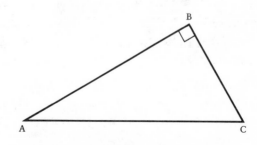

Using the diagram given at the foot of the previous page, find:

(a) BC if ∠A = 56°39′ and AB = 35 cm

(b) AB if ∠A = 43°57′ and BC = 80 cm

(c) BC if ∠C = 73°43′ and AB = 7.6 cm

(d) AB if ∠C = 27°47′ and BC = 27.3 cm

9   Find the sine of each of the following angles:

54°, 67°, 72°, 88°, 24°, 73°24′, 63°48′, 17°12′, 88°14′, 16°17′, 44°32′, 83°05′, 21°33′, 47°55′, 36°49′.

10   Evaluate each of the following:

10 sin 36°,   5 sin 64°,   8 sin 65°18′,   6 sin 72°42′,   7 sin 70°38′, 9 sin 45°53′, 30 sin 76°04′,   60 sin 27°14′,   0.8 sin 19°43′, 0.6 sin 40°39′.

 11

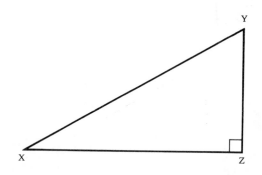

Using the diagram given above find YZ in each of the following cases:

(a) ∠X = 50°, XY = 10 cm   (b) ∠X = 72°, XY = 80 cm

(c) ∠X = 32°36′, XY = 8 cm   (d) ∠X = 52°42′, XY = 6 cm

(e) ∠X = 77°14′, XY = 50 cm   (f) ∠X = 37°20′, XY = 80 cm

(g) ∠X = 42°52′, XY = 7 cm   (h) ∠X = 7°48′, XY = 5 cm

12   Find the log sin of each of the following angles:

30°, 52°, 75°, 53°48′, 50°30′, 29°24′, 57°50′, 32°09′, 80°54′, 62°45′, 19°13′, 88°26′, 77°08′, 14°31′, 45°55′.

13   Find:

(a) 27 sin 66°   (b) 82 sin 72°

(c) 9.4 sin 72°18′   (d) 16 sin 32°48′

(e) 67 sin 44°32′   (f) 34 sin 66°32′

(g) 5.42 sin 37°45′   (h) 4.89 sin 82°14′

14 Evaluate:

(a) $\dfrac{12}{\sin 77°}$

(b) $\dfrac{8}{\sin 65°}$

(c) $\dfrac{7.2}{\sin 73°48'}$

(d) $\dfrac{65}{\sin 74°47'}$

(e) $\dfrac{9.28}{\sin 55°59'}$

(f) $\dfrac{17.6}{\sin 9°13'}$

(g) $\dfrac{67.4}{\sin 53°08'}$

(h) $\dfrac{9.98}{\sin 7°57'}$

(i) $\dfrac{18.4}{\sin 47°23'}$

(j) $\dfrac{954}{\sin 70°33'}$

15

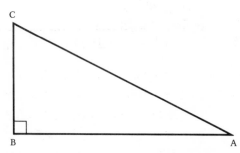

Using the diagram given above find AC if:

(a) ∠A = 76°, BC = 12 cm   (b) ∠A = 53°, BC = 73 cm

(c) ∠A = 85°24', BC = 14 cm   (d) ∠A = 64°13', BC = 6.66 cm

(e) ∠A = 52°44', BC = 3.76 cm   (f) ∠A = 32°19', BC = 5.49 cm

(g) ∠A = 79°34', BC = 57.3 cm   (h) ∠A = 15°52', BC = 72.5 cm

16

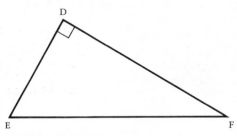

Using the diagram given above find:

(a) ED if ∠F = 67°17' and EF = 33.72 cm,

(b) DF if ∠E = 58°38' and EF = 17.83 cm,

(c) EF if ∠E = 62°32' and DF = 5.73 cm,

(d) EF if ∠F = 43°17' and DE = 9.78 cm.

17 Find the cosine of each of the following angles:
73°, 38°, 63°, 47°, 72°54', 36°36', 84°48', 16°49', 7°43', 83°06', 46°52', 67°31', 39°43', 80°04', 19°10'.

18 Evaluate each of the following:

$30 \cos 45°$, $8 \cos 57°$, $5 \cos 62°$, $7 \cos 73°18'$, $50 \cos 70°24'$, $6 \cos 44°02'$, $12 \cos 79°13'$, $0.8 \cos 45°45'$, $0.5 \cos 76°50'$, $40 \cos 52°23'$.

19

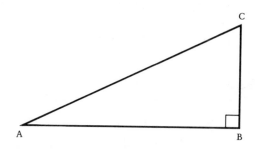

Using the diagram given above find AB if:

(a) $\angle A = 70°$, $AC = 10$ cm   (b) $\angle A = 64°$, $AC = 70$ cm
(c) $\angle A = 84°18'$, $AC = 5$ cm   (d) $\angle A = 44°48'$, $AC = 8$ cm
(e) $\angle A = 67°45'$, $AC = 70$ cm   (f) $\angle A = 76°50'$, $AC = 40$ cm
(g) $\angle A = 47°23'$, $AC = 0.4$ cm   (h) $\angle A = 72°37'$, $AC = 7$ cm

20 Find the log cos of each of the following angles:

$56°$, $82°$, $37°$, $65°24'$, $73°48'$, $63°52'$, $53°36'$, $37°08'$, $80°13'$, $39°49'$, $70°10'$, $33°46'$, $66°22'$, $78°04'$, $12°16'$.

21 Find:

(a) $13 \cos 46°$ (b) $56 \cos 72°$
(c) $2.4 \cos 58°42'$ (d) $77 \cos 80°24'$
(e) $56 \cos 66°22'$ (f) $6.2 \cos 23°44'$
(g) $89.7 \cos 80°33'$ (h) $44.8 \cos 70°32'$

22 Evaluate:

(a) $\dfrac{54}{\cos 27°}$ (b) $\dfrac{80}{\cos 78°}$ (c) $\dfrac{9.5}{\cos 73°24'}$

(d) $\dfrac{78}{\cos 67°42'}$ (e) $\dfrac{90.4}{\cos 77°36'}$ (f) $\dfrac{18.9}{\cos 78°35'}$

(g) $\dfrac{17.9}{\cos 70°33'}$ (h) $\dfrac{75.9}{\cos 49°45'}$ (i) $\dfrac{345}{\cos 78°55'}$

(j) $\dfrac{45.67}{\cos 14°37'}$

23

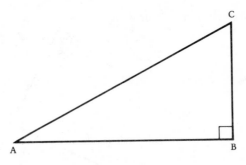

Using the diagram given above find AC if:

(a) ∠A = 86°, AB = 45 cm   (b) ∠A = 65°, AB = 37 cm

(c) ∠A = 27°54′, AB = 17 cm   (d) ∠A = 70°42′, AB = 7.9 cm

(e) ∠A = 37°23′, AB = 9.9 cm   (f) ∠A = 54°54′, AB = 88.8 cm

(g) ∠A = 64°49′, AB = 77 cm   (h) ∠A = 22°47′, AB = 764 cm

24

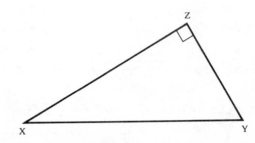

Using the diagram given above find:

(a) XZ if ∠X = 48°55′ and XY = 16.54 cm

(b) ZY if ∠Y = 39°45′ and XY = 77.25 cm

(c) XY if ∠Y = 68°47′ and ZY = 28.45 cm

(d) XY if ∠X = 54°23′ and XZ = 9.67 cm

25

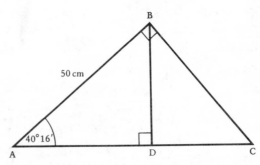

In a triangle ABC, D is the foot of the perpendicular from B to AD, ∠BAC = 40°16′, AB = 50 cm and ∠ABC = 90°. Find BD, AD and BC.

26

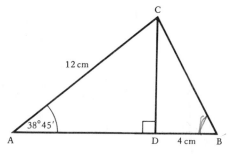

In a triangle ABC, D is the foot of the perpendicular from C to AB. If ∠CAB = 38°45′, AC = 12 cm and DB = 4 cm calculate CD, AD and ∠CBD.

27

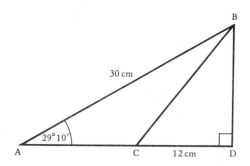

ABC is a triangle and D is the foot of the perpendicular from B to AC produced. If ∠BAC = 29°10′, AB = 30 cm and CD = 12 cm, calculate BD, AC and ∠BCD.

28

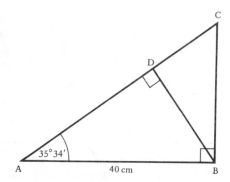

Given the above diagram where AB = 40 cm, ∠ABC = ∠ADB = 90° and ∠BAC = 35°34′. Calculate BD, AD, ∠ACB and DC.

29

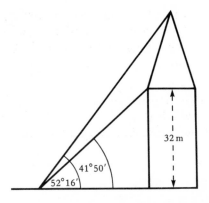

A church tower 32 metres high is surmounted by a vertical spire. From a point on the ground, in the horizontal plane through the base of the tower, the angles of elevation of the base and top of the spire are 41°50′ and 52°16′ respectively. How tall is the spire? (Neglect the width of the tower.)

30 A man walks 70 metres away from the base of a vertical building and finds that the elevation of its top is 30°47′. How high is the building? He continues his walk away from the building in the same straight line until he reaches another point from which the elevation of the top is 25°32′. How far has he walked from the foot of the building?

31

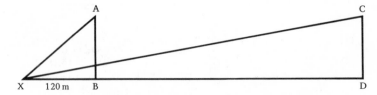

The diagram shows the two similar supporting towers of a suspension bridge. When the tops of the towers A and C are viewed from a point X, situated 120 m from the base of AB such that X, B and D are in a horizontal straight line, their angles of elevation are 39°48′ and 6°12′ respectively. Calculate the heights of the towers and the horizontal distance between them, giving your answers correct to the nearest metre.

32 The angle of depression of a boat which is directly out to sea as observed from the top of a vertical cliff 50 m high is 32°39′. Find the distance of the boat from the foot of the cliff.

33 A girl observes that the angle of depression of the base of a tree outside her window is 23°14′ and the angle of elevation of its top is 53°43′. If she sits 5 metres above ground level, find the height of the tree correct to three significant figures.

34 From the top of a building 30 metres high the angles of depression of the near side and far side of a road which runs parallel to the building, are 63°40′ and 58°50′ respectively. How wide is the road?

35 The angles of depression of the bow and stern of a ship from the bridge, which is 20 metres above the level of the deck, are 22°30′ and 13°53′ respectively. How long is the deck?

Statistics   26

1 The ninety staff in a school are divided by subject as follows: 25 teach science (including mathematics), 10 teach English, 15 teach practical subjects, 22 teach other specialist subjects including history, geography and foreign languages, and 18 are general subjects teachers. Illustrate this information in: (a) a pie chart, (b) a horizontal bar chart, (c) a histogram. (Clear labelling is essential.)

2 One hundred and eighty third form pupils have to choose one subject from an option group. 72 choose art, 8 music, 24 metal-work, 50 biology and the remainder choose history. Illustrate this information in: (a) a pie chart, (b) a horizontal bar chart, (c) a histogram.

3 Find the mean, mode and median of each of the following:
   (a) 6, 7, 4, 7, 4, 5, 4, 4, 3, 4, 5, 7.
   (b) 14, 8, 10, 10, 5, 21, 16.
   (c) 33, 37, 35, 34, 33, 36, 39, 33.

4 Find the mean, mode and median of nine successive rounds of a golfer whose scores were: 69, 70, 73, 83, 84, 69, 70, 72, 74.

5 The heights of seven boys (to the nearest centimetre) are 172, 169, 174, 165, 170, 172, 182. Calculate: (a) the mean height, (b) the median height, (c) the modal height.

6 The table shows the frequency of the number of letters occurring in the words of a sentence selected from a book.

Number of letters in a word	1	2	3	4	5	6	7	8	9
Frequency	2	4	7	2	5	2	0	3	1

(a) How many words are there in the sentence?
(b) How many letters are there in the sentence?
(c) Find the mean number of letters per word.
(d) Find the modal number of letters per word.
(e) Find the median number of letters per word.

7 The table shows the distribution of marks out of 10 obtained in a test given to the whole of the first year intake in a school.

Marks	0	1	2	3	4	5	6	7	8	9	10
Number of pupils	2	5	9	14	20	37	42	63	35	18	14

Calculate: (a) the total number of pupils sitting the test;
(b) the mode, median and mean score.

8 The number of goals scored by a First Division Football Team in twenty consecutive matches was: 0, 2, 1, 3, 6, 0, 0, 1, 2, 1, 3, 1, 1, 2, 3, 4, 1, 4, 0, 3.
Complete the table:

Score	Tally	Number
6	/	1
5		
4		
3		
2		
1		
0		

(a) Draw a histogram to illustrate this information.
(b) Find the modal score, the median score and the mean score.

9 In an archery competition the scores of the forty competitors in the first round were: 2, 3, 1, 2, 2, 3, 3, 1, 4, 3, 2, 3, 0, 4, 3, 2, 2, 1, 3, 2, 2, 3, 4, 1, 1, 3, 3, 3, 2, 4, 2, 3, 3, 2, 1, 5, 2, 4, 1, 3.

Complete the table:

Score	Tally	Number
0		
1	~~IIII~~ II	7
2		
3		
4		
5		

(a) Draw a histogram to illustate this information.

(b) Find the mode, median and mean score.

10 A die is thrown thirty-seven times and the following scores are obtained: 4, 3, 1, 6, 6, 4, 4, 2, 5, 3, 5, 4, 3, 6, 3, 4, 4, 5, 3, 3, 1, 6, 4, 1, 2, 1, 6, 4, 5, 3, 2, 6, 3, 1, 4, 6, 4.

Complete the table:

Score	Tally	Number
1	~~IIII~~	5
2		
3		
4		
5		
6		

(a) Draw a histogram to illustrate this information.

(b) Find the mode, median and mean score.

Part 2: Revision Papers 1–25

Revision Paper

1   Simplify:
    (a) $8x + 4x$,   (b) $8x - 4x$,   (c) $8x \times 4x$,
    (d) $8x \div (-2x)$.

2   Solve the equations:
    (a) $3x + 2 = 1$,   (b) $\frac{x}{3} + 2 = 1$.

3   (a)   Remove the brackets and simplify:
       (i) $(3a + 4b)(3a - 4b)$,   (ii) $(3a - 4b)^2$.
    (b)   Find the value of a when $b = -4$ given that $a = 3 - 5b$.

4   Find: $\log 73.29$, antilog $\bar{1}.5263$, $\dfrac{1}{247.3}$, $\sqrt{6.273}$, $\sin 49°05'$,
    $\log \cos 53°40'$.

5

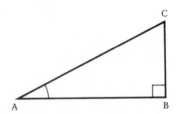

    (a)   ABC is a triangle with $\angle ABC = 90°$. Referring to angle A
state which trigonometric ratios are given by:
    (i) $\dfrac{CB}{AC}$,   (ii) $\dfrac{AB}{AC}$,   (iii) $\dfrac{CB}{AB}$.
    (b)   If, using the same diagram,
        $AC = 40$ cm and $BC = 20$ cm find: (i) $\angle CAB$, (ii) AB.

6   Find the interior angle of a regular octagon.

7   Given: $U = \{$whole numbers $\leqslant 12\}$
                $A = \{$prime numbers$\}$
                $B = \{$odd numbers$\}$
    list the elements of A, B' and $A \cap B$.

8   Find the equation of the straight line with gradient -3 which
passes through the point $(4, 1)$.

9   Factorise:
    (a) $x^2 - 6x - 27$,   (b) $x^2 - 6x$,   (c) $x(x - 6) - (x - 6)$.

10 Solve the simultaneous linear equations:

$$3x + y = 17$$
$$7x - y = 23$$

11 Construct a triangle ABC in which AB = 14 cm, AC = 12 cm and ∠BAC = 30°. Construct the perpendicular CD from C to AB. Measure and record its length.

12 Find the angles denoted by the letters a, b, c, d and e.

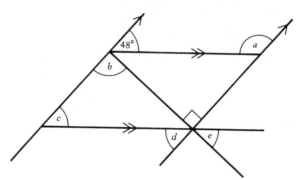

13 (a) Solve the equations:
(i) $9x^2 - 4x = 0$, (ii) $9x^2 - 4 = 0$,
(iii) $x^2 + 8x + 12 = 0$.

(b) A polygon with n sides has $\dfrac{n}{2}(n-3)$ diagonals. Find the number of sides of a polygon which has: (i) 35 diagonals, (ii) 77 diagonals.

14

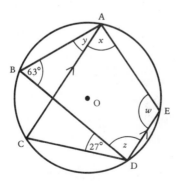

A, B, C, D and E are points on the circumference of a circle centre O such that AC is parallel to ED, ∠ABD = 63° and ∠BDC = 27°. Find the angles marked w, x, y and z. What can you deduce about the straight line BE?

15

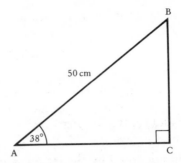

ABC is a triangle in which AB = 50 cm, ∠BAC = 38° and ∠ACB = 90°. Use trigonometric ratios to find AC and BC.

Revision Paper

2

1 Simplify:
   (a) $10a + 5a$, (b) $10a \times 5a$, (c) $10a - 5a$,
   (d) $10a \div 5a$.

2 Factorise:
   (a) $6ab + 3bc$, (b) $a(b+c) - d(b+c)$,
   (c) $x^2 - x - 6$, (d) $25a^2 - 4b^2$.

3 If x is a positive whole number calculate:
   (a) the values of x which satisfy $5x - 3 < 19$.
   (b) the maximum value of x if $4x + 3 < 24$,
   (c) the minimum value of x if $3x + 2 > 20$.

4 Remove the brackets and simplify:
   (a) $3(a + 2b) + 5(2a + b)$,
   (b) $(a + 2b)(2a + b)$,
   (c) $3(a + 2b) - 5(a - 2b)$.

5 Find: $\sqrt{27.26}$, 4.936^2, $\dfrac{1}{0.5173}$, $\cos 36°40'$.

6 Solve the equations:
   (a) $5x - 3 = 12$, (b) $\dfrac{3x+1}{2} = 8$, (c) $x^2 = \dfrac{25}{4}$.

7

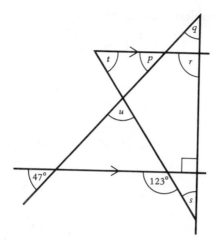

Find the angles denoted by the letters p, q, r, s, t and u.

8

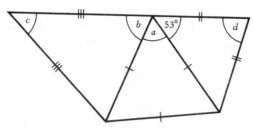

Find the angles denoted by the letters.

9

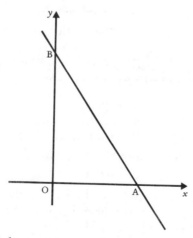

AB is a straight line with a gradient of -2, A being the point $(6, 0)$. Find:

(a) the coordinates of B,

(b) the equation of AB.

10 Solve the simultaneous equations:

$$\begin{pmatrix} 4 & -3 \\ 1 & -2 \end{pmatrix} \begin{pmatrix} x \\ y \end{pmatrix} = \begin{pmatrix} 25 \\ 10 \end{pmatrix}$$

11

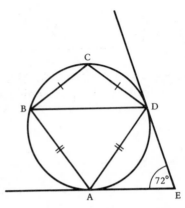

ABCD is a cyclic quadrilateral with the tangents at A and D intersecting at E. If CB = CD, AB = AD and $\angle$AED = $72°$ calculate $\angle$ADE, $\angle$ADB, $\angle$BAD, $\angle$BCD and $\angle$CBD.

12

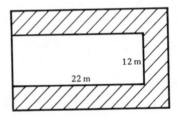

A lawn measuring 22 metres by 12 metres is surrounded on three sides by a path of width x metres as shown in the diagram. If the area of the path is $120\,m^2$ form an equation in x and solve it. What is the total perimeter of the path?

13 (a) If: $\mathcal{E}$ = {positive integers less than 15}
                     A = {multiples of 3}
                     B = {multiples of 4}

list the elements in the following sets:

$$A, \quad B, \quad A \cap B, \quad (A \cup B)'$$

(b) In a group of twenty children twelve have a pen, fourteen a pencil, but three have neither. How many children have both a pen and a pencil?

14 Draw a circle centre O with a radius of 7.5 cm and mark any diameter AB. Construct a perpendicular to AB at O to cut the circle in two points C and D. What name is given to the figure ABCD? Measure and record the length of one side of this figure.

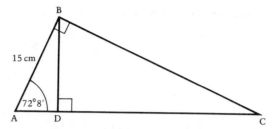

ABC is a triangle with ∠BAC = 72°8′, AB = 15 cm and ∠ABC = 90°. If D is the foot of the perpendicular from B to AC calculate:

(a) BD,   (b) AD,   (c) DC.

Revision Paper   3

1 Find the value of $x^2 + 3yz$ if:
   (a) $x = 2$, $y = \frac{1}{3}$, $z = 1$.
   (b) $x = -3$, $y = 2$, $z = -1$.

2 Factorise:
   (a) $12abc - 3bcd$,   (b) $x^2 + 7x + 6$,   (c) $4x^2 - 49$,
   (d) $9x - 18x^2$.

3 Solve the equations:

   (a) $3(x-2) - (x+4) = 1$,   (b) $\dfrac{x}{2} - \dfrac{2}{3} = 0$,   (c) $\frac{1}{2}(x+3) = 5$.

4 If:
            $\mathscr{E}$ = {positive whole numbers less than 14}
            A = {even numbers}
            B = {multiples of 3}
   List the elements of the sets:
   (a) A,   (b) B,   (c) $A \cup B$,   (d) A',   (e) $A \cap B$.

5 Find the equation of the straight line which passes through the point $(-3, 2)$ and has gradient $\frac{1}{2}$. Does the point $(2, -3)$ lie on this line?

6 Find: $\tan 72°$, $\log \cos 50°40'$, 3.926^2, $\sqrt{26}$.

7

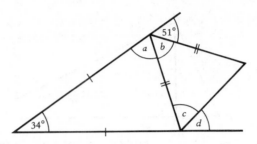

Find the angles denoted by the letters a, b, c and d.

8   If $X = \begin{pmatrix} -2 & 1 \\ 3 & 4 \end{pmatrix}$, $Y = \begin{pmatrix} 2 & 1 \\ 3 & -2 \end{pmatrix}$ and $Z = \begin{pmatrix} 0 & 2 \\ 3 & 5 \end{pmatrix}$ find:

(a) the determinant of Z,   (b) $X + Y + Z$,   (c) XY,   (d) YX.

9   (a) If $a = \begin{pmatrix} 3 \\ 2 \end{pmatrix}$, $b = \begin{pmatrix} -4 \\ 3 \end{pmatrix}$ and $c = \begin{pmatrix} 5 \\ -1 \end{pmatrix}$ find:

(i) $a + b$,   (ii) $a - 2b$,   (iii) $a + b - c$.

(b) ABC is a triangle such that A is the point $(-1, 2)$ B is the point $(4, -1)$ and $AC = \begin{pmatrix} 3 \\ 2 \end{pmatrix}$. Find:

(i) the gradient of AB,
(ii) the vector BA,
(iii) the coordinates of C.

10

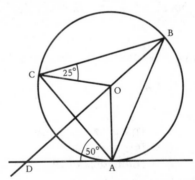

A, B and C are three points on the circumference of a circle centre O. BO produced meets the tangent to the circle at A, in D. If $\angle CAD = 50°$ and $\angle BCO = 25°$ calculate $\angle CBA$, $\angle COA$, $\angle ABO$, $\angle OAB$, and $\angle OAC$. What can you conclude about BA and BC?

11   Given the formula $A = 4\pi r^2$ change the subject to r. If $A = 154$ and $\pi = \frac{22}{7}$ find r.

12 A ladder 8 metres long rests with one end on level ground and the other at a point on a vertical wall 7 metres above the ground. Find:

(a) the angle between the ladder and the ground,

(b) the distance from the foot of the ladder to the base of the wall.

13

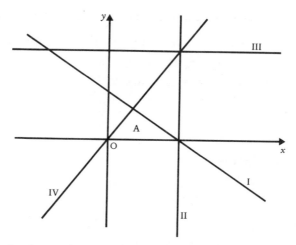

The graph shows four straight lines, labelled I, II, III and IV, whose equations are $x = 2$, $y = 4$, $y = 2x$ and $x + y = 2$.

(a) State clearly the equation of each.

(b) Shade the area which satisfies all the inequalities
$$x > 0, \quad x < 2, \quad y < 4, \quad y > 2x, \quad y > 2 - x.$$

(c) Give all the inequalities necessary to define the region A.

14

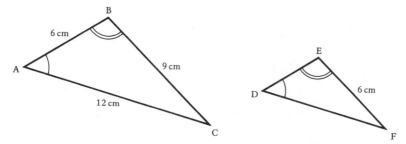

ABC, DEF are triangles with equal angles marked. AB = 6 cm, AC = 12 cm, BC = 9 cm and EF = 6 cm. Find:

(a) DE and DF,   (b) the ratio $\dfrac{\triangle ABC}{\triangle DEF}$.

103

15 The velocity (v metres per second) of a particle at different times (t seconds) from its starting time is given in the table.

t	0	1	2	3	4	5	6	7	8	9
v	70	84	93	99	102	102	98	87	64	20

Plot this data on a graph using 2 cm as unit on the t-axis and 2 cm ≡ 10 units on the v-axis.

From your graph find:

(a) the maximum velocity and the time at which it occurs,

(b) the velocity after $1\frac{1}{2}$ seconds,

(c) when the velocity is $50 \, \text{m s}^{-1}$.

Revision Paper

4

1 Find the value of $4x^2$ if:

(a) $x = 2$, (b) $x = -3$, (c) $x = -\frac{1}{2}$.

2 Express each of the following algebraically:

(a) the sum of a and b multiplied by c,

(b) the product of x and y added to their sum,

(c) the square root of the sum of the squares of c and d.

3 Find the equation of the straight line passing through the points $(5, -2)$ and $(-3, -4)$.

4 Find:

$$\cos 46°34', \quad \frac{1}{0.5216}, \quad 0.7243^2, \quad \log \tan 53°04'.$$

5 Factorise: $9a^2 - 1$, $x^2 - 3x - 10$, $ax + 3a + 3x + 9$.

6 Given that $\frac{1}{u} + \frac{1}{v} = \frac{1}{f}$ find the value of f when $u = 4$ and $v = 5$.

7 Solve the linear equations:

(a) $\dfrac{5x}{3} - 3 = 4$,

(b) $\dfrac{x-3}{2} + \dfrac{x}{7} = 3$,

(c) $2(x + 3) - 3(2x + 1) + 23 = 0$.

8 Solve the second-degree equations:

(a) $(2x - 3)(x + 7) = 0$,

(b) $8x^2 - 3x = 0$,

(c) $5x^2 + 13x - 6 = 0$.

9 If:

$$\& = \{\text{positive integers less than 14}\}$$
$$A = \{\text{multiples of 4}\}$$
$$B = \{\text{multiples of 3}\}$$

List the elements of the sets:

(a) $A \cup B$, (b) B', (c) $A' \cap B'$.

10 Solve $\begin{pmatrix} 3 & -2 \\ 7 & 3 \end{pmatrix} \begin{pmatrix} x \\ y \end{pmatrix} = \begin{pmatrix} 19 \\ 6 \end{pmatrix}$.

11 Construct a rhombus with diagonals of length 8 cm and 6 cm. Measure and record the length of a side.

12

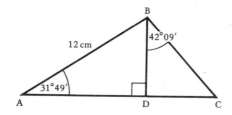

ABC is a triangle with D the foot of the perpendicular from B to AC. If $\angle BAC = 31°49'$, AB = 12 cm and $\angle DBC = 42°09'$, calculate:

(a) BD, (b) AD, (c) DC.

13 ABC is a triangle with a point X on AB and Y on AC such that XY is parallel to BC. If AX = 2 cm, XB = 3 cm and AY = 3 cm calculate:

(a) the length of CY,

(b) the ratio of the area of triangle AXY to the area of triangle ABC.

14

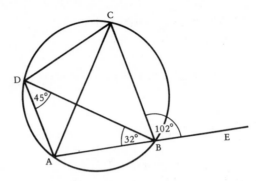

The side AB of a cyclic quadrilateral ABCD is produced to E. If $\angle CBE = 102°$, $\angle ADB = 45°$ and $ABD = 32°$ find $\angle BDC$, $\angle BCD$, $\angle BAD$ and $\angle DBC$.

15 The function f maps x onto $f(x)$ where $f(x) = 2 - 4x$. If A is the set $\{-2, 0, 2, 3\}$ onto what set is A mapped by f? Find x if it is mapped onto 26 by f.

Revision Paper   5

1 Simplify:
   (a) $5 - 2x + 3x^2 + 5x - 2x^2$.
   (b) $3(x + 2) + x(x - 5)$.

2 Factorise: (a) $8x^2 - 2x$,   (b) $16 - x^2$,   (c) $2x^2 - 5x - 3$.

3 If $a = 5 \times 10^2$ and $b = 2 \times 10^3$ write in standard form:
   (a) $a + b$,   (b) ab.

4

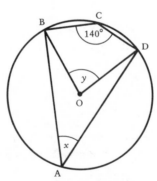

ABCD is a quadrilateral inscribed in a circle centre O. If $\angle BCD = 140°$ calculate the angles denoted by the letters x and y.

5   Given: $\&$ = {prime numbers less than 13}
            A = {prime factors of 30}
            B = {prime factors of 50}

List the sets A and B and draw a Venn diagram to illustrate them.
Find $A \cup B$ and $A \cap B$.

6   Solve the equations:

(a) $3x + 5y = 5$,
      $x - 5y = 15$.

(b) $\begin{pmatrix} 3 & 0 \\ 2 & 1 \end{pmatrix} \begin{pmatrix} x \\ y \end{pmatrix} = \begin{pmatrix} 15 \\ 7 \end{pmatrix}$.

7   If $a = \frac{1}{2}$ and $b = 2$, find the value of:

(a) $4a + b$ (b) $5ab$.

8   If $g(x) = 5x^2$ calculate:

(a) $g(2)$,   (b) $g(-3)$,   (c) $g(2x)$,   (d) $g(2x-1)$.

9   If $\mathbf{a} = \begin{pmatrix} 3 \\ 2 \end{pmatrix}$ and $\mathbf{b} = \begin{pmatrix} 2 \\ -3 \end{pmatrix}$ find:

(a) $\mathbf{a} + 2\mathbf{b}$,   (b) $3\mathbf{a} - \mathbf{b}$.

10   Given that $A = \begin{pmatrix} 2 & 1 \\ 4 & -3 \end{pmatrix}$, $B = \begin{pmatrix} 1 & 0 \\ 0 & 2 \end{pmatrix}$ and $C = \begin{pmatrix} 3 & -1 \\ 4 & 2 \end{pmatrix}$
calculate:

(a) $A + B$,   (b) $B + 2C$,   (c) A^2,   (d) A^{-1}.

11

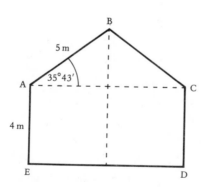

The diagram shows the cross-section through a shed. $AB = BC$
= 5 metres, $AE = CD = 4$ metres and $\angle BAC = 35°43'$. Calculate:

(a) AC,   (b) the height of the ridge B above the ground.

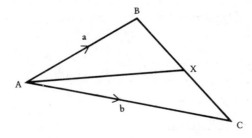

12

ABC is a triangle with **AB** = **a**, **AC** = **b** and X the midpoint of BC. Find, in terms of **a** and **b**:

(a) **XB**,   (b) **AX**.

13 Solve the equations:

(a) $\dfrac{x}{7} - 2 = 5$,   (b) $3(x - 2) - 2(x + 2) = 9$.

14 Find the equation of the straight line passing through the points $(5, 6)$ and $(-3, -4)$.

15

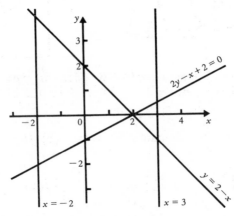

The diagram shows four straight lines with equations $y = 2 - x$, $2y - x + 2 = 0$, $x = 3$ and $x = -2$.

(a) Shade the area thus //////////, which satisfies all the inequalities:

$$x < 3, \quad y > 2 - x, \quad y < \tfrac{1}{2}x - 1.$$

(b) Shade the area thus \\\\\\\\\\\\, which satisfies all the inequalities:

$$x > -2, \quad y < 2 - x, \quad x < 0, \quad y > 0.$$

Revision Paper

1   Given $s = ut + \frac{1}{2}at^2$ calculate:
    (a) s when $u = 5$, $t = 4$ and $a = 9.8$,
    (b) a when $s = 550$, $u = 6$ and $t = 10$.

2   Solve the equations:
    (a) $\dfrac{5x - 2}{3} = 6$,   (b) $5(x - 2) + 2(x + 3) = 3$.

3   Find:

    0.573^2, $\dfrac{1}{347.2}$, $\sqrt{92.67}$, $\cos 57°26'$, antilog $\bar{1}.4972$,
    $\log \tan 32°15'$.

4   On the given Venn diagrams, shade the areas representing:
    (a) B',   (b) $(A \cap B) \cup C$.

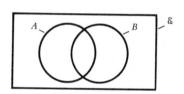
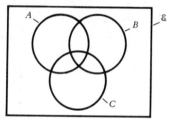

5   Construct a trapezium ABCD with AB parallel to DC such that
    AB = 12 cm, AD = 7 cm, DC = 5 cm and $\angle DAB = 60°$. Measure
    and record the length of BC.

6   If $f(x) = \dfrac{1}{2x^2}$ calculate: (a) $f(\frac{1}{2})$, (b) $f(-3)$.

7   If $\mathbf{a} = \begin{pmatrix} 4 \\ 2 \end{pmatrix}$, $\mathbf{b} = \begin{pmatrix} 3 \\ -1 \end{pmatrix}$ and $\mathbf{c} = \begin{pmatrix} -2 \\ 4 \end{pmatrix}$ find:

    (a) $\mathbf{a} + \mathbf{b} + \mathbf{c}$,   (b) $3\mathbf{a} + 2\mathbf{b} - \mathbf{c}$,   (c) $\mathbf{x}$ if $\mathbf{a} + \mathbf{x} = \frac{1}{2}(\mathbf{b} - \mathbf{c})$.

8   (a) Multiply $3x^2 - 4x + 1$ by $2x - 5$.
    (b) Divide $6x^3 + 23x^2 + 18x - 5$ by $2x + 5$.

9   Solve the simultaneous equations: $2x + y = 9$,
                                          $x - y = 6$.

10 An open rectangular tank has a base measuring 15 cm by 12 cm
    and is 8 cm deep. Calculate the longest stick (of negligible thick-
    ness) which will fit diagonally into the tank. Give your answer
    correct to three significant figures.

11 Rearrange the equation $5x - 2y + 9 = 0$ in the form $y = mx + c$. Write down the values of m and c.

12 N is a positive whole number such that when added to its square the answer is 56. Find N.

13 Express $\dfrac{5x + 2y}{3} - \dfrac{2x + 4y}{5}$ as a single fraction in its lowest terms.

14

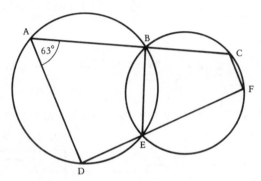

The diagram shows two circles which intersect at B and E. ABC and DEF are straight lines and $\angle BAD = 63°$. Calculate:

(a) $\angle BED$,   (b) $\angle BCF$.

15

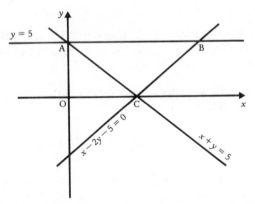

The diagram shows the graphs of the straight lines $x + y = 5$, $x - 2y - 5 = 0$ and $y = 5$.

(a) Find the coordinates of A, B and C.

(b) For the line $x - 2y - 5 = 0$ find the value of y when $x = 2$.

(c) Shade the area which satisfies all the inequalities
$$x > 0, \quad x + y < 5 \quad \text{and} \quad x - 2y > 5.$$

Revision Paper

7

1. If $5x = 2y$ find $x : y$.

2. Simplify $\dfrac{4x - 3}{2} - \dfrac{x}{3}$.

3. Factorise:
   (a) $x^2 - x - 20$, (b) $12x^2 - 7x$, (c) $x^2 - 7x - 18$.

4.

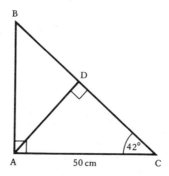

ABC is a triangle in which $\angle BAC = 90°$ and D is the foot of the perpendicular from A to BC. If $\angle BCA = 42°$ and $AC = 50\,\text{cm}$ use trigonometry to find:

(a) DC, (b) AD, (c) AB.

5. A boy has £2.26 in 50p, 10p and 2p coins. He has two fewer 50p coins than 10p coins, and 8 more 2p coins than 10p coins. How many of each did he have?

6. Find the largest possible positive integer which satisfies the inequality $2(10 - x) > x + 3$.

7. (a) Evaluate the determinant $\begin{vmatrix} 5 & 6 \\ -5 & 4 \end{vmatrix}$.

   (b) If $A = \begin{pmatrix} -4 & 2 \\ 3 & -6 \end{pmatrix}$ and $B = \begin{pmatrix} 2 & 2 \\ 4 & 1 \end{pmatrix}$ find:

   (i) $A - B$, (ii) AB, (iii) BA, (iv) B^2.

8. Find the interior angle of a regular polygon with fifteen sides.

9. Using ruler and compasses only, construct a quadrilateral ABCD in which $AD = 12\,\text{cm}$, $AB = 7\,\text{cm}$, $BC = 5\,\text{cm}$, $AC = 10\,\text{cm}$ and $\angle BAD = 60°$. Measure and record the length of CD. Find the point which is equidistant from A, B and D using a constructional method. How far is this point from C?

10

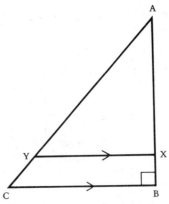

X and Y are points on the sides AB and AC of a triangle ABC such that XY is parallel to BC. AX = 4 cm, AB = 5 cm, AY = 5 cm and ∠ABC = 90°. Calculate:

(a) YC, (b) XY, (c) BC, (d) $\dfrac{\triangle AYX}{\triangle BYX}$.

11

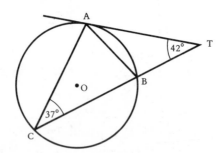

TA is a tangent and TBC a secant, to a circle centre O. If ∠ATB = 42° and ∠ACB = 37° find:

(a) ∠TAB, (b) ∠CAT, (c) ∠CAB, (d) ∠ABC.

12 Solve the equations:

$$\begin{pmatrix} 5 & -2 \\ 4 & 3 \end{pmatrix}\begin{pmatrix} x \\ y \end{pmatrix} = \begin{pmatrix} 27 \\ -6 \end{pmatrix}$$

13 Plot the points A, B, C and D on a graph given that $\mathbf{AB} = \begin{pmatrix} 2 \\ 3 \end{pmatrix}$, $\mathbf{DC} = \begin{pmatrix} 6 \\ 9 \end{pmatrix}$, A is the point (1, 4) and D the point (3, 0). Hence find:

(a) the coordinates of B,

(b) the vector **CB**,

(c) the vector **AC**.

(d) what kind of quadrilateral is ABCD?

14   & = {the letters of the alphabet which appear in the word
        DISTANCE}

    A = {the letters in the word ADIDAS}

    B = {the letters in the word SAINT}

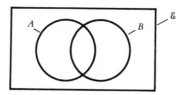

Place each of these letters in the correct space in the given Venn diagram and write down the letters belonging to the following sets:

(a) $A \cap B$,   (b) A',   (c) $(A \cup B)'$.

15

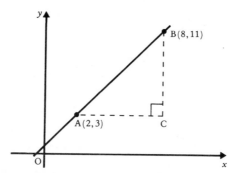

The points $A(2, 3)$, $B(8, 1)$ and C are shown in the diagram, AC and BC being parallel to the x and y axes respectively. Calculate:

(a) the coordinates of C,   (b) the slope of AB,

(c) the length of AB,   (d) the equation of the line AB.

Revision Paper   8

1   Find the value of $(2a - 3b)^2$ when:

    (a) $a = 4$, $b = 1$.

    (b) $a = 2$, $b = 3$.

    (c) $a = -2$, $b = -3$.

2   (a) Multiply $5x^2 - 3x - 4$ by $3x + 4$.

    (b) Divide $8 + 6x - 29x^2 + 15x^3$ by $4 - 3x$.

3 (a)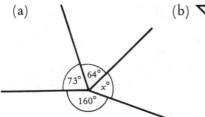

Find x.

(b)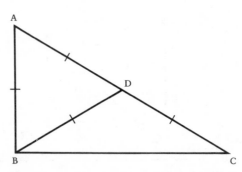

Find y.

4 Express the following algebraically:
(a) c is added to the product of a^2 and b^2,
(b) the square of b is subtracted from the sum of a and c.

5

ABC is a triangle with D a point on AC such that AB = AD = BD = DC. Find the value of $\angle ABD$, $\angle BDC$, $\angle DCB$ and $\angle ABC$.

6 (a) Remove the brackets and simplify:
(i) $3(x-2)$, (ii) $5(a+3)+2(a-6)$, (iii) $(5x+2)(3-4x)$
(b) Simplify $\dfrac{x-2}{5}+\dfrac{2x-3}{3}$.

7 Find the equation of the straight line passing through the points $(-3, -2)$ and $(4, 3)$.

8 (a) Solve the equations:
(i) $\dfrac{6x-5}{2} = 7$, (ii) $\dfrac{(x-1)}{2} - \dfrac{(x+3)}{3} = 2$.
(b) If $x = 4$ is a solution of the equation $3x = 2(a-4)$ find the value of a.

114

9 Copy and complete the following tables:

x	-4	0	1
$y = \frac{1}{2}(x+2)$			1.5

x	0	1	4
$y = 2(3-x)$	6		

Using 2 cm as unit on each axis draw the graphs of $y = \frac{1}{2}(x+2)$ and $y = 2(3-x)$ on the same axes.

Use your graph to solve the simultaneous equations

$$x - 2y + 2 = 0$$
$$2x + y - 6 = 0$$

10 Construct a triangle ABC such that $\angle ABC = 90°$ and $\tan A = \frac{4}{7}$. Measure and record the value of angle A. Without using tables, find the value of:

(a) $\sin^2 A$,   (b) $2 \sin A \cos A$.

(Leave your answer in fractions.)

11 Find the image of each of the points $A(2,1)$, $B(3,2)$ and $C(4,1)$ when transformed using the matrix $\begin{pmatrix} 1 & 0 \\ 0 & -1 \end{pmatrix}$. Plot these on a diagram and deduce the effect of the transformation matrix.

Find the point D which transforms into the point D′ with coordinates $(-3,-4)$. Plot D and D′ on the diagram indicating clearly which is which.

12

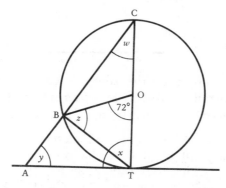

AT is a tangent, CT a diameter, and ABC a secant to a circle centre O. If $\angle BOT = 72°$ calculate the angles denoted by the letters w, x, y and z.

115

13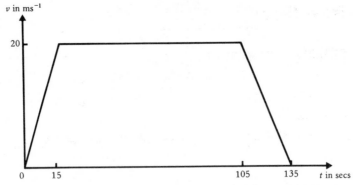

The diagram shows a velocity–time graph for a car which starts from rest, accelerates to 20 metres per second in 15 seconds, travels at uniform speed for $1\frac{1}{2}$ minutes, and finally comes to rest with a constant retardation over a further 30 seconds.

Use the graph to find:

(a) the maximum speed attained,

(b) the initial acceleration in m s^{-2},

(c) the retardation in m s^{-2},

(d) the distance travelled when moving at uniform speed,

(e) the total distance travelled.

14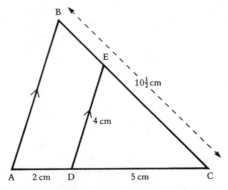

D and E are points on the sides CA, CB of a triangle ABC such that ED is parallel to BA. If CD = 5 cm, DA = 2 cm, CB = $10\frac{1}{2}$ cm and ED = 4 cm use similar triangles to find CE and AB.

15 From a house A a man walks 80 metres in a direction N75°E (075°) to a point B. At B he changes direction and walks 140 metres to C which is in a direction N27°W (333°). From C he walks 120 metres in a direction S32°W (212°) to D. Draw a scale diagram to represent his route taking 1 cm = 10 metres. Use your diagram to find the distance and direction of A from D.

Revision Paper

9

1 Simplify:
   (a) $9a - 3a$,   (b) $9a \times 3a$,   (c) $9a \div 3a$,
   (d) $(9a^2)^2 \div 27a^3$.

2 Factorise:
   (a) $x^2 + 14x + 45$,   (b) $9a^2 - b^2$,   (c) $a^3 - 2a^2 + a - 2$.

3 Find:

   $\cos 73°40'$, $\sin 37°04'$, $\dfrac{1}{3040}$, 0.6723^2, $\sqrt{726.4}$.

4 (a)   (b)

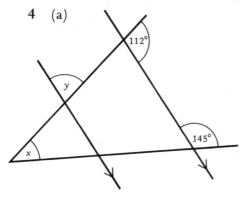
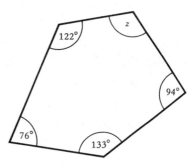

   Find x and y.   Find z.

5 Find x, y and z if:

$$x - 3 = 2$$
$$x + y = 7$$
$$x + 2y + z = 3$$

6

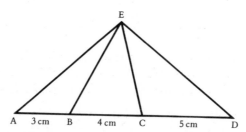

A, B, C and D are four points in a straight line such that
AB = 3 cm, BC = 4 cm and CD = 5 cm. E is a point above the
line which is joined to each of the points A, B, C and D. If the
area of triangle EBC is 10 cm², find the area of each of the
triangles ABE, ECD and AED.

117

7 Solve the equations:

(a) $9x - 3x + x - 7 = 30,$

(b) $\dfrac{3x - 2}{7} = \dfrac{2}{5},$

(c) $5(2x + 1) + 3(x - 7) = 5.$

8 If $X = \begin{pmatrix} -4 & 2 \\ 5 & -3 \end{pmatrix}$, $Y = \begin{pmatrix} 5 & 3 \\ 2 & -4 \end{pmatrix}$ and I is the 2×2 unit matrix find:

(a) $2X + I,$ (b) $2Y - 3X,$ (c) $X + I + Y,$ (d) $YX,$

(e) $XY.$

9 (a) If $7a = 13b$ find the ratio of a to b.

(b) Sally has £x, Alison twice as much as Sally, and Elizabeth twice as much as Sally and Alison together. If they have £54 between them how much does each have?

10 Construct a regular octagon ABCDEFGH whose vertices lie on a circle of radius 7 cm. Measure and record the length of a side of this octagon.

11 A field is bounded by four straight hedges. From one corner A the distances and bearings of the other three corners B, C and D are respectively 65 metres S64°E (116°), 120 metres N46°E (046°) and 80 metres N24°W (336°).

Draw a scale diagram to represent this field using 1 cm = 10 metres. From your diagram determine:

(a) the distance between B and D,

(b) the direction of C from D.

12

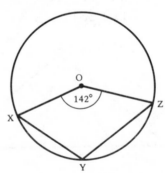

X, Y and Z are three points on a circle centre O such that $\angle XOZ = 142°$. Find $\angle XYZ$.

13 Solve the equation $\dfrac{x + 1}{2} - \dfrac{x + 3}{5} = 6\frac{2}{5}.$

14

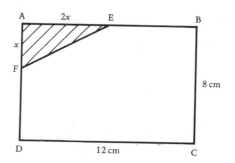

From a rectangle ABCD measuring 12 cm by 8 cm a triangular corner-piece AEF is removed.

AF = x cm and AE = $2x$ cm. If the remaining area is 60 cm² form an equation in x and solve it.

What is the area of the triangular piece which has been removed?

15 A farmer uses 140 metres of fencing to form a rectangular enclosure. When the length of the rectangle is x metres the area (A) enclosed is $x(70-x)$ square metres. Complete the following table which gives the area for given values of x.

x	0	10	20	30	35	40	50	60	70
$A = x(70-x)$	0	600	1000		1225	1200	1000		0

Taking 2 cm = 10 units on the x-axis and 2 cm = 100 units on the A-axis plot a graph which shows the relationship between x and A.

From your graph determine:

(a) the maximum area which may be enclosed,

(b) the area enclosed when $x = 18$,

(c) the value of x when $A = 500$.

Revision Paper

10

1 Solve the equations:

(a) $\dfrac{3x-7}{2} = 4$,

(b) $\dfrac{5(2x-3)}{11} - \dfrac{2(x-4)}{3} = 3$,

(c) $\frac{1}{2}(3x-4) - \frac{1}{3}(2x+7) = 4$.

2 Factorise:
   (a) $x^2 - 13x - 30$,   (b) $2x^2 + 15x + 7$,   (c) $6x^2 + 7x + 2$.

3 Solve the equations:
   (a) $(x - 3)(x + 7) = 0$,
   (b) $(2x + 1)(x + 7) = 0$,
   (c) $8x - x^2 = 0$.

4

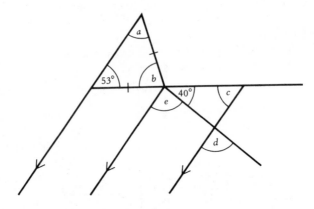

   Find the angles denoted by the letters a, b, c, d and e.

5 Construct a rectangle ABCD, using ruler and compasses only, such that AB = 12 cm and BC = 8 cm. Measure and record the length of DB.

6 If $A = \begin{pmatrix} 5 & -2 \\ 3 & 4 \end{pmatrix}$ and $B = \begin{pmatrix} 6 & 5 \\ -2 & 5 \end{pmatrix}$ find:
   (a) $3A$,   (b) $3A + B$,   (c) $A - I$,   (d) AB.
   (I is the 2 × 2 unit matrix.)

7 Find the equation of the straight line with gradient $-\frac{1}{3}$ which passes through the point $(5, -2)$.

8 (a) Multiply $2a + 3$ by $3a^2 - 4a + 1$.
   (b) Divide $10 - 7x + 13x^2 - 6x^3$ by $2 - x$.

9 A function f is defined by $f(x) = 5x - 2$ and a function g is defined by $g(x) = \dfrac{2}{x^2}$.

   Find: $f(2)$, $g(-3)$, $f[g(2)]$, $g(1)$.

10

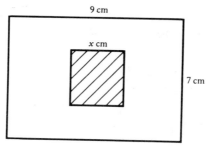

A rectangular sheet of metal measuring 9 cm by 7 cm has a square hole, of side x cm, removed from its centre. If the area remaining is 47 cm² find x.

11

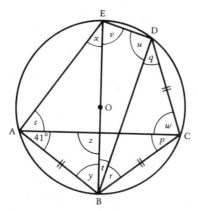

ABCDE is a pentagon inscribed in a circle centre O with AB = BC = CD. If EB is a diameter and $\angle BAC = 41°$ find, without giving reasons, the angles denoted by the letters $p, q, r, s, t, u, v, w, x, y$ and z.

12

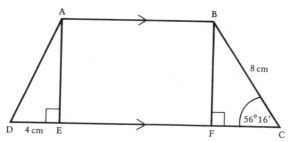

ABCD is a trapezium with AB parallel to DC, and E and F the respective perpendiculars from A and B to DC. If $\angle BCD = 56°16'$, BC = 8 cm and DE = 4 cm. Calculate:

(a) BF,   (b) FC,   (c) $\angle ADE$,   (d) AD.

121

13

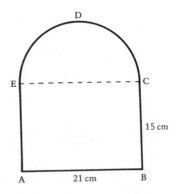

The diagram represents the cross-section of a metal bar 2 metres long. It shows a rectangle, measuring 21 cm by 15 cm surmounted by a semi-circle. Calculate:

(a) the area of cross-section in cm²,

(b) the volume of the bar in m³,

(c) the mass of the bar if 1 m³ of the metal has a mass of 1020 kilograms.

(Take $\pi = \frac{22}{7}$.)

14 On Monday a greengrocer buys 3 boxes of apples, 2 of bananas and 3 of oranges. On Wednesday he buys 5 of apples, 3 of bananas and 3 of oranges, and on Friday 7 of apples, 4 of bananas and 6 of oranges. The cost price of the fruit per box is: apples £8, bananas £9 and oranges £12.

Give this data in matrix form, and multiply the two matrices together to give the total cost price per day. Put a ring around the number which gives the cost price for Wednesday.

15 The following equations represent four straight lines:

$$2y = 3x + 1 \qquad \text{(i)}$$
$$y = 4 - x \qquad \text{(ii)}$$
$$3y + 3x = 7 \qquad \text{(iii)}$$
$$x - 3y = 0 \qquad \text{(iv)}$$

Which two of these lines are parallel?

Which line passes through the origin?

Find the coordinates of the points where the line which passes through the origin intersects each of the two parallel lines.

Revision Paper

1   Find the value of $(a-2b)^2+c^2$ when:
    (a) $a=1$, $b=2$, $c=3$,
    (b) $a=3$, $b=2$, $c=-1$.

2   (a) If $5x=9y$ find the ratio of x to y.

    (b) If $\frac{3}{4}=\frac{6}{x}$ find x.

    (c) Given $\dfrac{x+7}{3}=\dfrac{2x+1}{5}$ find x.

3   Construct, using ruler and compasses only, a triangle ABC in which $\angle ABC = 60°$, AB $= 12$ cm and BC $= 8$ cm. Measure and record the length of AC.

    Construct the inscribed circle to this triangle. Measure and record its radius.

4   Remove the brackets and simplify:
    (a) $3(2a-b)-4(a+2b)$,
    (b) $(2a-b)(a+2b)$,
    (c) $(2a-b)^2$.

5   Factorise:
    (a) $ax+2ay-2bx-4by$,
    (b) a^2+4a+4,
    (c) $2a^2-9a-18$.

6   (a) Use the table of squares to find 5.062^2.
    (b) Use square root tables to find $\sqrt{78.24}$.
    (c) Use the theorem of Pythagoras together with suitable tables to find AB in the given right-angled triangle ABC. Give your answer correct to three significant figures.

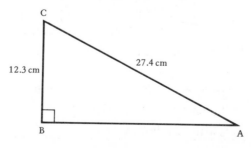

7

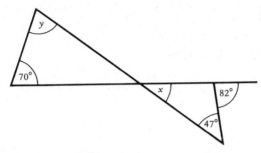

Find the angles denoted by the letters x and y.

8

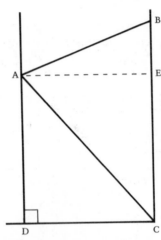

A boy looks out from his bedroom window at a building on the other side of the street. He observes that the angle of elevation of the top of the building opposite is $43°14'$ and the angle of depression of its bottom is $57°36'$. If the street is level and 30 metres wide find:

(a) the height of the boy above street level,

(b) the height of the building opposite.

9 The mass of a rat at different ages is given in the following table.

Age (A) in days	10	20	40	60	80	100	120	140
Mass (m) in gms	20	40	90	170	300	350	380	395

Draw a graph to represent these data and use it to estimate:

(a) when the rat has a mass of 200g,

(b) its mass after 90 days.

10 A girl has twenty coins in her purse with a total value of £1.04. If there are x 10p coins, three more 5p coins than there are 10p's, and the remainder are 2p coins, form an equation in x and solve it to find how many of each there are.

11 Given $a = x + y$ and $b = x - y$, find:
(a) $a + b$,   (b) $a^2 + b^2$,   (c) $a^2 + 2ab + b^2$.

12

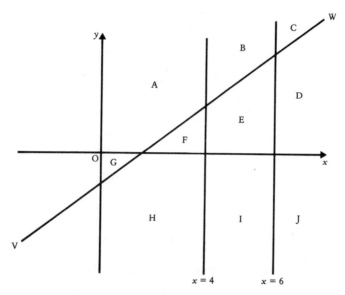

The straight line VW has equation $y = 2x - 5$ and intersects the lines $x = 4$ and $x = 6$ as shown. The letters A, B, C, D, E, F, G, H, I and J represent regions of the graph for $x > 0$.

(a) Which of these regions are defined by:
    (i) $y > 0$, $y < 2x - 5$, $x > 4$,
    (ii) $x > 4$, $x < 6$, $y > 2x - 5$.

(b) Using inequalities define the regions:
    (i) E + F + D,   (ii) B.

13

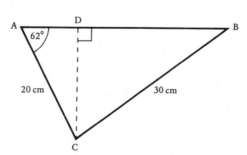

125

The diagram represents the cross-section through an animal feeding trough of length 6 metres. The plank AC is 20 cm wide and slopes at 62° to the horizontal and the plank CB is 30 cm wide. Find:

(a) the depth (DC) of the trough,

(b) the angle between CB and the horizontal,

(c) the width AB,

(d) the volume of liquid it will hold in metres³ correct to three significant figures.

14

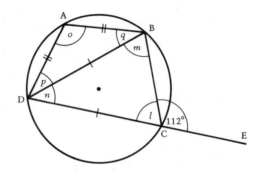

The side DC of a cyclic quadrilateral ABCD is produced to E. If AB = AD, BD = CD and ∠BCE = 112° calculate the angles marked l, m, n, o, p and q.

15 Complete the following tables which give:

(a) the value of x^2 for given values of x,

(b) the value of $2x + 9$ for given values of x.

x	-4	-3	-2	-1	0	1	2	3	4
x^2	16		4	1	0	1		9	16

x	-2	0	3
$2x + 9$	5	9	

Use these data to plot the graphs of $y = x^2$ and $y = 2x + 9$ for values of x between -4 and 4. Use 2 cm ≡ unit on the x-axis and 2 cm ≡ 2 units on the y-axis.

Write down the values of x at the points of intersection of the graphs. What equation are these the roots of?

Revision Paper

12

1 Factorise:
   (a) $3x^2 - 27$,
   (b) $x^2 - 11x + 30$,
   (c) $2x^2 + 13x - 7$.

2 Solve the equations:
   (a) $\dfrac{x-5}{3} = 6$
   (b) $4(3x - 1) - 2(5x + 4) = 3$,
   (c) $\dfrac{x}{5} - \dfrac{x}{6} = \dfrac{1}{2}$.

3 Simplify:
   (a) $\dfrac{x-2}{3} - \dfrac{x+7}{4}$,
   (b) $5(3a - 2b) + 3(a - 4b)$,
   (c) $(5a^2b)^3 \div (2ab^3)^2$.

4 (a) Find the interior angle of a regular polygon with 20 sides.
   (b) Find the equation of the straight line through the origin which has gradient $-\frac{2}{3}$.

5

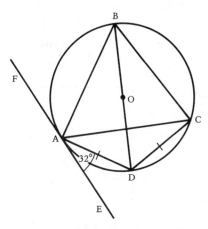

ABCD is a cyclic quadrilateral with AD = DC. The diagonal BD passes through the centre of the circle and the tangent FAE at A is such that $\angle DAE = 32°$.

Find $\angle ABD$, $\angle BCD$, $\angle CAD$, $\angle DBC$, $\angle BAD$ and $\angle BAF$.

127

6 If $A = \begin{pmatrix} 4 & -5 \\ 2 & 3 \end{pmatrix}$ find the determinant of A and hence find its inverse.

Use this inverse to solve:

$$\begin{pmatrix} 4 & -5 \\ 2 & 3 \end{pmatrix}\begin{pmatrix} x \\ y \end{pmatrix} = \begin{pmatrix} 21 \\ 5 \end{pmatrix}$$

7 Solve the equations:
   (a) $(2x + 7)(x - 4) = 0$,
   (b) $x^2 - x - 6 = 0$,
   (c) $\frac{1}{4}x^2 = 9$.

8 Find $\log 527.6$, antilog $\bar{2}.3725$, $\tan 50°13$, 0.9261^2.

9

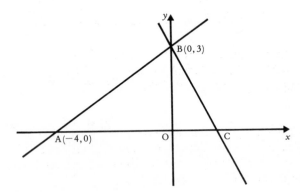

The diagram shows two straight lines AB and BC. The equation of the line BC is $3x + 2y = 6$ and A is the point $(-4, 0)$. Find:
   (a) the coordinates of C,
   (b) the gradient of AB,
   (c) the equation of AB,
   (d) the area of triangle ABC.

10

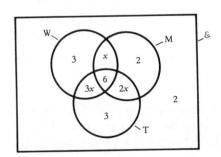

The Venn diagram shows the number of boys in a class of 34 who study one or more or none of the subjects Woodwork (W), Metalwork (M) and Technical Drawing (T). Form an equation in x and solve it.

How many boys:

(a) study just one of these subjects?

(b) do not study Woodwork?

(c) study Metalwork and Technical Drawing?

11

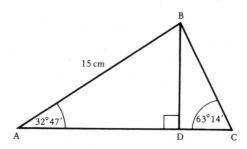

ABC is a triangle with D the foot of the perpendicular from B to AC. If AB = 15 cm, $\angle BAC = 32°47'$ and $\angle BCA = 63°14'$ calculate: (a) BD, (b) AD, (c) DC.

12 A packaging manufacturer produces rectangular cardboard boxes of varying depths but always with the sides in the same proportions. The area of cardboard used for boxes of different depths is given in the table.

Depth of box (D) in cm	10	15	20	25	30	35	40
Area of card- board (A) in m²	0.09	0.20	0.36	0.56	0.81	1.10	1.44

Taking 6 cm ≡ 10 units on the horizontal D-axis and 10 cm as unit on the vertical A-axis draw a graph to represent these data and use it to find:

(a) the depth of the box made from 1 m² of cardboard,

(b) the area of cardboard used to make a box with a depth of 22 cm.

13 Construct a parallelogram ABCD in which the diagonals AC and BD have lengths 10.2 cm and 8.2 cm respectively, and $\angle BEC = 45°$; E being the point of intersection of the diagonals.

14

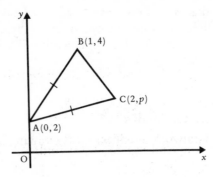

ABC is an isosceles triangle with AB = AC. A has coordinates $(0, 2)$, $B(1, 4)$ and $C(2, p)$. Find:

(a) the y coordinate of C,

(b) the gradient (m_1) of AB,

(c) the gradient (m_2) of AC,

(d) the value of $\dfrac{m_1 - m_2}{1 + m_1 m_2}$,

(e) the angle whose tangent has the value of the answer to (d).

(f) how does this angle compare with $\angle$BAC?

15

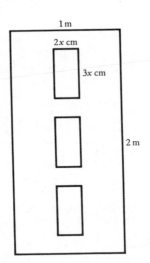

A DIY enthusiast wishes to fit three identical glass panels in a door 2 metres high and 1 metre wide. Each panel is $2x$ cm wide and one-and-a-half times as long. If the total area to be glazed is one quarter the area of the door, form an equation in x and solve it. Give your answer correct to the nearest whole number.

Revision Paper **13**

1 Given that $\dfrac{42 \times 8}{56} = 6$ find, without using tables:

    (a) $\dfrac{4.2 \times 0.8}{56}$,   (b) $42 \times 8 - 56 \times 6$.

2 Given $v = u + at$ and $v^2 = u^2 + 2as$ find:
    (a) v when $u = 12$, $a = 9.8$, $t = 5$,
    (b) v when $u = 8$, $a = 5$, $s = 8$,
    (c) s when $u = 12$, $v = 20$, $a = 64$.

3 (a) Solve the equations:
        (i) $x^2 - 4x - 21 = 0$,   (ii) $x(x-6) = 5(x-6)$.
    (b) If $x = 3$ is one solution of the equation $x^2 - 5x + a = 0$ find
    the value of a. Use this value of a to solve the equation
    completely.

4 Simplify:

    (a) $\dfrac{2(a-3b)}{3} - \dfrac{3(a+2b)}{5}$,   (b) $\dfrac{3}{a+b} - \dfrac{2}{a-b}$.

5 Factorise:
    (a) $2x + y - 2xz - yz$,   (b) $4x^2 - x$,   (c) $2x^2 - 5x - 3$.

6 Find: $\sqrt{39.26}$, 17.53^2, $\dfrac{1}{49.43}$, antilog 2.6174, log tan $56°27'$,
    cos $51°32'$.

7 Rearrange the formula

$$\frac{1}{R} = \frac{1}{R_1} + \frac{1}{R_2}$$

    to make R_1 the subject. Hence find R_1 if $R = 2$ and $R_2 = 3$.

8 Solve the equation $\dfrac{1}{x+1} + \dfrac{1}{x+2} = \dfrac{2}{x+3}$.

9 A housewife buys 3 lb of potatoes at x pence per lb and 2 lb of
    carrots at y pence per lb. How much change does she receive
    from a £5 note? Give your answer: (a) in pence, (b) in pounds.

10 Construct a triangle ABC in which AB = 14 cm, AC = 11.5 cm
    and BC = 9.5 cm. Construct the circumcircle to this triangle.
    Measure and record its radius.

11

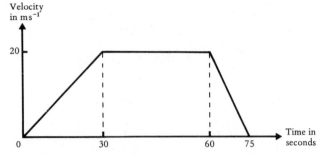

The diagram shows the velocity of a particle over a period of 75 seconds. Use this velocity–time graph to find:

(a) the initial acceleration,

(b) the distance travelled when moving at constant velocity,

(c) the total distance covered.

12

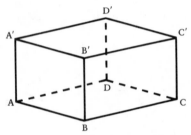

The diagram represents a rectangular shaped lounge which is 5 metres long, 3.5 metres wide and 2.8 metres high. Find the length of the diagonal AC and hence find the length of AC'.

13

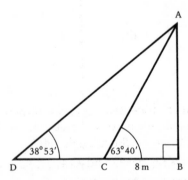

AB represents a flagpole. B, C and D are points on level ground such that ∠ACB = 63°40′ and ∠ADB = 38°53′. If CB = 8 metres, calculate, as accurately as your tables allow:

(a) the height AB of the flagpole,

(b) the distance of D from the foot of the flagpole.

132

14

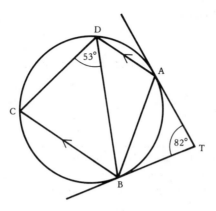

ABCD is a cyclic quadrilateral with AD parallel to BC and with the tangents at A and B intersecting at T. If ∠ATB = 82° and ∠BDC = 53° calculate each of the angles ∠BAT, ∠ADB, ∠DBC, ∠BCD, ∠BAD and ∠DBT.

15

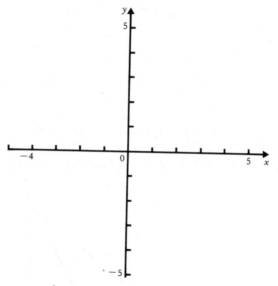

On graph paper draw two axes as shown and mark the scales 2 cm ≡ 1 unit on each axis. Mark the points A(1, 4), B(5, 0) and C(−1, −2). Draw the triangle ABC.

Mark the points D(0, −1) and E(4, 3). Join DE.

Mark the points F(−3, 2) and G(3, 0). Join FG.

Let DE and FG intersect at H. Write down the coordinates of H.

With centre H and radius HA draw a circle. Measure and record its radius. How would you describe this circle?

Revision Paper 14

1 (a) Write the next two terms in the series $1, \dfrac{a}{2}, \dfrac{a^2}{3}, \dfrac{a^3}{4}, \ldots$

   (b) Express $\dfrac{4x-3}{6} - \dfrac{2x+5}{5}$ as a single fraction in its lowest terms.

2 Remove the brackets and simplify:
   (a) $5(x+2y) - 2(x-2y)$,
   (b) $(5x+2y)^2$,
   (c) $(5x+2y)(5x-2y)$.

3 (a) Solve the equations:
     (i) $7x^2 - 3x = 0$,   (ii) $(7x+3)(2x-5) = 0$.
   (b) By multiplying out the brackets, collecting terms and factorising, solve the equation $2(x^2-4) = (x-4)(x-2)$.

4 Rearrange the equation $5x + 2y - 4 = 0$ in the form $y = mx + c$. Hence find the gradient and y-intercept for the given line.

5 In a class of 33 pupils, 18 like soccer (S), 12 like rugby (R), and 8 do not like either.

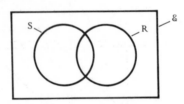

   Fill in the correct number in each of the regions in the given Venn diagram. Hence find how many pupils:
   (a) like both sports,
   (b) like one and only one of the two sports,
   (c) do not like rugby.

6 If $a = 3 \times 10^2$ and $b = 2 \times 10^3$ find: (a) ab, (b) $a+b$.

7 Ashton, Brintley and Cottam are three towns on a map. From Ashton, Brintley is 8 miles in a direction of N52°E (052°) and Cottam is 4 miles in a direction S35°W (215°).

   Taking 1 cm ≡ 1 mile make a scale drawing to show the positions of these three towns. Use your drawing to find the distance and direction of Cottam from Brintley.

8

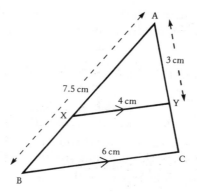

ABC is a triangle with X and Y points on the sides AB and AC respectively such that XY is parallel to BC. If AB = 7.5 cm, AY = 3 cm, XY = 4 cm and BC = 6 cm, use similar triangles to find AX and AC.

Find also $\dfrac{\triangle AXY}{\triangle ABC}$ and $\dfrac{\triangle AXY}{\triangle BXY}$.

9 Draw a circle with radius 4.8 cm and mark a point T 8 cm from its centre. Construct the two tangents from T to the circle. Measure and record the angle between them.

10 A cricketer averages x runs per innings for 10 completed innings and y runs per innings for his next 5 completed innings. Find an expression for his average over the 15 completed innings.

11

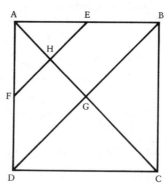

ABCD is a square of side $2x$ cm with the diagonals intersecting at G. E and F are the mid-points of AB and AD respectively, and EF cuts AC at H.

(a) Find the area of each of the following in terms of x:

   (i) $\triangle DGC$, (ii) $\triangle AFE$, (iii) $\triangle AHE$, (iv) trapezium FEBD.

(b) If the area of trapezium FHGD is 48 cm² form an equation in x and solve it.

12 A river is 70 metres wide. The table shows the depth of water in the river at different distances from one bank.

Distance from bank in metres (S)	0	10	20	30	40	50	60	65	70
Depth of water in metres (D)	0	2.2	4	5.6	6.8	7	6	4	0

Taking 4 cm ≡ 10 metres for S and 2 cm ≡ 1 metre for D, draw a graph to represent this data and use it to estimate:

(a) the depth 25 metres from the bank,

(b) where the river is 5 metres deep,

(c) the distance from the bank where the river has its maximum depth.

13

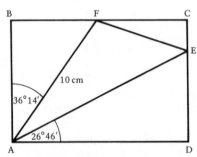

ABCD is a rectangle with AD = 12 cm. E is a point on CD and F a point on BC such that ∠EAD = 26°46′, ∠BAF = 36°14′ and AF = 10 cm. Find:

(a) BF, (b) AB, (c) ED, (d) CE, (e) FC, (f) ∠CFE.

14 If $\sin x = 0.6273$ find:

(a) x, (b) $\cos x$, (c) $(\sin x)^2$, (d) $(\cos x)^2$,

(e) $(\sin x)^2 + (\cos x)^2$,

giving your answer correct to three significant figures.

15 Refer to the diagram near the top of the opposite page.

(a) Write down the coordinates of A and B.

(b) Operate the matrix $\begin{pmatrix} 0 & -1 \\ 1 & 0 \end{pmatrix}$ on AB and draw its image, marking it A_1B_1.

(c) Join OA, OB, OA_1, OB_1. Describe the effect of this matrix operating on triangle OAB.

(d) Operate the matrix $\begin{pmatrix} 1 & 0 \\ 0 & -1 \end{pmatrix}$ on AB and draw its image, marking it A_2B_2. Describe the effect of this matrix operating on AB.

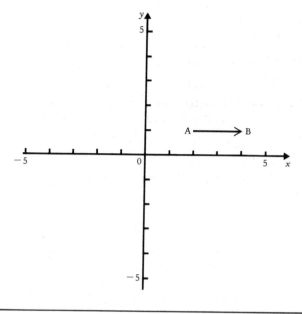

Revision Paper 15

1 $\mathscr{E} = \{x : 0 < x < 17\}$
   $A = \{\text{Factors of } 12\}$
   $B = \{\text{Prime numbers}\}$
   Find: (a) $A \cup B$, (b) $n(A \cap B)$, (c) $(A \cup B)'$.

2 Find:
   (a) $\cos 44°16'$, (b) $\log \sin 31°24'$, (c) $\sqrt{261.7}$, (d) $\dfrac{1}{5.726}$.

3
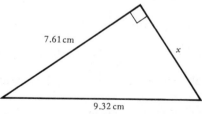

   Use the result of Pythagoras to find x in the given right-angled triangle, giving your answer correct to three significant figures.

4 (a) Add $5a + 2b - c$, $2a - 5b + 3c$, $a + b + c$.
   (b) Subtract $8x + 2y - z$ from $12x - 5y + 3z$.

5 In a group of 23 pupils, 14 have a dog and 8 have a cat, while 3 have neither. If x children have both, form an equation in x and solve it. Illustrate this information on a Venn diagram.

6

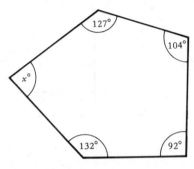

Find the unknown angle in the given pentagon.

7 If $y = \dfrac{3(x-5)}{7}$ find:

(a) y when $x = 54$,   (b) x when $y = 27$.

8 If f is defined by $f(x) = 3x + 1$ and g is defined by $g(x) = 5 - 2x$. Find:

(a) $f(4)$,   (b) $g(5)$,   (c) $f[g(5)]$,   (d) x if $g(x) = 13$.

Show also that $f(x + y) = f(x) + f(y) - 1$.

9

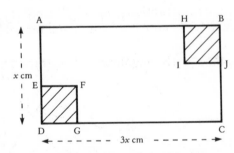

ABCD is a rectangle with AB $= 3x$ cm and BC $= x$ cm. BHIJ and DGFE are squares, each of side 4 cm, which are removed from the corners as shown in the diagram.

Find, in terms of x, the length of the perimeter of the figure AHIJCGFEA.

If the value of the perimeter is 48 cm find x and hence evaluate the area of the figure.

10

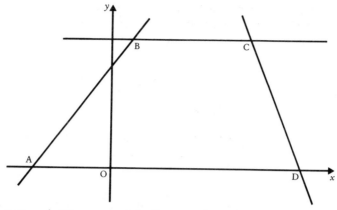

AB, BC and CD are straight lines with equations $x - 2y + 4 = 0$, $y = 3$ and $x + y - 6 = 0$ respectively. Find the coordinates of each of the points A, B, C and D. What special name is given to this quadrilateral?

11

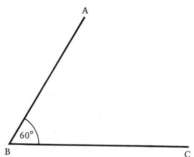

Given AB = 8 cm, BC = 10 cm and $\angle ABC = 60°$.

Find, using a constructional method, a point X which is 5.2 cm from BC and 4.7 from AB. Measure and record the distance BX.

12

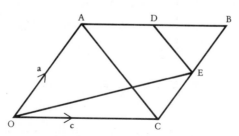

OABC is a parallelogram with D and E the mid-points of AB and BC respectively. **OA** = **a** and **OC** = **c**. Write down, in terms of **a** and **c**:

(a) **AD** and **CE**,   (b) **OE** and **CA**,

(c) **ED**,   (d) Compare the vectors **ED** and **CA**.

What relationship is there between these two lines?

13 Solve the equations:
$$x - 3 = 0$$
$$2x + y = 11$$
$$x + y + z = 0$$

14 (a) If $A = \begin{pmatrix} 3 & -5 \\ 7 & -3 \end{pmatrix}$ find the determinant and inverse of A.

(b) Solve the simultaneous equations:
$$3x - 5y + 11 = 0$$
$$7x - 3y + 4 = 0$$

15

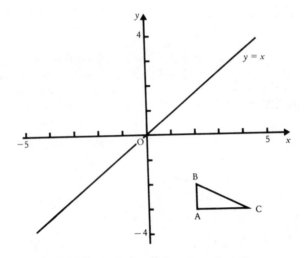

The triangle ABC is:
(a) rotated anticlockwise through 180° about B to give $A_1B_1C_1$,
(b) reflected in the line $y = x$ to give $A_2B_2C_2$,
(c) reflected in the x-axis to give $A_3B_3C_3$.
Mark each of these triangles on the diagram distinguishing clearly between them.

Revision Paper 16

1 (a) Multiply $2x^2 + 5x - 3$ by $2x - 3$.
(b) Divide $5x^3 + 27x^2 + 8x - 10$ by $x + 5$.

2 The angles of a triangle are $2x°$, $3x°$ and $4x°$. Find them.

3   If $\& = \{1, 2, 3, 4, 5, 6, 7, 8, 9, 10.\}$,
    $A = \{3, 6, 9\}$, $B = \{5, 10\}$, $C = \{2, 3, 5, 7\}$.
    (a) List the elements in $(A \cup B) \cap C$.
    (b) Write down the value of $n(A \cup B)$.
    (c) List the elements in $(B \cup C)'$.

4   Find the equation of the straight line passing through the points
    $(-3, 0)$ and $(0, -5)$.

5   Solve the simultaneous linear equations:
    $$2x + 5y = 2, \qquad 3x + 8y = 4.$$

6   Three-fifths of John's money is equal to Harry's, and eight-
    ninths of Harry's is equal to Tom's. If they have a total of
    £38.40 between them, how much does each have?

7   If x is an even number, what is the sum of the next odd number
    and the next even number?

8   Solve:
    (a) $4(2x - 9) - 3(x - 7) - 6x = 7$,
    (b) $\dfrac{x}{3} - \dfrac{x}{4} + \dfrac{x}{5} = \dfrac{17}{20}$,   (c) $\dfrac{2x + 7}{6x + 1} = \dfrac{3}{5}$.

9   Simplify:
    (a) $2a^3 \times 8a^2$,   (b) $12x^9 \div 3x^6$,
    (c) $(-2a^2 b)^2 \times 3ab^4$,   (d) $\dfrac{1}{x + 5} - \dfrac{1}{x + 4}$.

10 A greengrocer buys 6 bags of red potatoes and 5 bags of white
    potatoes for £25. The following day he buys 4 bags of red
    together with 8 bags of white for £26. If he pays £x for the reds
    and £y for the whites on both occasions form two linear
    equations in x and y and solve them to find the price of each
    bag.

11 Solve the equations:
    (a) $(4x - 3)(4x + 3) = 0$,
    (b) $x^2 - 13x + 42 = 0$,
    (c) $2x^2 - 21x + 10 = 0$.

12

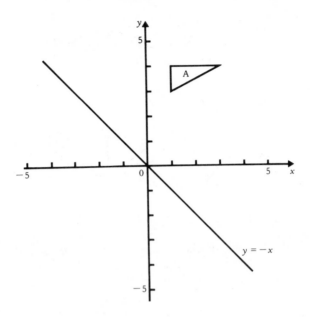

(a) (i) Draw the image of A when it is reflected in the x-axis and mark it B.
   (ii) What matrix will represent this transformation?

(b) (i) Draw the image of A when it is reflected in the given line $y = -x$, and mark it C.
   (ii) What matrix will represent this transformation?

(c) (i) Draw the position of A when rotated anticlockwise about the origin through 90°. Mark it D.
   (ii) What matrix will cause this rotation?

13 A, B and C are three towns. The bearing of B from A is North 62° East (062°) and the bearing of C from A is North 35° West (325°). AB = 16 kilometres and AC = 22 kilometres. Using 1 cm ≡ 2 km, make a scale diagram of the positions of the three towns and from your drawing find:

(a) the bearing of C from B,

(b) the distance, correct to the nearest kilometre, of C from B.

14 In the figure opposite, A, B, C and D are points on a circle, centre O, with TA the tangent at A and TBC a straight line. If ∠BAT = 36° calculate, without giving reasons, each of the angles ∠ACB, ∠ABC, ∠ATC and ∠ADB.

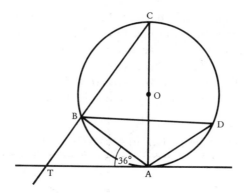

15 The temperatures taken at two-hourly intervals on a certain day are given in the following table:

Time	Mid-night	2 a.m.	4 a.m.	6 a.m.	8 a.m.	10 a.m.	Noon
Temperature in °C	2.4	1.7	1.2	2.4	7.4	12.2	15.8

Time	2 p.m.	4 p.m.	6 p.m.	8 p.m.	10 p.m.	Mid-night	
Temperature in °C	17.2	16.8	15	10.6	6	3	

Draw a graph to show this data taking $2\,cm \equiv 2\,hours$ and $2\,cm \equiv 2°C$. From your graph determine:

(a) the temperature at 9 a.m.,

(b) the times at which the temperature was 9°C.

Revision Paper

17

1 Simplify:

(a) $24a \times 3a$, (b) $24a \div 6a^2$, (c) $(-12a) \times (-2a)$.

2 Find the value of $2\pi R\,(R + H)$ when $\pi = \frac{22}{7}$, $R = 10$ and $H = 11$.

3 (a) Multiply $3a^2 - 5a - 2$ by $4a - 3$.

(b) Divide $9x^3 + 18x^2 + 14x + 3$ by $3x + 1$.

4 Factorise:

(a) $9 - 49x^2$, (b) $6 - 2a - 3b + ab$, (c) $y^2 - 10y + 9$.

5 In a cricket match between England and Australia, Australia lead on the first innings by 103 runs. In the second innings Australia score twice as many as England scored in the first, and England score three times as many as they did in their first innings, thereby winning the match by 53 runs. Find the number of runs scored by each side in each innings.

6 (a) Find:
   (i) $\sin 73°04'$,   (ii) $\log \cos 37°43'$,   (iii) 0.2222^2.

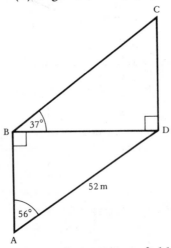

   (b) In the diagram ABCD represents a field. The diagonal BD is perpendicular to AB and DC, $\angle BAD = 56°$, $\angle CBD = 37°$ and $AD = 52$ metres. Find:

   (i) AB,   (ii) BD,
   (iii) CD,   (iv) the area of the field in square metres.

7

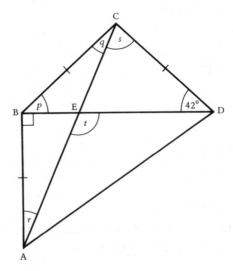

144

ABCD is a quadrilateral with AB = BC = CD and the diagonals intersecting at E. If ∠ABD = 90° and ∠BDC = 42° find the angles denoted by the letters p, q, r, s and t.

8

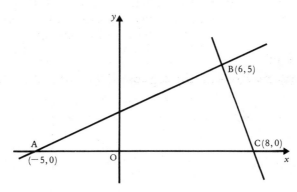

A, B and C are three points with co-ordinates $(-5, 0)$, $(6, 5)$ and $(8, 0)$ respectively. Find:

(a) the gradient of AB,

(b) the equation of AB,

(c) the gradient of BC,

(d) the area of the triangle ABC.

9 Given that $\dfrac{56 \times 36}{42} = 48$ find:

(a) $5.6 \times 36 - 4.8 \times 42$,   (b) $\dfrac{4.8 \times 4.2}{0.36}$

10 The depth of water in a harbour at different times is shown in the following table:

Time	6 a.m.	7 a.m.	8 a.m.	9 a.m.	10 a.m.	11 a.m.	Noon
Depth of water in metres	5.1	3.8	3.1	3.2	3.7	4.7	6.3

Time	1 p.m.	2 p.m.	3 p.m.	4 p.m.	5 p.m.	6 p.m.	
Depth of water in metres	8.0	8.9	8.9	8.4	7.3	5.3	

Draw a graph to represent this data using 2 cm ≡ 1 hour for the horizontal time axis and 2 cm ≡ 1 metre for the vertical depth axis.

Use your graph to find:

(a) the times when the depth of water is 7 metres,

(b) the depth of water at 10.30 a.m.

145

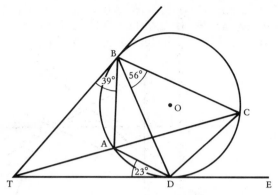

ABCD is a cyclic quadrilateral with the tangents at B and D intersecting at T. TAC is a straight line. If $\angle ADT = 23°$, $\angle CBD = 56°$ and $\angle TBA = 39°$ find each of the angles $\angle CDE$, $\angle ABD$, $\angle ADC$, $\angle ADB$, $\angle BTD$, $\angle BCA$, $\angle BAC$ and $\angle BTA$.

12 (a) ABCD is a quadrilateral with A the point $(3, -2)$, C the

point $(7, 4)$. $\mathbf{AB} = \begin{pmatrix} 3 \\ 4 \end{pmatrix}$ and $\mathbf{CD} = \begin{pmatrix} 6 \\ 0 \end{pmatrix}$.

Find the coordinates of B and D, and the vectors $\mathbf{AD}$ and $\mathbf{DB}$.

(b) OAB is a triangle such that $\overrightarrow{OA} = 3m + 4n$ and $\overrightarrow{OB} = 5m - 2n$. Find the vector $\overrightarrow{OM}$ in terms of m and n if M is the middle point of AB. Find also the vector $\overrightarrow{OC}$ given that $\dfrac{OC}{OM} = \dfrac{2}{1}$, C being a point on OM.

13 Complete the following table which gives the value of $2x^2$ for values of x from -4 to $+4$:

x	-4	-3	-2	-1	0	1	2	3	4
$2x^2$	32	18		2	0	2	8		32

Taking 2 cm as unit for x, and three units for y plot the graph of $y = 2x^2$ for values of x from -4 to $+4$.

Draw on the same axes the graph of $y = 3(4-x)$ by finding the y values corresponding to $x = -3$, $x = 0$ and $x = 4$.

Give the values of x where the graphs cut.

What equation has these x values as roots?

14

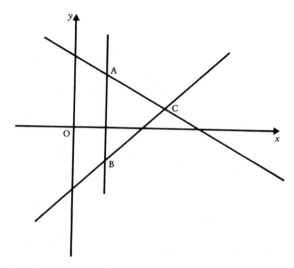

Triangle ABC is formed by three straight lines which have equations $y = x - 2$, $x = 1$, and $3y + x = 10$. State clearly the equation of each of the lines AB, BC and CA, and find the coordinates of the points A, B and C.

Shade the area which satisfies all the inequalities:

$$y > x - 2, \quad x > 1, \quad 3y < 10 - x.$$

15

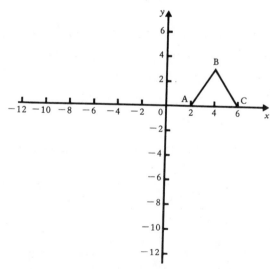

A, B, C are three points with coordinates $A(2, 0)$, $B(4, 3)$ and $C(6, 0)$.

(a) On graph paper draw axes for x and y from -12 to $+6$, taking 1 cm as unit on each axis. Plot the given points and join them to form triangle ABC.

(b) Draw the reflection of ABC in:
   (i) the x-axis; mark it $A_1B_1C_1$,
   (ii) the y-axis; mark it $A_2B_2C_2$.
In each case give:
   (i) the new coordinates of A, B and C,
   (ii) the matrix which will perform this transformation.
(c) Draw the new position of ABC when operated on by the matrix $\begin{pmatrix} -2 & 0 \\ 0 & -2 \end{pmatrix}$. Mark it $A_3B_3C_3$. Compare the area of $A_3B_3C_3$ with that of ABC.

Revision Paper 18

1 Find the value of $\dfrac{a^2+b^2}{2c}$ if:

  (a) $a = 4, b = 3, c = 5$,
  (b) $a = 2, b = -1, c = -5$.

2 Simplify:
  (a) $\dfrac{2x}{y} \times \dfrac{x^2}{y^3}$,   (b) $\dfrac{2x}{y} \div \dfrac{x^2}{y^3}$,   (c) $\dfrac{2x}{y} - \dfrac{x^2}{y^3}$.

3 (a) If $7x = 3y$ find the ratio of x to y.
  (b) Factorise $x^2 - y^2$ and use your result to find the value of $64^2 - 36^2$.

4 Solve the equations:
  (a) $2x - 3 = 9$,
  (b) $x + 3(x + 1) = 19$,
  (c) $\dfrac{x}{4} - \dfrac{x}{5} = \dfrac{3}{10}$.

5 (a) Solve the simultaneous equations:
$$4x - 3y = 7$$
$$7x + 3y = 37$$

  (b) Find the gradient of the straight line which passes through the points $(-5, 2)$ and $(6, -4)$.

6 (a) Find:

    $\log \tan 73°$, antilog 1.4927, 16.34^2, $\dfrac{1}{27.25}$.

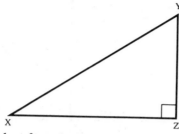

(b) Use the result of Pythagoras to find XY if $\angle$XZY = 90°, XZ = 23 cm and YZ = 14 cm.

7 Solve the equations:

(a) $(x-5)(x+1) = 0$, (b) $5x^2 - 6x = 0$, (c) $x^2 - 36 = 0$.

8

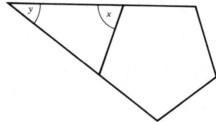

Two sides of a regular pentagon are produced to meet as shown in the diagram. Find the angles marked x and y.

9 If $3x + 2y = 5$ rearrange to make y the subject. Use this value of y to find y^2, multiplying out any brackets. What is the value of y^2 when $x = -5$?

10

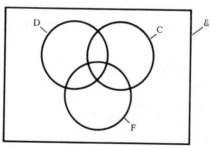

Twenty-one pupils were asked if they had attended a disco (D), a cinema (C) or a football match (F) during the previous week. Everyone had attended at least one, but no one all three. Copy the Venn diagram and shade the areas which represent the *two* empty sets.

It was also recorded that: 5 had been to a cinema, 15 had been to a disco, 9 had attended a football match, 1 had been to both a cinema and had attended a football match, and 3 had been to see a football match but had not gone to either of the others. How many pupils attended a cinema and went to a disco?

11

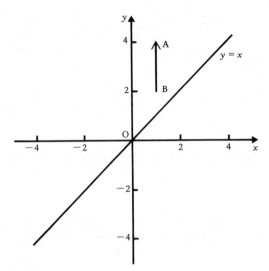

The arrow AB is:

(a) reflected in the y-axis to give A_1B_1,

(b) reflected in the line $y = x$ to give A_2B_2,

(c) rotated clockwise about the origin O through 180° to give A_3B_3.

Show these on the same diagram, indicating clearly the direction of the arrow in each case.

12 F is defined by $F(x) = 5x + 2$ and G is defined by $G(x) = x^2$. Find:

(a) $F(3)$, (b) $G(-3)$, (c) $F[G(3)]$, (d) $G[F(3)]$,

(e) x if $F(X) = -13$.

13 Plot the graphs of $y = 3x + 1$ and $y = 5 - 2x$ on the same axes taking values of x between -3 and $+4$. Take 2 cm as unit on the x-axis and as 2 units on the y-axis. Write down the coordinates of the point of intersection of the two lines.

14

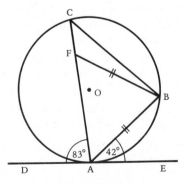

ABC is a triangle inscribed in a circle centre O with DAE the tangent at A. F is a point on AC such that BA = BF. If ∠DAC = 83° and ∠BAE = 42° calculate ∠ABC, ∠ACB, ∠AFB and ∠CBF.

15 Various values for the wavelength (W metres) and corresponding values for the frequency (f kilohertz) as found on a radio are given below:

Wavelength (W)	300	400	500	600	700	800
Frequency (f)	1000	750	600	500	425	375

Draw a graph to illustrate this data taking 2 cm ≡ 100 metres on the W-axis and 2 cm ≡ 100 kilohertz on the f-axis.

From your graph find:

(a) the wavelength corresponding to a frequency of 850 kilohertz,

(b) the frequency corresponding to a wavelength of 550 metres.

Revision Paper   19

1 Find the value of $a^2 + b^2 - 3abc$ if:

(a) $a = -2, b = 3, c = -1$,

(b) $a = \frac{1}{2}$ $b = 1, c = -\frac{1}{3}$.

2 (a) Simplify $\dfrac{4x-3}{5} - \dfrac{6x+3}{6}$.

(b) Multiply $9x - 1$ by $2x^2 + 4x - 5$.

(c) Divide $3a^3 + 4a^2b - 7ab^2 + 2b^3$ by $3a - 2b$.

3 Find:

$\cos 84°16'$, $\log \tan 52°15'$,   antilog $\bar{1}.6742$,
x if $\sqrt{\cos x} = 0.8425$.

4 Factorise:

(a) $8ab - 2bc$,   (b) $8a^2 - 2b^2$,

(c) $8a^2 - 2ab - b^2$,   (d) $5(a+b)c - 3(a+b)$.

5 (a) Find the equation of the straight line with gradient -2 which passes through the point $(5, -3)$.

(b) Write down the gradient of the line with equation $7x - 4y + 15 = 0$.

6 (a) By multiplying out the brackets, collecting terms and factorising, solve the equation $2x(x+4) = (x-5)(x+2)$.

(b) Solve the equation $2x^2 - 15x + 28 = 0$.

7 (a) If $A = \begin{pmatrix} 10 & 2 \\ 7 & 1 \end{pmatrix}$ and $B = \begin{pmatrix} 3 & 5 \\ 5 & 4 \end{pmatrix}$ find:

(i) $A - B$, (ii) AB, (iii) BA.

(b) Solve the simultaneous equations:

$$\begin{pmatrix} 2 & 5 \\ 1 & -3 \end{pmatrix}\begin{pmatrix} x \\ y \end{pmatrix} = \begin{pmatrix} 4 \\ -9 \end{pmatrix}$$

8

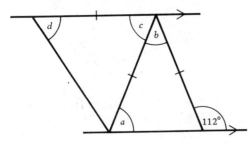

Find the angles marked with the letters a, b, c and d.

9 A local club books a 45-seater coach for a day-trip to London at a cost of £185. Twenty-five adults accompanied by twenty children intend making the trip, each adult to pay £x and each child £y. A family of five, mother, father and three children are unable to make the journey so the organiser increases each fare by 50p thereby collecting fares totalling £186.

Form two equations in x and y and solve them to find the original fares.

10

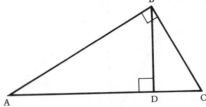

ABC is a triangle with $\angle ABC = 90°$ and D the foot of the perpendicular from B to AC. If AB = 15 cm and AD = 12 cm use the result of Pythagoras to find BD.

Show that the triangles ABD and BCD are similar and hence find BC and DC.

152

11 I walk for x seconds at b metres per second and cycle for y seconds at c metres per second. Find my average speed for the whole journey in:

(a) metres per second,   (b) kilometres per hour.

12

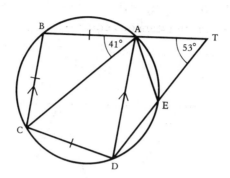

TAB, TED are two secants drawn from an external point T to a circle ABCDE. Given that AB = BC = CD, CB is parallel to DA, $\angle$BAC = 41° and $\angle$ATE = 53° find:

$\angle$BCA, $\angle$CDA, $\angle$ACD, $\angle$TAD, $\angle$AET and $\angle$EAT.

13 Draw a circle of radius 7 cm and construct a regular hexagon ABCDEF with all its vertices lying on the circle. Measure and record the length of:

(a) the side AB,   (b) the diagonal AD.

14

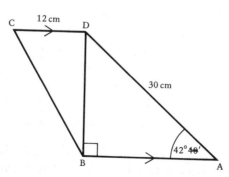

ABCD is a trapezium with AB parallel to DC. $\angle$ABD = 90°, $\angle$BAD = 42°40', AD = 30 cm and DC = 12 cm.

Calculate: (a) BD,   (b) AB,   (c) $\angle$BCD.

153

15 The following are the cross-sectional areas for a solid for varying distances from one end:

Distance (D) from one end in cm	10	22	41	70	86	102	130	145	160
Area (A) in cm²		150	192	210	173	115	80	35	20	12

Taking $2\,\text{cm} \equiv 20$ units on each axis draw a graph to represent this data and use it to estimate:

(a) the area at a distance of 60 cm from the given end,

(b) the distance from the end where the area is 100 cm².

Revision Paper   20

1 Simplify:

   (a) $12a \times 3a$,   (b) $12a \div 3a$,   (c) $\dfrac{12a \times 3a}{4a^2}$.

2 Express the following statements in algebraic form:

   (a) the sum of x and y is subtracted from the square of z,

   (b) the square root of the product of x and y is divided by z.

3 Factorise:

   (a) $3xyz + 2yz$,   (b) $3(x+y) + z(x+y)$,

   (c) $(x+y)z - (x+y)$.

4 Remove the brackets and simplify:

   (a) $4(a-b) - 3(a+b)$,   (b) $(4a-3b)^2$,

   (c) $(4a-3b)(2a+b)$.

5 Solve the equations:

   (a) $3x - 2 = 10$,   (b) $4(x-2) - 2(x-7) = 14$,

   (c) $\dfrac{5(x-2)}{3} = 2$.

154

6

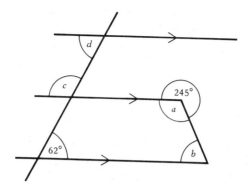

Find the angles denoted by the letters a, b, c and d.

7

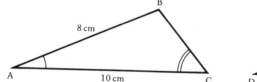

Similar triangles ABC, DEF represent the cross-sections of two wooden wedges. $\angle A = \angle D$ and $\angle C = \angle F$. If AC = 10 cm, AB = 8 cm, DF = 6 cm and EF = 2.5 cm, find:

(a) DE, (b) BC, (c) $\dfrac{\triangle ABC}{\triangle DEF}$.

8 Simplify $\dfrac{4x-3}{2} - \dfrac{5x-2}{3}$.

Use this result to solve the equation:

$$\frac{4x-3}{2} - \frac{5x-2}{3} = \frac{1}{6}$$

9 Construct a quadrilateral ABCD in which AB = 12.2 cm, AD = 8 cm, BD = 10.5 cm, AC = 14 cm and BC = CD. Measure and record the length of BC.

10

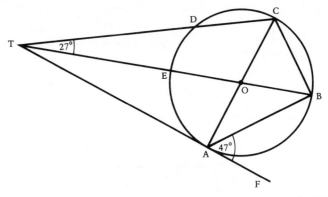

TA is a tangent to a circle centre O, and TEB and TDC are secants. If ∠BAF = 47° and ∠CTB = 27° find each of the angles ∠ABC, ∠ACB, ∠AOB, ∠ABO, and ∠ACT.

11

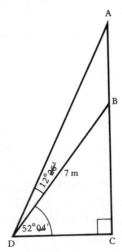

ABC is a vertical flag-pole which is supported by two wire stays DB and DA (D and C being in the same horizontal plane). If BD = 7 metres, ∠BDC = 52°04′ and ∠ADB = 12°46′ find, as accurately as your tables will permit:

(a) BC,   (b) DC,   (c) AC.

12   A greengrocer sells 7 lb bags of mixed vegetables for £1.16. Each bag contains 4 lb of carrots at x pence per lb and 3 lb of parsnips at y pence per lb. When the price of carrots increases by 2 p and parsnips by 6 p he decides to include only 2 lb of parsnips with 5 lb of carrots in each bag. In this way he is able to sell the 7 lb bag at £1.32.

Form two equations in x and y and solve them to find the original price per lb for each vegetable.

13

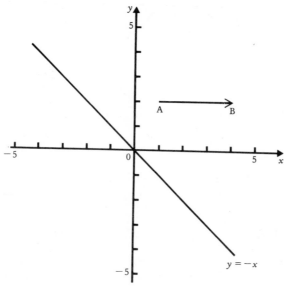

The arrow AB is:

(a) reflected in the x-axis to give A_1B_1. What matrix will perform this transformation?

(b) reflected in the line $y = -x$ to give A_2B_2. What matrix will perform this transformation?

(c) rotated about O through 90° anticlockwise to give A_3B_3. What matrix will perform this transformation?

Plot each of the new positions of AB on the same diagram, indicating clearly the direction of the arrow.

14

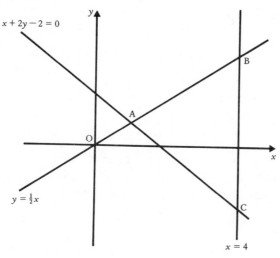

(*continued overleaf*)

Three straight lines with equations

$$x + 2y - 2 = 0$$
$$y = \tfrac{1}{2}x$$

and
$$x = 4$$

intersect at the points A, B and C.

Find the coordinates of each of these points.

Shade the area which satisfies all the inequalities:

$$x + 2y > 2, \qquad y < \tfrac{1}{2}x, \qquad x > 4.$$

15   The masses of ball-bearings of various diameters were as follows:

Diameter (D) in mm	5	10	15	20	25	28
Mass (m) in grams	0.5	5.5	18	42	82	115

Draw a graph to illustrate this data using $3\,\text{cm} \equiv 5\,\text{mm}$ on the D-axis and $2\,\text{cm} \equiv 10\,\text{g}$ on the m-axis. Use your graph to estimate:

(a) the diameter of a ball-bearing of mass 100g.

(b) the mass of a ball-bearing of diameter 18 mm.

Revision Paper   21

1   Find the mean, mode and median of the numbers 8, 4, 9, 10, 9, 9, 4, 3, 13, 6, 2, 9, clearly indicating which is which.

2   (a) If $5x + 4y = 20$ find the value of y when $x = 2$.

(b) Simplify $\dfrac{x-3}{5} - \dfrac{2x+7}{6}$.

3   (a) The interior angle of a regular polygon is $156°$. How many sides does it have?

(b) The angles of a pentagon are $2x°, 3x°, 3x°, \tfrac{5}{2}x°$ and $57°$. Form an equation in x and solve it.

4   Find:

$$\sqrt{46.62}, \qquad 31.23^2, \qquad \log 0.049, \qquad \frac{1}{63.27}.$$

5 Factorise:
   (a) $3xy - 9yz$,   (b) $a(b+c) + (b+c)$,
   (c) $a(2b-c) - 3(2b-c)$.

6 Solve the equations:
   (a) $5(x-2) - 3(x+7) = 14$,   (b) $\dfrac{3x-2}{2} + \dfrac{2x-5}{3} = \dfrac{8}{9}$,

   (c) $\dfrac{3x+1}{5x-2} = \dfrac{2}{5}$.

7 If $A = \begin{pmatrix} 5 & 7 \\ 4 & 2 \end{pmatrix}$ find:
   (a) the determinant of A,   (b) A^2,
   (c) $I - 2A$ where I is the 2×2 unit matrix.

8 Solve the equations:
   (a) $5x - x^2 = 0$,   (b) $5x^2 - 6x + 1 = 0$,   (c) $\dfrac{x^2}{4} - 9 = 0$.

9 Thirty-two children in a class were asked which of the subjects geography, cookery and woodwork they were studying. Their replies gave the following information:

   17 studied geography
   13 studied woodwork
   5 studied cookery only
   4 studied geography and cookery
   3 studied woodwork and cookery
   2 studied all three

Two pupils did not study any one of these subjects.

Assuming that x pupils studied geography and woodwork but not cookery, draw a Venn diagram to show this data. Form an equation in x and solve it. Use this value of x to determine:

(a) the number of pupils studying woodwork only,

(b) the number of pupils studying exactly two of these subjects.

10

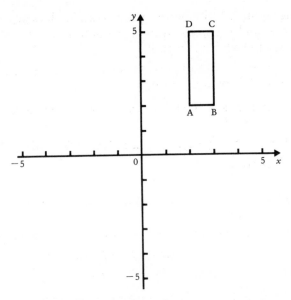

The rectangle ABCD is reflected in the y-axis to give the rectangle $A_1B_1C_1D_1$, in the x-axis to give the rectangle $A_2B_2C_2D_2$, and rotated about the origin through 180° to give the rectangle $A_3B_3C_3D_3$. Show, in the same diagram, the three new positions of the rectangle.

11

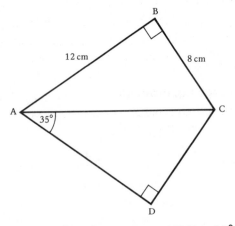

ABCD is a quadrilateral with $\angle ABC = \angle ADC = 90°$.
If AB = 12 cm, BC = 8 cm and $\angle CAD = 35°$ find:
(a) $\angle BAC$,   (b) AC,   (c) CD,   (d) AD.

12 A ship leaves a port P and sails for 8 kilometres on a course N57°E (057°). It then changes course to S28°E (152°) and sails for $15\frac{1}{2}$ kilometres.

160

Using $1\,\text{cm} \equiv 1\,\text{kilometre}$ make a scale drawing of the ship's journey and use your diagram to determine the course it must now set to sail directly to P.

How long will the final section of the journey take if the ship travels at 10 km per hour.

13 A function f is defined by $f(x) = 2x - 1$. Write down the values of:

(a) $f(2)$, (b) $f(-3)$, (c) x if $f(x) = 9$, (d) $f(2x)$,
(e) $f[f(x)]$.

14 (a) If $A = \begin{pmatrix} 7 & 6 \\ 5 & -2 \end{pmatrix}$ find the determinant of A.

(b) Use the method of determinants to solve the equations:
$$7x + 6y - 17 = 0$$
$$5x - 2y - 9 = 0$$

15 The road test for a new motor car recorded speeds at various times after starting as given in the following table.

Time (t) in seconds	0	4	8	12	16	20	24	28	32	36
Speed (v) in mph	0	30	53	70	81	90	97	102	105	107

Taking $2\,\text{cm} \equiv 4\,\text{seconds}$ on the t-axis and $2\,\text{cm} \equiv 10\,\text{mph}$ on the v-axis plot this data and draw a smooth curve through the points.

Use your graph to estimate:

(a) the time which passes before the car reaches 100 mph,
(b) the speed after 15 seconds.

Revision Paper   22

1 Find the value of $a(b - 2c)$ if:
(a) $a = -2, b = 6, c = 3$,   (b) $a = 1, b = 2, c = 3$.

2 (a) Multiply $5x^2 - 3x + 2$ by $2x - 3$.
(b) Divide $6x^3 - 19x + 21x - 9$ by $2x - 3$.

3

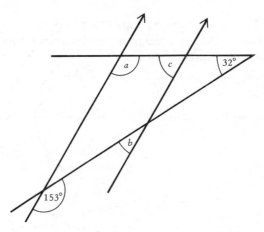

Find the angles marked by the letters a, b and c.

4 Solve the equations:

(a) $5x + 7 - 3(2x + 1) + 2 = 0$,

(b) $\dfrac{7x - 2}{3} - \dfrac{2x + 5}{5} = 6\frac{1}{15}$.

5

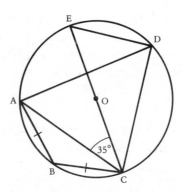

ABCDE is a pentagon inscribed in a circle centre O such that EC is a diameter and AB = BC. If $\angle$ACE = 35° find the value of each of the angles $\angle$EDC, $\angle$EDA, $\angle$ADC, $\angle$ABC, $\angle$BAC and $\angle$EAB.

6 ABC is a triangle in which $\angle$ABC = 90°, AC = 16 cm and AB = 12 cm. Use the theorem of Pythagoras, together with suitable tables, to find the value of BC as accurately as your tables allow.

7

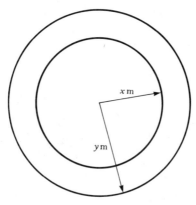

A circular path has an internal radius of x metres and an external radius of y metres. Find an expression for the area of the path in terms of x, y and π. If the path is 2 metres wide and if the area of the path is equal to $\frac{7}{9}$ ths the area of the enclosed central region, form an equation in x and solve it. $(\pi = \frac{22}{7}.)$

8 Solve the simultaneous equations:

$$7x - 8y = 5$$
$$4x + 3y = 18$$

9

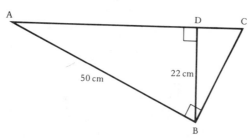

ABC represents the cross-section through a horse-trough which is 2 metres long. $\angle ABC = 90°$, $AB = 50$ cm and the depth of the trough at its deepest point is 22 cm. Calculate:

(a) the width of the trough AC,

(b) the length of the other sloping side BC,

(c) the volume contained in the trough when full in m³.

10 I have a certain number (x) of 10p coins, twice that number of 5p coins, and three times that number of 2p coins. In all I have £1.56. Form an equation in x and solve it. How many 2p coins do I have?

11 The time of sunrise at Greenwich on various dates, each two weeks apart, is given in the following table:

Date (D)	March 28th	April 11th	April 25th	May 9th	May 23rd	June 6th	June 20th	July 4th	July 14th
Time (T)	6.45	6.15	5.45	5.18	4.57	4.45	4.42	4.51	5.03

Using $1\,\text{cm} \equiv 1\,\text{week}$ on the D-axis and $4\,\text{cm} \equiv 1\,\text{hour}$ on the T-axis, plot these points and join them with a smooth curve. From the graph determine:

(a) the time of sunrise on 16th May,

(b) on which date the sun rises at 6.00 a.m.

12 A and B are two look-out posts on the opposite sides of a river with parallel banks. The river flows north-south and at 1 p.m. a ship S is in a direction N21°E (021°) from A while it is 1600 metres from B in a direction N40°W (320°). Find the width of the river.

If the ship moves at $10\,\text{km h}^{-1}$ in a direction parallel to the bank of the river, at what time will it be immediately opposite A and B?

13

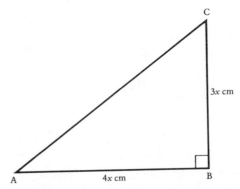

ABC is a triangle with sides $3x$ and $4x$ cm as shown in the diagram, and $\angle ABC = 90°$. Use Pythagoras' result to find AC in terms of x.

If the perimeter of the triangle is 48 cm form an equation in x and solve it. Use this value of x to find the area of the triangle in square centimetres.

14 Draw the given Venn diagram (opposite) three times and use them to illustrate by shading each of the sets:

(a) $A \cup B$,   (b) $A' \cap B$,   (c) $A' \cap B'$.

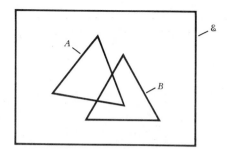

15 Use suitable tables to find the following as accurately as possible:

(a) $\sqrt{157.6}$, (b) 3.927^2, (c) $\sqrt{157.6} + 3.927^2$,

(d) $\dfrac{1}{\sqrt{157.6} + 3.927^2}$.

Revision Paper   23

1 There are 20 girls in a class, 10 of whom take needlework and 12 of whom take cookery. If 4 take neither, how many study one subject?

2 If $A = 2x + 1$ and $B = x - 3$ find expressions for:
(a) $A + B$, (b) $3A - 2B$, (c) A^2, (d) $A^2 - B^2$.

3 If $v = rw^2$ find:
(a) v when $r = 4$ and $w = 3\frac{1}{2}$,
(b) w when $v = 45$ and $r = 5$.

4 Expand:
(a) $(5p + q)(3p - q)$, (b) $(5p - 3q)^2$,
(c) $(p - q)(p^2 + pq + q^2)$.

5 Factorise:
(a) $9a^2 - 3a$, (b) $ac + 2b - bc - 2a$,
(c) $(a + b)(c - 2) + (a + b)$, (d) $a^2 + 13a + 36$.

6 Solve:
(a) $5t + 3 = 2t - 15$, (b) $\dfrac{3t - 4}{7} = 5$,
(c) $2t + 3 + 3(t + 2) = 16$.

7 Solve:
(a) $t(t - 1) = 0$, (b) $(3t - 4)(t + 2) = 0$,
(c) $t^2 + t - 20 = 0$, (d) $2t^2 + 11t - 21 = 0$.

165

8 Find:

$$\cos 63°26', \qquad \log \sin 34°40', \qquad 0.26^2, \qquad \frac{1}{635.2},$$

$$\sqrt{635.2}, \qquad \text{antilog } \bar{1}.7261.$$

9

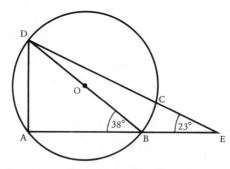

Chords AB and DC are drawn in a circle centre O such that BD is a diameter; the chords when produced intersect in E as shown. If $\angle ABD = 38°$ and $\angle AED = 23°$ find $\angle BAD$, $\angle ADB$ and $\angle BDE$.

10

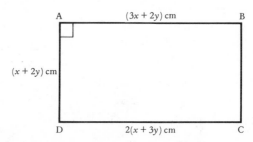

The diagram shows a rectangle ABCD with the sides given in terms of two unknown quantities x and y. Compare AB and DC to find the value of y in terms of x.

If the perimeter of the rectangle is 20 cm form an equation in x and solve it. Hence find:

(a) the sides of the rectangle,   (b) its area.

11

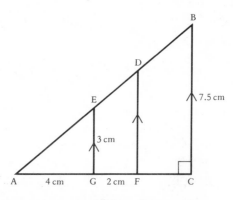

166

ABC is a triangle with $\angle ACB = 90°$. E and D are points on AB and G and F are points on AC such that EG and DF are parallel to BC. If AG = 4 cm, EG = 3 cm, GF = 2 cm and BC = 7.5 cm use similar triangles to find DF and AC. Find also $\dfrac{\triangle ADF}{\triangle AEG}$.

12

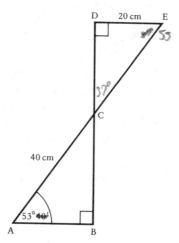

In the diagram ACE and BCD are straight lines, AC = 40 cm, DE = 20 cm and $\angle BAC = 53°40'$. Calculate:

(a) BC,   (b) AB,   (c) DC.

13 Fill in the blanks in each of the following:

(a) $\dfrac{3a}{12} = \dfrac{}{4}$,

(b) $\dfrac{16a^3}{4a^4} = \dfrac{4}{}$,

(c) $(a+b)^2 = a^2 + + b^2$

(d) $(5a+2b)(2a-5b) = 10a^2 - - 10b^2$.

14 Simplify $\dfrac{5(x+3)}{2} - \dfrac{3(x-2)}{4}$.

Hence solve the equation $\dfrac{5(x+3)}{2} - \dfrac{3(x-2)}{4} = 7$.

15 Construct a quadrilateral ABCD in which AB = 14 cm, BC = 10.5 cm, AD = DC = 8 cm and $\angle ABC = 60°$. Measure and record the length of each diagonal.

Revision Paper 24

1 Solve the equation $\dfrac{5-2x}{2-3x} = 8$.

2 Factorise:
   (a) $x^2 + 5x - 14$, (b) $2x^2 + 6x + 4$, (c) $xz - 2x + yz - 2y$.

3 (a) Multiply $3 - 4a$ by $a^2 - 2a + 1$.
   (b) Divide $2a^3 + a^2 - 8a + 3$ by $2a - 3$.

4 Plot the points A$(5, 2)$, B$(-1, 1)$ and C$(1, -3)$ using 2 cm as unit on each axis. Construct the perpendicular bisectors of AB and BC, marking their point of intersection X. With centre X, radius XA describe a circle. Does this circle pass through any of the marked points? Measure and record its radius.

5 Find the number of sides of a regular polygon in which the interior angle is five times the exterior angle.

6 Express $\dfrac{x}{2} + \dfrac{2x}{3} - \dfrac{3x}{4}$ as a single fraction.

7 (a) Solve the simultaneous equations:
$$3x + y = 7$$
$$2x - y = 8$$
   (b) Given
$$2x + y = 6$$
$$3x + 4y = 9$$
   find $x + y$ without solving the equations.

8 Given $a = 2.7 \times 10^6$ and $b = 9 \times 10^5$ express in standard form:
   (a) $a + b$, (b) $a \times b$, (c) $\dfrac{a}{b}$.

9

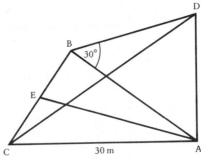

A vertical flagpole stands at A, one corner of a horizontal equilateral triangle ABC of side 30 metres. From B the elevation of the top of the flagpole is 30°. How high is the pole? If E is the midpoint of BC, find AE and the elevation of the top of the pole from E.

10 The sides of a right-angled triangle are $x-2$, $2x$ and $2(x+1)$. Find x.

11

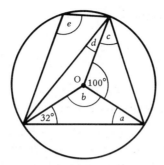

If O is the centre of the given circle calculate the angles marked a, b, c, d and e.

12 John goes to the post office and buys x stamps costing 12p each, twice as many costing 14p each, and half as many costing 3p each as he had bought at 12p. He presented a £5 note and received 2p change. How many of each did he buy?

13 If $A = \dfrac{\pi d}{4}(d+h)$ find:

    (a) A when $\pi = \frac{22}{7}$, $d = 9$ and $h = 5$,

    (b) h when $A = 82\frac{1}{2}$, $\pi = \frac{22}{7}$ and $d = 5$.

14

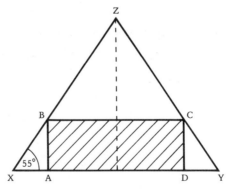

The diagram shows the cross-section of a roof XYZ, the shaded area ABCD representing the cross-section of a room within the roof space.

If $ZX = ZY = 7\frac{1}{2}$ metres, $\angle ZXY = 55°$ and $\dfrac{XB}{BZ} = \dfrac{2}{3}$ find:

    (a) the height of the ridge Z above XY,

    (b) the width of the roof XY,

    (c) the height (AB) and the width (AD) of the room.

15

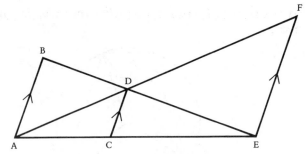

AB, CD and EF are three parallel lines cut by three transversals, ADF, BDE and ACE. If AC = 4 cm, CD = 2 cm, AD = 5 cm and EF = 5 cm use the properties of similar triangles to find:

(a) CE,   (b) AB,   (c) DF.

Find also   (i) $\dfrac{\triangle ADC}{\triangle AFE}$ and   (ii) $\dfrac{\triangle ADC}{\triangle DCE}$.

Revision Paper   **25**

1   Given $\mathcal{E}$ = {the letters of the alphabet used in the word
                        COMPREHENSIVE.}
            A = {the letters used in the word SCIENCE}
            B = {the letters used in the word PROVISION}
  List the elements in the following sets:
            $A,\quad B',\quad (A \cup B)',\quad A \cap B.$

2   Solve:
    (a) $3(x - 12) + 2(3x - 5) = 17,$ (b) $x + \dfrac{x}{3} = 12,$

    (c) $0.25x = 4.$

3   If
$$\frac{1}{x} = \frac{1}{y} + \frac{1}{z}$$
  find:
    (a) the value of x when $y = 2$ and $z = 3,$
    (b) the value of x when $y = 2$ and $z = -3,$
    (c) the value of z when $x = 2$ and $y = \frac{1}{2}.$

4 (a) If the angles of a triangle are $x°$, $(x + 20)°$ and $(2x - 8)°$ find them.

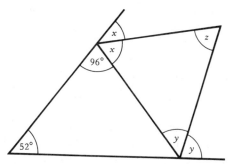

(b) Find each of the angles x, y and z.

5 Construct a rectangle ABCD with AB = 10 cm and BC = 7 cm. Using ruler and compasses only find the midpoint M of AC. With centre M radius AM describe a circle. What points will it pass through?

6 Solve $\dfrac{x + 1}{7} - \dfrac{3(x - 2)}{14} = 1.$

7

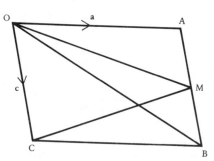

OABC is a parallelogram with M the mid-point of AB.
If **OA** = **a** and **OC** = **c** express each of the vectors **OB, OM, MC** in terms of **a** and **c**.

8   A questionnaire on 'Holidays' given to a form of 35 pupils gave the following information:

18 took a holiday in the United Kingdom (UK)
15 went abroad for a holiday (A)
5 did not have a holiday

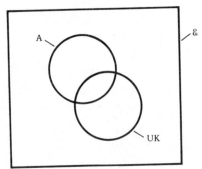

How many pupils took a holiday both abroad and in the United Kingdom?

9   A ladder, 12.5 metres long rests on level ground at a distance 4.4 metres from the base of a vertical wall. The other end leans against the wall. How high is the top of the ladder above the ground?

If a man ascends three-quarters the way up the ladder how far is he:

(a) above the ground,   (b) from the wall?

10 Find:

antilog 2.3010,   log 5721,   tan 63°04′,   log cos 72°51′,

$\sqrt{736.2}$, 17.21^2,   sin 67°05′, $\dfrac{1}{0.3472}$.

11 Simplify:

(a) $\dfrac{a^2 \times a^3}{a^4}$,   (b) $\dfrac{(5a^3)^2}{2a^2}$,   (c) $\dfrac{(-3a)^3}{4a^2}$.

12 EDF is a tangent at D to a circle centre O in which is inscribed a quadrilateral ABCD.

If DAB = 105° and ∠ADE = 42° calculate ∠BCD, ∠CDF, ∠BDE, ∠BDA, ∠DBA and ∠CBD.

172

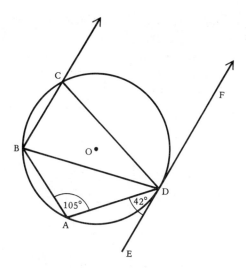

13 John is a fairly light smoker who spends £38.40 a year on cigars. When the price of a cigar rises by 2p he must buy 8 fewer cigars a year if he is to spend exactly the same amount. How many cigars a year does he smoke at present and how much does each cost?

14 If $x = \dfrac{2at}{1+t^2}$ and $y = \dfrac{a(1-t^2)}{1+t^2}$ find $x^2 + y^2$ in as simple a form as possible.

15

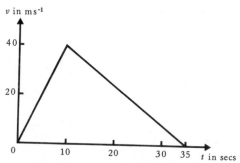

A particle starts from rest and accelerates uniformly until it attains a speed of $40 \, \text{m s}^{-1}$. Immediately, it begins to retard uniformly finally coming to rest 35 sec after it started. Find:
(a) the acceleration in m s^{-2},
(b) the retardation in m s^{-2},
(c) the total distance travelled.

Useful Facts and Formulae

Parallel Lines, Angles and Triangles

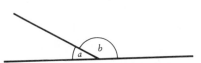

Adjacent angles on a straight line

$$a + b = 180°$$

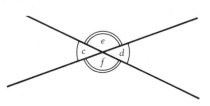

Vertically opposite angles are equal

$$c = d, \ e = f$$

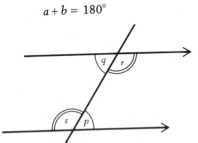

Alternate or Z angles are equal

$$p = q, \ r = s$$

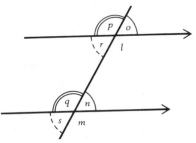

Corresponding angles are equal

$$l = m, \ n = o, \ p = q, \ r = s$$

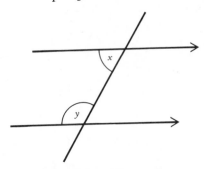

Interior opposite angles on the same side of a transversal are supplementary

$$x + y = 180°$$

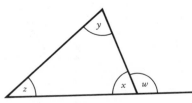

Angles of a triangle total 180°

$$x + y + z = 180°$$

Exterior angle of a triangle equals the sum of the two inside and opposite angles

$$w = y + z$$

Polygons

There are the same number of sides as angles.

The sum of all the exterior angles is 360°.

If the polygon is *regular* all the angles are equal.

The sum of all the interior angles is $(2N - 4)$ right angles where N is the number of sides.

If the polygon is *regular,* all these angles are equal.

The Equation of a Straight Line

$y = mx + c$ where m is the gradient and c the y-intercept.

Pythagoras' Theorem

If ABC is a right-angled triangle with sides a, b and c where c is the hypotenuse then

$$c^2 = a^2 + b^2$$

The Circle

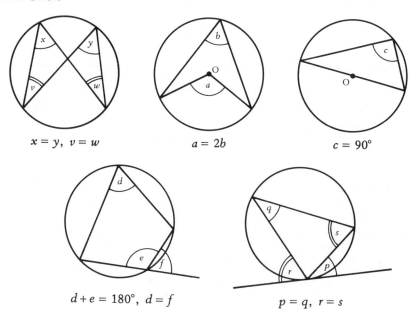

$x = y$, $v = w$ $a = 2b$ $c = 90°$

$d + e = 180°$, $d = f$ $p = q$, $r = s$

Similar triangles

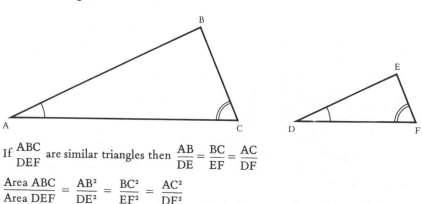

If $\dfrac{ABC}{DEF}$ are similar triangles then $\dfrac{AB}{DE} = \dfrac{BC}{EF} = \dfrac{AC}{DF}$

$$\dfrac{\text{Area ABC}}{\text{Area DEF}} = \dfrac{AB^2}{DE^2} = \dfrac{BC^2}{EF^2} = \dfrac{AC^2}{DF^2}$$

175

Trigonometry

$$\sin A = \frac{\text{Opposite side}}{\text{Hypotenuse}} = \frac{a}{c}$$

$$\cos A = \frac{\text{Adjacent side}}{\text{Hypotenuse}} = \frac{b}{c}$$

$$\tan A = \frac{\text{Opposite side}}{\text{Adjacent side}} = \frac{a}{b}$$

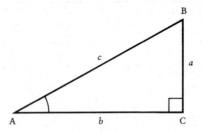

Indices

$$x^m \times x^n = x^{m+n} \qquad\qquad (x^m)^n = x^{mn} \qquad\qquad x^0 = 1$$

$$\frac{x^m}{x^n} = x^{m-n} \qquad\qquad x^{\frac{m}{n}} = \sqrt[n]{x^m} \qquad\qquad x^{-m} = \frac{1}{x^m}$$

Factors

$$a^2 + 2ab + b^2 = (a+b)^2$$

$$a^2 - 2ab + b^2 = (a-b)^2$$

$$a^2 - b^2 = (a+b)(a-b)$$

Determinants and Matrices

The determinant of $A = \begin{vmatrix} a & b \\ c & d \end{vmatrix} = ad - bc$

To *add* matrices: add the corresponding elements.

To *subtract* matrices: subtract the corresponding elements.

Multiplication of matrices

$$\begin{pmatrix} a & b \\ c & d \end{pmatrix} \begin{pmatrix} p & q \\ r & s \end{pmatrix} = \begin{pmatrix} ap+br & aq+bs \\ cp+dr & cq+ds \end{pmatrix}$$

Inverse of a matrix

If $A = \begin{pmatrix} a & b \\ c & d \end{pmatrix}$, $\quad A^{-1} = \frac{1}{|A|} \begin{pmatrix} d & -b \\ -c & a \end{pmatrix}$

Sets

$\&$ or U stands for the universal set

A' is the complement of a set A i.e. the elements of $\&$ which are not in A

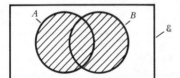

$A \cup B$ is the union of two sets

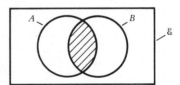

$A \cap B$ is the intersection of two sets

$n(A)$ means the number of elements in the set A.

TABLE OF SQUARES

x	0	1	2	3	4	5	6	7	8	9	1	2	3	4	5	6	7	8	9
1.0	1.000	1.020	1.040	1.061	1.082	1.103	1.124	1.145	1.166	1.188	2	4	6	8	10	13	15	17	19
1.1	1.210	1.232	1.254	1.277	1.300	1.323	1.346	1.369	1.392	1.416	2	5	7	9	11	14	16	18	21
1.2	1.440	1.464	1.488	1.513	1.538	1.563	1.588	1.613	1.638	1.664	2	5	7	10	12	15	17	20	22
1.3	1.690	1.716	1.742	1.769	1.796	1.823	1.850	1.877	1.904	1.932	3	5	8	11	13	16	19	22	24
1.4	1.960	1.988	2.016	2.045	2.074	2.103	2.132	2.161	2.190	2.220	3	6	9	12	14	17	20	23	26
1.5	2.250	2.280	2.310	2.341	2.372	2.403	2.434	2.465	2.496	2.528	3	6	9	12	15	19	22	25	28
1.6	2.560	2.592	2.624	2.657	2.690	2.723	2.756	2.789	2.822	2.856	3	7	10	13	16	20	23	26	30
1.7	2.890	2.924	2.958	2.993	3.028	3.063	3.098	3.133	3.168	3.204	3	7	10	14	17	21	24	28	31
1.8	3.240	3.276	3.312	3.349	3.386	3.423	3.460	3.497	3.534	3.572	4	7	11	15	18	22	26	30	33
1.9	3.610	3.648	3.686	3.725	3.764	3.803	3.842	3.881	3.920	3.960	4	8	12	16	19	23	27	31	35
2.0	4.000	4.040	4.080	4.121	4.162	4.203	4.244	4.285	4.326	4.368	4	8	12	16	20	25	29	33	37
2.1	4.410	4.452	4.494	4.537	4.580	4.623	4.666	4.709	4.752	4.796	4	9	13	17	21	26	30	34	39
2.2	4.840	4.884	4.928	4.973	5.018	5.063	5.108	5.153	5.198	5.244	4	9	13	18	22	27	31	36	40
2.3	5.290	5.336	5.382	5.429	5.476	5.523	5.570	5.617	5.664	5.712	5	9	14	19	23	28	33	38	42
2.4	5.760	5.808	5.856	5.905	5.954	6.003	6.052	6.101	6.150	6.200	5	10	15	20	24	29	34	39	44
2.5	6.250	6.300	6.350	6.401	6.452	6.503	6.554	6.605	6.656	6.708	5	10	15	20	25	31	36	41	46
2.6	6.760	6.812	6.864	6.917	6.970	7.023	7.076	7.129	7.182	7.236	5	11	16	21	26	32	37	42	48
2.7	7.290	7.344	7.398	7.453	7.508	7.563	7.618	7.673	7.728	7.784	5	11	16	22	27	33	38	44	49
2.8	7.840	7.896	7.952	8.009	8.066	8.123	8.180	8.237	8.294	8.352	6	11	17	23	28	34	40	46	51
2.9	8.410	8.468	8.526	8.585	8.644	8.703	8.762	8.821	8.880	8.940	6	12	18	24	29	35	41	47	53
3.0	9.000	9.060	9.120	9.181	9.242	9.303	9.364	9.425	9.486	9.548	6	12	18	24	30	37	43	49	55
3.1	9.610	9.672	9.734	9.797	9.860	9.923	9.986	10.05	10.11	10.18	6	13	19	25	31	38	44	50	57
3.2	10.24	10.30	10.37	10.43	10.50	10.56	10.63	10.69	10.76	10.82	1	1	2	3	3	4	5	5	6
3.3	10.89	10.96	11.02	11.09	11.16	11.22	11.29	11.36	11.42	11.49	1	1	2	3	3	4	5	5	6
3.4	11.56	11.63	11.70	11.76	11.83	11.90	11.97	12.04	12.11	12.18	1	1	2	3	3	4	5	6	6
3.5	12.25	12.32	12.39	12.46	12.53	12.60	12.67	12.74	12.82	12.89	1	1	2	3	4	4	5	6	6
3.6	12.96	13.03	13.10	13.18	13.25	13.32	13.40	13.47	13.54	13.62	1	1	2	3	4	4	5	6	7
3.7	13.69	13.76	13.84	13.91	13.99	14.06	14.14	14.21	14.29	14.36	1	2	2	3	4	4	5	6	7
3.8	14.44	14.52	14.59	14.67	14.75	14.82	14.90	14.98	15.05	15.13	1	2	2	3	4	5	5	6	7
3.9	15.21	15.29	15.37	15.44	15.52	15.60	15.68	15.76	15.84	15.92	1	2	2	3	4	5	6	6	7
4.0	16.00	16.08	16.16	16.24	16.32	16.40	16.48	16.56	16.65	16.73	1	2	2	3	4	5	6	6	7
4.1	16.81	16.89	16.97	17.06	17.14	17.22	17.31	17.39	17.47	17.56	1	2	2	3	4	5	6	7	7
4.2	17.64	17.72	17.81	17.89	17.98	18.06	18.15	18.23	18.32	18.40	1	2	3	3	4	5	6	7	8
4.3	18.49	18.58	18.66	18.75	18.84	18.92	19.01	19.10	19.18	19.27	1	2	3	3	4	5	6	7	8
4.4	19.36	19.45	19.54	19.62	19.71	19.80	19.89	19.98	20.07	20.16	1	2	3	4	4	5	6	7	8
4.5	20.25	20.34	20.43	20.52	20.61	20.70	20.79	20.88	20.98	21.07	1	2	3	4	5	5	6	7	8
4.6	21.16	21.25	21.34	21.44	21.53	21.62	21.72	21.81	21.90	22.00	1	2	3	4	5	6	7	7	8
4.7	22.09	22.18	22.28	22.37	22.47	22.56	22.66	22.75	22.85	22.94	1	2	3	4	5	6	7	8	9
4.8	23.04	23.14	23.23	23.33	23.43	23.52	23.62	23.72	23.81	23.91	1	2	3	4	5	6	7	8	9
4.9	24.01	24.11	24.21	24.30	24.40	24.50	24.60	24.70	24.80	24.90	1	2	3	4	5	6	7	8	9
5.0	25.00	25.10	25.20	25.30	25.40	25.50	25.60	25.70	25.81	25.91	1	2	3	4	5	6	7	8	9
5.1	26.01	26.11	26.21	26.32	26.42	26.52	26.63	26.73	26.83	26.94	1	2	3	4	5	6	7	8	9
5.2	27.04	27.14	27.25	27.35	27.46	27.56	27.67	27.77	27.88	27.98	1	2	3	4	5	6	7	8	9
5.3	28.09	28.20	28.30	28.41	28.52	28.62	28.73	28.84	28.94	29.05	1	2	3	4	5	6	7	9	10
5.4	29.16	29.27	29.38	29.48	29.59	29.70	29.81	29.92	30.03	30.14	1	2	3	4	5	7	8	9	10

TABLE OF SQUARES (continued)

x	0	1	2	3	4	5	6	7	8	9	1	2	3	4	5	6	7	8	9
5.5	30.25	30.36	30.47	30.58	30.69	30.80	30.91	31.02	31.14	31.25	1	2	3	4	6	7	8	9	10
5.6	31.36	31.47	31.58	31.70	31.81	31.92	32.04	32.15	32.26	32.38	1	2	3	5	6	7	8	9	10
5.7	32.49	32.60	32.72	32.83	32.95	33.06	33.18	33.29	33.41	33.52	1	2	3	5	6	7	8	9	10
5.8	33.64	33.76	33.87	33.99	34.11	34.22	34.34	34.46	34.57	34.69	1	2	4	5	6	7	8	9	11
5.9	34.81	34.93	35.05	35.16	35.28	35.40	35.52	35.64	35.76	35.88	1	2	4	5	6	7	8	10	11
6.0	36.00	36.12	36.24	36.36	36.48	36.60	36.72	36.84	36.97	37.09	1	2	4	5	6	7	9	10	11
6.1	37.21	37.33	37.45	37.58	37.70	37.82	37.95	38.07	38.19	38.32	1	2	4	5	6	7	9	10	11
6.2	38.44	38.56	38.69	38.81	38.94	39.06	39.19	39.31	39.44	39.56	1	3	4	5	6	8	9	10	11
6.3	39.69	39.82	39.94	40.07	40.20	40.32	40.45	40.58	40.70	40.83	1	3	4	5	6	8	9	10	11
6.4	40.96	41.09	41.22	41.34	41.47	41.60	41.73	41.86	41.99	42.12	1	3	4	5	6	8	9	10	12
6.5	42.25	42.38	42.51	42.64	42.77	42.90	43.03	43.16	43.30	43.43	1	3	4	5	7	8	9	10	12
6.6	43.56	43.69	43.82	43.96	44.09	44.22	44.36	44.49	44.62	44.76	1	3	4	5	7	8	9	11	12
6.7	44.89	45.02	45.16	45.29	45.43	45.56	45.70	45.83	45.97	46.10	1	3	4	5	7	8	9	11	12
6.8	46.24	46.38	46.51	46.65	46.79	46.92	47.06	47.20	47.33	47.47	1	3	4	5	7	8	10	11	12
6.9	47.61	47.75	47.89	48.02	48.16	48.30	48.44	48.58	48.72	48.86	1	3	4	6	7	8	10	11	13
7.0	49.00	49.14	49.28	49.42	49.56	49.70	49.84	49.98	50.13	50.27	1	3	4	6	7	8	10	11	13
7.1	50.41	50.55	50.69	50.84	50.98	51.12	51.27	51.41	51.55	51.70	1	3	4	6	7	9	10	11	13
7.2	51.84	51.98	52.13	52.27	52.42	52.56	52.71	52.85	53.00	53.14	1	3	4	6	7	9	10	12	13
7.3	53.29	53.44	53.58	53.73	53.88	54.02	54.17	54.32	54.46	54.61	1	3	4	6	7	9	10	12	13
7.4	54.76	54.91	55.06	55.20	55.35	55.50	55.65	55.80	55.95	56.10	1	3	4	6	7	9	10	12	13
7.5	56.25	56.40	56.55	56.70	56.85	57.00	57.15	57.30	57.46	57.61	2	3	5	6	8	9	11	12	14
7.6	57.76	57.91	58.06	58.22	58.37	58.52	58.68	58.83	58.98	59.14	2	3	5	6	8	9	11	12	14
7.7	59.29	59.44	59.60	59.75	59.91	60.06	60.22	60.37	60.53	60.68	2	3	5	6	8	9	11	12	14
7.8	60.84	61.00	61.15	61.31	61.47	61.62	61.78	61.94	62.09	62.25	2	3	5	6	8	9	11	13	14
7.9	62.41	62.57	62.73	62.88	63.04	63.20	63.36	63.52	63.68	63.84	2	3	5	6	8	10	11	13	14
8.0	64.00	64.16	64.32	64.48	64.64	64.80	64.96	65.12	65.29	65.45	2	3	5	6	8	10	11	13	14
8.1	65.61	65.77	65.93	66.10	66.26	66.42	67.59	66.75	66.91	67.08	2	3	5	7	8	10	11	13	15
8.2	67.24	67.40	67.57	67.73	67.90	68.06	68.23	68.39	68.56	68.72	2	3	5	7	8	10	12	13	15
8.3	68.89	69.06	69.22	69.39	69.56	69.72	69.89	70.06	70.22	70.39	2	3	5	7	8	10	12	13	15
8.4	70.56	70.73	70.90	71.06	71.23	71.40	71.57	71.74	71.91	72.08	2	3	5	7	8	10	12	14	15
8.5	72.25	72.42	72.59	72.76	72.93	73.10	73.27	73.44	73.62	73.79	2	3	5	7	9	10	12	14	15
8.6	73.96	74.13	74.30	74.48	74.65	74.82	75.00	75.17	75.34	75.52	2	3	5	7	9	10	12	14	16
8.7	75.69	75.86	76.04	76.21	76.39	76.56	76.74	76.91	77.09	77.26	2	4	5	7	9	11	12	14	16
8.8	77.44	77.62	77.79	77.97	78.15	78.32	78.50	78.68	78.85	79.03	2	4	5	7	9	11	12	14	16
8.9	79.21	79.39	79.57	79.74	79.92	80.10	80.28	80.46	80.64	80.82	2	4	5	7	9	11	13	14	16
9.0	81.00	81.18	81.36	81.54	81.72	81.90	82.08	82.26	82.45	82.63	2	4	5	7	9	11	13	14	16
9.1	82.81	82.99	83.17	83.36	83.54	83.72	83.91	84.09	84.27	84.46	2	4	5	7	9	11	13	15	16
9.2	84.64	84.82	85.01	85.19	85.38	85.56	85.75	85.93	86.12	86.30	2	4	6	7	9	11	13	15	17
9.3	86.49	86.68	86.86	87.05	87.24	87.42	87.61	87.80	87.98	88.17	2	4	6	7	9	11	13	15	17
9.4	88.36	88.55	88.74	88.92	89.11	89.30	89.49	89.68	89.87	90.06	2	4	6	8	9	11	13	15	17
9.5	90.25	90.44	90.63	90.82	91.01	91.20	91.39	91.58	91.78	91.97	2	4	6	8	10	11	13	15	17
9.6	92.16	92.35	92.54	92.74	92.93	93.12	93.32	93.51	93.70	93.90	2	4	6	8	10	12	14	15	17
9.7	94.09	94.28	94.48	94.67	94.87	95.06	95.26	95.45	95.65	95.84	2	4	6	8	10	12	14	16	18
9.8	96.04	96.24	96.43	96.63	96.83	97.02	97.22	97.42	97.61	97.81	2	4	6	8	10	12	14	16	18
9.9	98.01	98.21	98.41	98.60	98.80	99.00	99.20	99.40	99.60	99.80	2	4	6	8	10	12	14	16	18

SQUARE ROOT TABLES

Main values — each cell shows $\sqrt{N}$ (upper) and $\sqrt{10N}$ (lower).

	0	1	2	3	4	5	6	7	8	9
10	1000 / 3162	1005 / 3178	1010 / 3194	1015 / 3209	1020 / 3225	1025 / 3240	1030 / 3256	1034 / 3271	1039 / 3286	1044 / 3302
11	1049 / 3317	1054 / 3332	1058 / 3347	1063 / 3362	1068 / 3376	1072 / 3391	1077 / 3406	1082 / 3421	1086 / 3435	1091 / 3450
12	1095 / 3464	1100 / 3479	1105 / 3493	1109 / 3507	1114 / 3521	1118 / 3536	1122 / 3550	1127 / 3564	1131 / 3578	1136 / 3592
13	1140 / 3606	1145 / 3619	1149 / 3633	1153 / 3647	1158 / 3661	1162 / 3674	1166 / 3688	1170 / 3701	1175 / 3715	1179 / 3728
14	1183 / 3742	1187 / 3755	1192 / 3768	1196 / 3782	1200 / 3795	1204 / 3808	1208 / 3821	1212 / 3834	1217 / 3847	1221 / 3860
15	1225 / 3873	1229 / 3886	1233 / 3899	1237 / 3912	1241 / 3924	1245 / 3937	1249 / 3950	1253 / 3962	1257 / 3975	1261 / 3987
16	1265 / 4000	1269 / 4012	1273 / 4025	1277 / 4037	1281 / 4050	1285 / 4062	1288 / 4074	1292 / 4087	1296 / 4099	1300 / 4111
17	1304 / 4123	1308 / 4135	1311 / 4147	1315 / 4159	1319 / 4171	1323 / 4183	1327 / 4195	1330 / 4207	1334 / 4219	1338 / 4231
18	1342 / 4243	1345 / 4254	1349 / 4266	1353 / 4278	1356 / 4290	1360 / 4301	1364 / 4313	1367 / 4324	1371 / 4336	1375 / 4347
19	1378 / 4359	1382 / 4370	1386 / 4382	1389 / 4393	1393 / 4405	1396 / 4416	1400 / 4427	1404 / 4438	1407 / 4450	1411 / 4461
20	1414 / 4472	1418 / 4483	1421 / 4494	1425 / 4506	1428 / 4517	1432 / 4528	1435 / 4539	1439 / 4550	1442 / 4561	1446 / 4572
21	1449 / 4583	1453 / 4593	1456 / 4604	1459 / 4615	1463 / 4626	1466 / 4637	1470 / 4648	1473 / 4658	1476 / 4669	1480 / 4680
22	1483 / 4690	1487 / 4701	1490 / 4712	1493 / 4722	1497 / 4733	1500 / 4743	1503 / 4754	1507 / 4764	1510 / 4775	1513 / 4785
23	1517 / 4796	1520 / 4806	1523 / 4817	1526 / 4827	1530 / 4837	1533 / 4848	1536 / 4858	1539 / 4868	1543 / 4879	1546 / 4889
24	1549 / 4899	1552 / 4909	1556 / 4919	1559 / 4930	1562 / 4940	1565 / 4950	1568 / 4960	1572 / 4970	1575 / 4980	1578 / 4990
25	1581 / 5000	1584 / 5010	1587 / 5020	1591 / 5030	1594 / 5040	1597 / 5050	1600 / 5060	1603 / 5070	1606 / 5079	1609 / 5089
26	1612 / 5099	1616 / 5109	1619 / 5119	1622 / 5128	1625 / 5138	1628 / 5148	1631 / 5158	1634 / 5167	1637 / 5177	1640 / 5187
27	1643 / 5196	1646 / 5206	1649 / 5215	1652 / 5225	1655 / 5235	1658 / 5244	1661 / 5254	1664 / 5263	1667 / 5273	1670 / 5282
28	1673 / 5292	1676 / 5301	1679 / 5310	1682 / 5320	1685 / 5329	1688 / 5339	1691 / 5348	1694 / 5357	1697 / 5367	1700 / 5376
29	1703 / 5385	1706 / 5394	1709 / 5404	1712 / 5413	1715 / 5422	1718 / 5431	1720 / 5441	1723 / 5450	1726 / 5459	1729 / 5468
30	1732 / 5477	1735 / 5486	1738 / 5495	1741 / 5505	1744 / 5514	1746 / 5523	1749 / 5532	1752 / 5541	1755 / 5550	1758 / 5559
31	1761 / 5568	1764 / 5577	1766 / 5586	1769 / 5595	1772 / 5604	1775 / 5612	1778 / 5621	1780 / 5630	1783 / 5639	1786 / 5648
32	1789 / 5657	1792 / 5666	1794 / 5675	1797 / 5683	1800 / 5692	1803 / 5701	1806 / 5710	1808 / 5718	1811 / 5727	1814 / 5736

Mean differences (proportional parts) — upper value for $\sqrt{N}$, lower for $\sqrt{10N}$.

	1	2	3	4	5	6	7	8	9
10	0/2	1/3	1/5	2/6	2/8	3/9	3/11	4/12	4/14
11	0/1	1/3	1/4	2/6	2/7	3/9	3/10	4/12	4/13
12	0/1	1/3	1/4	2/6	2/7	3/9	3/10	4/11	4/13
13	0/1	1/3	1/4	2/5	2/7	3/8	3/9	3/11	4/12
14	0/1	1/3	1/4	2/5	2/7	3/8	3/9	3/10	4/12
15	0/1	1/3	1/4	2/5	2/6	2/8	3/9	3/10	4/11
16	0/1	1/2	1/4	2/5	2/6	2/7	3/9	3/10	4/11
17	0/1	1/2	1/4	2/5	2/6	2/7	3/8	3/10	3/11
18	0/1	1/2	1/3	1/5	2/6	2/7	3/8	3/9	3/10
19	0/1	1/2	1/3	1/5	2/6	2/7	3/8	3/9	3/10
20	0/1	1/2	1/3	1/4	2/6	2/7	2/8	3/9	3/10
21	0/1	1/2	1/3	1/4	2/5	2/6	2/8	3/9	3/10
22	0/1	1/2	1/3	1/4	2/5	2/6	2/7	3/8	3/10
23	0/1	1/2	1/3	1/4	2/5	2/6	2/7	3/8	3/9
24	0/1	1/2	1/3	1/4	2/5	2/6	2/7	3/8	3/9
25	0/1	1/2	1/3	1/4	2/5	2/6	2/7	2/8	3/9
26	0/1	1/2	1/3	1/4	2/5	2/6	2/7	2/8	3/9
27	0/1	1/2	1/3	1/4	2/5	2/6	2/7	2/8	3/9
28	0/1	1/2	1/3	1/4	2/5	2/6	2/7	2/7	3/8
29	0/1	1/2	1/3	1/4	1/5	2/6	2/6	2/7	3/8
30	0/1	1/2	1/3	1/4	1/5	2/5	2/6	2/7	3/8
31	0/1	1/2	1/3	1/4	1/4	2/5	2/6	2/7	3/8
32	0/1	1/2	1/3	1/4	1/4	2/5	2/6	2/7	3/8

The first significant figure and the position of the decimal point must be determined by the user.

SQUARE ROOT TABLES (continued)

Main values — each cell shows $\sqrt{N}$ (upper) and $\sqrt{10N}$ (lower).

	0	1	2	3	4	5	6	7	8	9
33	1817 / 5745	1819 / 5753	1822 / 5762	1825 / 5771	1828 / 5779	1830 / 5788	1833 / 5797	1836 / 5805	1838 / 5814	1841 / 5822
34	1844 / 5831	1847 / 5840	1849 / 5848	1852 / 5857	1855 / 5865	1857 / 5874	1860 / 5882	1863 / 5891	1865 / 5899	1868 / 5908
35	1871 / 5916	1873 / 5925	1876 / 5933	1879 / 5941	1881 / 5950	1884 / 5958	1887 / 5967	1889 / 5975	1892 / 5983	1895 / 5992
36	1897 / 6000	1900 / 6008	1903 / 6017	1905 / 6025	1908 / 6033	1910 / 6042	1913 / 6050	1916 / 6058	1918 / 6066	1921 / 6075
37	1924 / 6083	1926 / 6091	1929 / 6099	1931 / 6107	1934 / 6116	1936 / 6124	1939 / 6132	1942 / 6140	1944 / 6148	1947 / 6156
38	1949 / 6164	1952 / 6173	1954 / 6181	1957 / 6189	1960 / 6197	1962 / 6205	1965 / 6213	1967 / 6221	1970 / 6229	1972 / 6237
39	1975 / 6245	1977 / 6253	1980 / 6261	1982 / 6269	1985 / 6277	1987 / 6285	1990 / 6293	1992 / 6301	1995 / 6309	1997 / 6317
40	2000 / 6325	2002 / 6332	2005 / 6340	2007 / 6348	2010 / 6356	2012 / 6364	2015 / 6372	2017 / 6380	2020 / 6387	2022 / 6395
41	2025 / 6403	2027 / 6411	2030 / 6419	2032 / 6427	2035 / 6434	2037 / 6442	2040 / 6450	2042 / 6458	2045 / 6465	2047 / 6473
42	2049 / 6481	2052 / 6488	2054 / 6496	2057 / 6504	2059 / 6512	2062 / 6519	2064 / 6527	2066 / 6535	2069 / 6542	2071 / 6550
43	2074 / 6557	2076 / 6565	2078 / 6573	2081 / 6580	2083 / 6588	2086 / 6596	2088 / 6603	2090 / 6611	2093 / 6618	2095 / 6626
44	2098 / 6633	2100 / 6641	2102 / 6648	2105 / 6656	2107 / 6663	2110 / 6671	2112 / 6678	2114 / 6686	2117 / 6693	2119 / 6701
45	2121 / 6708	2124 / 6716	2126 / 6723	2128 / 6731	2131 / 6738	2133 / 6745	2135 / 6753	2138 / 6760	2140 / 6768	2142 / 6775
46	2145 / 6782	2147 / 6790	2149 / 6797	2152 / 6804	2154 / 6812	2156 / 6819	2159 / 6826	2161 / 6834	2163 / 6841	2166 / 6848
47	2168 / 6856	2170 / 6863	2173 / 6870	2175 / 6877	2177 / 6885	2179 / 6892	2182 / 6899	2184 / 6907	2186 / 6914	2189 / 6921
48	2191 / 6928	2193 / 6935	2195 / 6943	2198 / 6950	2200 / 6957	2202 / 6964	2205 / 6971	2207 / 6979	2209 / 6986	2211 / 6993
49	2214 / 7000	2216 / 7007	2218 / 7014	2220 / 7021	2223 / 7029	2225 / 7036	2227 / 7043	2229 / 7050	2232 / 7057	2234 / 7064
50	2236 / 7071	2238 / 7078	2241 / 7085	2243 / 7092	2245 / 7099	2247 / 7106	2249 / 7113	2252 / 7120	2254 / 7127	2256 / 7134
51	2258 / 7141	2261 / 7148	2263 / 7155	2265 / 7162	2267 / 7169	2269 / 7176	2272 / 7183	2274 / 7190	2276 / 7197	2278 / 7204
52	2280 / 7211	2283 / 7218	2285 / 7225	2287 / 7232	2289 / 7239	2291 / 7246	2293 / 7253	2296 / 7259	2298 / 7266	2300 / 7273
53	2302 / 7280	2304 / 7287	2307 / 7294	2309 / 7301	2311 / 7308	2313 / 7314	2315 / 7321	2317 / 7328	2319 / 7335	2322 / 7342
54	2324 / 7348	2326 / 7355	2328 / 7362	2330 / 7369	2332 / 7376	2335 / 7382	2337 / 7389	2339 / 7396	2341 / 7403	2343 / 7409

Mean differences (proportional parts) — upper value for $\sqrt{N}$, lower for $\sqrt{10N}$.

	1	2	3	4	5	6	7	8	9
33	0/1	1/2	1/3	1/3	1/4	2/5	2/6	2/7	2/8
34	0/1	1/2	1/3	1/3	1/4	2/5	2/6	2/7	2/8
35	0/1	1/2	1/3	1/3	1/4	2/5	2/6	2/7	2/8
36	0/1	1/2	1/2	1/3	1/4	2/5	2/6	2/7	2/8
37	0/1	1/2	1/2	1/3	1/4	2/5	2/6	2/6	2/7
38	0/1	1/2	1/2	1/3	1/4	2/5	2/6	2/6	2/7
39	0/1	0/2	1/2	1/3	1/4	1/5	2/6	2/6	2/7
40	0/1	0/2	1/2	1/3	1/4	1/5	2/5	2/6	2/7
41	0/1	0/2	1/2	1/3	1/4	1/5	2/5	2/6	2/7
42	0/1	0/2	1/2	1/3	1/4	1/5	2/5	2/6	2/7
43	0/1	0/2	1/2	1/3	1/4	1/5	2/5	2/6	2/7
44	0/1	0/2	1/2	1/3	1/4	1/5	2/5	2/6	2/7
45	0/1	0/1	1/2	1/3	1/4	1/4	2/5	2/6	2/7
46	0/1	0/1	1/2	1/3	1/4	1/4	2/5	2/6	2/7
47	0/1	0/1	1/2	1/3	1/4	1/4	2/5	2/6	2/6
48	0/1	0/1	1/2	1/3	1/4	1/4	2/5	2/6	2/6
49	0/1	0/1	1/2	1/3	1/4	1/4	2/5	2/6	2/6
50	0/1	0/1	1/2	1/3	1/4	1/4	2/5	2/6	2/6
51	0/1	0/1	1/2	1/3	1/4	1/4	2/5	2/6	2/6
52	0/1	0/1	1/2	1/3	1/3	1/4	2/5	2/6	2/6
53	0/1	0/1	1/2	1/3	1/3	1/4	2/5	2/6	2/6
54	0/1	0/1	1/2	1/3	1/3	1/4	1/5	2/5	2/6

The first significant figure and the position of the decimal point must be determined by the user.

178

Square roots (rows 78–99). Each cell gives two values: √(7.8x … 9.9x) / √(78.x … 99.x).

	0	1	2	3	4	5	6	7	8	9
78	2793/8832	2795/8837	2796/8843	2798/8849	2800/8854	2802/8860	2804/8866	2805/8871	2807/8877	2809/8883
79	2811/8888	2812/8894	2814/8899	2816/8905	2818/8911	2820/8916	2821/8922	2823/8927	2825/8933	2827/8939
80	2828/8944	2830/8950	2832/8955	2834/8961	2835/8967	2837/8972	2839/8978	2841/8983	2843/8989	2844/8994
81	2846/9000	2848/9006	2850/9011	2851/9017	2853/9022	2855/9028	2857/9033	2858/9039	2860/9044	2862/9050
82	2864/9055	2865/9061	2867/9066	2869/9072	2871/9077	2872/9083	2874/9088	2876/9094	2877/9099	2879/9105
83	2881/9110	2883/9116	2884/9121	2886/9127	2888/9132	2890/9138	2891/9143	2893/9149	2895/9154	2897/9160
84	2898/9165	2900/9171	2902/9176	2903/9182	2905/9187	2907/9192	2909/9198	2910/9203	2912/9209	2914/9214
85	2915/9220	2917/9225	2919/9230	2921/9236	2922/9241	2924/9247	2926/9252	2927/9257	2929/9263	2931/9268
86	2933/9274	2934/9279	2936/9284	2938/9290	2939/9295	2941/9301	2943/9306	2944/9311	2946/9317	2948/9322
87	2950/9327	2951/9333	2953/9338	2955/9343	2956/9349	2958/9354	2960/9359	2961/9365	2963/9370	2965/9375
88	2966/9381	2968/9386	2970/9391	2972/9397	2973/9402	2975/9407	2977/9413	2978/9418	2980/9423	2982/9429
89	2983/9434	2985/9439	2987/9445	2988/9450	2990/9455	2992/9460	2993/9466	2995/9471	2997/9476	2998/9482
90	3000/9487	3002/9492	3003/9497	3005/9503	3007/9508	3008/9513	3010/9518	3012/9524	3013/9529	3015/9534
91	3017/9539	3018/9545	3020/9550	3022/9555	3023/9560	3025/9566	3027/9571	3028/9576	3030/9581	3032/9586
92	3033/9592	3035/9597	3036/9602	3038/9607	3040/9612	3041/9618	3043/9623	3045/9628	3046/9633	3048/9638
93	3050/9644	3051/9649	3053/9654	3055/9659	3056/9664	3058/9670	3059/9675	3061/9680	3063/9685	3064/9690
94	3066/9695	3068/9701	3069/9706	3071/9711	3072/9716	3074/9721	3076/9726	3077/9731	3079/9737	3081/9742
95	3082/9747	3084/9752	3085/9757	3087/9762	3089/9767	3090/9772	3092/9778	3094/9783	3095/9788	3097/9793
96	3098/9798	3100/9803	3102/9808	3103/9813	3105/9818	3106/9823	3108/9829	3110/9834	3111/9839	3113/9844
97	3114/9849	3116/9854	3118/9859	3119/9864	3121/9869	3122/9874	3124/9879	3126/9884	3127/9889	3129/9894
98	3130/9899	3132/9905	3134/9910	3135/9915	3137/9920	3138/9925	3140/9930	3142/9935	3143/9940	3145/9945
99	3146/9950	3148/9955	3150/9960	3151/9965	3153/9970	3154/9975	3156/9980	3158/9985	3159/9990	3161/9995

Mean differences (columns 1–9; top/bottom line):

	1	2	3	4	5	6	7	8	9
78	0/1	0/1	1/2	1/2	1/3	1/3	1/4	1/5	2/5
79	0/1	0/1	1/2	1/2	1/3	1/3	1/4	1/5	2/5
80	0/1	0/1	1/2	1/2	1/3	1/3	1/4	1/4	2/5
81	0/1	0/1	1/2	1/2	1/3	1/3	1/4	1/4	2/5
82	0/1	0/1	1/2	1/2	1/3	1/3	1/4	1/4	2/5
83	0/1	0/1	1/2	1/2	1/3	1/3	1/4	1/4	2/5
84	0/1	0/1	1/2	1/2	1/3	1/3	1/4	1/4	2/5
85	0/1	0/1	1/2	1/2	1/3	1/3	1/4	1/4	2/5
86	0/1	0/1	1/2	1/2	1/3	1/3	1/4	1/4	2/5
87	0/1	0/1	1/2	1/2	1/3	1/3	1/4	1/4	2/5
88	0/1	0/1	1/2	1/2	1/3	1/3	1/4	1/4	2/5
89	0/1	0/1	1/2	1/2	1/3	1/3	1/4	1/4	2/5
90	0/1	0/1	1/2	1/2	1/3	1/3	1/4	1/4	2/5
91	0/1	0/1	1/2	1/2	1/3	1/3	1/4	1/4	2/5
92	0/1	0/1	0/2	1/2	1/3	1/3	1/4	1/4	1/5
93	0/1	0/1	0/2	1/2	1/3	1/3	1/4	1/4	1/5
94	0/1	0/1	0/2	1/2	1/3	1/3	1/4	1/4	1/5
95	0/1	0/1	0/2	1/2	1/3	1/3	1/4	1/4	1/5
96	0/1	0/1	0/2	1/2	1/3	1/3	1/4	1/4	1/5
97	0/1	0/1	0/2	1/2	1/3	1/3	1/4	1/4	1/5
98	0/1	0/1	0/2	1/2	1/3	1/3	1/4	1/4	1/5
99	0/1	0/1	0/2	1/2	1/3	1/3	1/4	1/4	1/5

The first significant figure and the position of the decimal point must be determined by the user.

Square roots (rows 55–77). Each cell gives two values: √(5.5x … 7.7x) / √(55.x … 77.x).

	0	1	2	3	4	5	6	7	8	9
55	2345/7416	2347/7423	2349/7430	2352/7436	2354/7443	2356/7450	2358/7457	2360/7463	2362/7470	2364/7477
56	2366/7483	2369/7490	2371/7497	2373/7503	2375/7510	2377/7517	2379/7523	2381/7530	2383/7537	2385/7543
57	2387/7550	2390/7556	2392/7563	2394/7570	2396/7576	2398/7583	2400/7589	2402/7596	2404/7603	2406/7609
58	2408/7616	2410/7622	2412/7629	2415/7635	2417/7642	2419/7649	2421/7655	2423/7662	2425/7668	2427/7675
59	2429/7681	2431/7688	2433/7694	2435/7701	2437/7707	2439/7714	2441/7720	2443/7727	2445/7733	2447/7740
60	2449/7746	2452/7752	2454/7759	2456/7765	2458/7772	2460/7778	2462/7785	2464/7791	2466/7797	2468/7804
61	2470/7810	2472/7817	2474/7823	2476/7829	2478/7836	2480/7842	2482/7849	2484/7855	2486/7861	2488/7868
62	2490/7874	2492/7880	2494/7887	2496/7893	2498/7899	2500/7906	2502/7912	2504/7918	2506/7925	2508/7931
63	2510/7937	2512/7944	2514/7950	2516/7956	2518/7962	2520/7969	2522/7975	2524/7981	2526/7987	2528/7994
64	2530/8000	2532/8006	2534/8012	2536/8019	2538/8025	2540/8031	2542/8037	2544/8044	2546/8050	2548/8056
65	2550/8062	2551/8068	2553/8075	2555/8081	2557/8087	2559/8093	2561/8099	2563/8106	2565/8112	2567/8118
66	2569/8124	2571/8130	2573/8136	2575/8142	2577/8149	2579/8155	2581/8161	2583/8167	2585/8173	2587/8179
67	2588/8185	2590/8191	2592/8198	2594/8204	2596/8210	2598/8216	2600/8222	2602/8228	2604/8234	2606/8240
68	2608/8246	2610/8252	2612/8258	2613/8264	2615/8270	2617/8276	2619/8283	2621/8289	2623/8295	2625/8301
69	2627/8307	2629/8313	2631/8319	2632/8325	2634/8331	2636/8337	2638/8343	2640/8349	2642/8355	2644/8361
70	2646/8367	2648/8373	2650/8379	2651/8385	2653/8390	2655/8396	2657/8402	2659/8408	2661/8414	2663/8420
71	2665/8426	2666/8432	2668/8438	2670/8444	2672/8450	2674/8456	2676/8462	2678/8468	2680/8473	2681/8479
72	2683/8485	2685/8491	2687/8497	2689/8503	2691/8509	2693/8515	2694/8521	2696/8526	2698/8532	2700/8538
73	2702/8544	2704/8550	2706/8556	2707/8562	2709/8567	2711/8573	2713/8579	2715/8585	2717/8591	2718/8597
74	2720/8602	2722/8608	2724/8614	2726/8620	2728/8626	2729/8631	2731/8637	2733/8643	2735/8649	2737/8654
75	2739/8660	2740/8666	2742/8672	2744/8678	2746/8683	2748/8689	2750/8695	2751/8701	2753/8706	2755/8712
76	2757/8718	2759/8724	2760/8729	2762/8735	2764/8741	2766/8746	2768/8752	2769/8758	2771/8764	2773/8769
77	2775/8775	2777/8781	2778/8786	2780/8792	2782/8798	2784/8803	2786/8809	2787/8815	2789/8820	2791/8826

Mean differences (columns 1–9; top/bottom line):

	1	2	3	4	5	6	7	8	9
55	0/1	0/1	1/2	1/3	1/3	1/4	1/5	2/5	2/6
56	0/1	0/1	1/2	1/3	1/3	1/4	1/5	2/5	2/6
57	0/1	0/1	1/2	1/3	1/3	1/4	1/5	2/5	2/6
58	0/1	0/1	1/2	1/3	1/3	1/4	1/5	2/5	2/6
59	0/1	0/1	1/2	1/3	1/3	1/4	1/5	2/5	2/6
60	0/1	0/1	1/2	1/3	1/3	1/4	1/5	2/5	2/6
61	0/1	0/1	1/2	1/3	1/3	1/4	1/4	2/5	2/6
62	0/1	0/1	1/2	1/3	1/3	1/4	1/4	2/5	2/6
63	0/1	0/1	1/2	1/3	1/3	1/4	1/4	2/5	2/6
64	0/1	0/1	1/2	1/3	1/3	1/4	1/4	2/5	2/6
65	0/1	0/1	1/2	1/2	1/3	1/4	1/4	2/5	2/6
66	0/1	0/1	1/2	1/2	1/3	1/4	1/4	2/5	2/6
67	0/1	0/1	1/2	1/2	1/3	1/4	1/4	2/5	2/5
68	0/1	0/1	1/2	1/2	1/3	1/4	1/4	2/5	2/5
69	0/1	0/1	1/2	1/2	1/3	1/4	1/4	2/5	2/5
70	0/1	0/1	1/2	1/2	1/3	1/4	1/4	2/5	2/5
71	0/1	0/1	1/2	1/2	1/3	1/4	1/4	2/5	2/5
72	0/1	0/1	1/2	1/2	1/3	1/4	1/4	2/5	2/5
73	0/1	0/1	1/2	1/2	1/3	1/4	1/4	2/5	2/5
74	0/1	0/1	1/2	1/2	1/3	1/3	1/4	1/5	2/5
75	0/1	0/1	1/2	1/2	1/3	1/3	1/4	1/5	2/5
76	0/1	0/1	1/2	1/2	1/3	1/3	1/4	1/5	2/5
77	0/1	0/1	1/2	1/2	1/3	1/3	1/4	1/5	2/5

The first significant figure and the position of the decimal point must be determined by the user.

TABLE OF RECIPROCALS OF NUMBERS FROM 1—10

	0	1	2	3	4	5	6	7	8	9	1	2	3	4	5	6	7	8	9
1.0	1.0000	0.9901	0.9804	0.9709	0.9615	0.9524	0.9434	0.9346	0.9259	0.9174									
1.1	0.9091	0.9009	0.8929	0.8850	0.8772	0.8696	0.8621	0.8547	0.8475	0.8403.									
1.2	0.8333	0.8264	0.8197	0.8130	0.8065	0.8000	0.7937	0.7874	0.7813	0.7752									
1.3	0.7692	0.7634	0.7576	0.7519	0.7463	0.7407	0.7353	0.7299	0.7246	0.7194									
1.4	0.7143	0.7092	0.7042	0.6993	0.6944	0.6897	0.6849	0.6803	0.6757	0.6711									
1.5	0.6667	0.6623	0.6579	0.6536	0.6494	0.6452	0.6410	0.6369	0.6329	0.6289	4	8	12	17	21	25	29	33	37
1.6	0.6250	0.6211	0.6173	0.6135	0.6098	0.6061	0.6024	0.5988	0.5952	0.5917	4	7	11	15	18	22	26	29	33
1.7	0.5882	0.5848	0.5814	0.5780	0.5747	0.5714	0.5682	0.5650	0.5618	0.5587	3	7	10	13	16	20	23	26	29
1.8	0.5556	0.5525	0.5495	0.5464	0.5435	0.5405	0.5376	0.5348	0.5319	0.5291	3	6	9	12	15	18	20	23	26
1.9	0.5263	0.5236	0.5208	0.5181	0.5155	0.5128	0.5102	0.5076	0.5051	0.5025	3	5	8	11	13	16	18	21	24
2.0	0.5000	0.4975	0.4950	0.4926	0.4902	0.4878	0.4854	0.4831	0.4808	0.4785	2	5	7	10	12	14	17	19	21
2.1	0.4762	0.4739	0.4717	0.4695	0.4673	0.4651	0.4630	0.4608	0.4587	0.4566	2	4	6	9	11	13	15	17	19
2.2	0.4545	0.4525	0.4505	0.4484	0.4464	0.4444	0.4425	0.4405	0.4386	0.4367	2	4	6	8	10	12	14	16	18
2.3	0.4348	0.4329	0.4310	0.4292	0.4274	0.4255	0.4237	0.4219	0.4202	0.4184	2	4	5	7	9	11	13	14	16
2.4	0.4167	0.4149	0.4132	0.4115	0.4098	0.4082	0.4065	0.4049	0.4032	0.4016	2	3	5	7	8	10	12	13	15
2.5	0.4000	0.3984	0.3968	0.3953	0.3937	0.3922	0.3906	0.3891	0.3876	0.3861	2	3	5	6	8	9	11	12	14
2.6	0.3846	0.3831	0.3817	0.3802	0.3788	0.3774	0.3759	0.3745	0.3731	0.3717	1	3	4	6	7	9	10	11	13
2.7	0.3704	0.3690	0.3676	0.3663	0.3650	0.3636	0.3623	0.3610	0.3597	0.3584	1	3	4	5	7	8	9	11	12
2.8	0.3571	0.3559	0.3546	0.3534	0.3521	0.3509	0.3497	0.3484	0.3472	0.3460	1	2	4	5	6	7	9	10	11
2.9	0.3448	0.3436	0.3425	0.3413	0.3401	0.3390	0.3378	0.3367	0.3356	0.3344	1	2	3	5	6	7	8	9	10
3.0	0.3333	0.3322	0.3311	0.3300	0.3289	0.3279	0.3268	0.3257	0.3247	0.3236	1	2	3	4	5	6	8	9	10
3.1	0.3226	0.3215	0.3205	0.3195	0.3185	0.3175	0.3165	0.3155	0.3145	0.3135	1	2	3	4	5	6	7	8	9
3.2	0.3125	0.3115	0.3106	0.3096	0.3086	0.3077	0.3067	0.3058	0.3049	0.3040	1	2	3	4	5	6	7	8	9
3.3	0.3030	0.3021	0.3012	0.3003	0.2994	0.2985	0.2976	0.2967	0.2959	0.2950	1	2	3	4	4	5	6	7	8
3.4	0.2941	0.2933	0.2924	0.2915	0.2907	0.2899	0.2890	0.2882	0.2874	0.2865	1	2	3	3	4	5	6	7	8
3.5	0.2857	0.2849	0.2841	0.2833	0.2825	0.2817	0.2809	0.2801	0.2793	0.2786	1	2	2	3	4	5	6	6	7
3.6	0.2778	0.2770	0.2762	0.2755	0.2747	0.2740	0.2732	0.2725	0.2717	0.2710	1	2	2	3	4	5	5	6	7
3.7	0.2703	0.2695	0.2688	0.2681	0.2674	0.2667	0.2660	0.2653	0.2646	0.2639	1	1	2	3	4	4	5	6	6
3.8	0.2632	0.2625	0.2618	0.2611	0.2604	0.2597	0.2591	0.2584	0.2577	0.2571	1	1	2	3	3	4	5	5	6
3.9	0.2564	0.2558	0.2551	0.2545	0.2538	0.2532	0.2525	0.2519	0.2513	0.2506	1	1	2	3	3	4	4	5	6
4.0	0.2500	0.2494	0.2488	0.2481	0.2475	0.2469	0.2463	0.2457	0.2451	0.2445	1	1	2	2	3	4	4	5	5
4.1	0.2439	0.2433	0.2427	0.2421	0.2415	0.2410	0.2404	0.2398	0.2392	0.2387	1	1	2	2	3	3	4	5	5
4.2	0.2381	0.2375	0.2370	0.2364	0.2358	0.2353	0.2347	0.2342	0.2336	0.2331	1	1	2	2	3	3	4	4	5
4.3	0.2326	0.2320	0.2315	0.2309	0.2304	0.2299	0.2294	0.2288	0.2283	0.2278	1	1	2	2	3	3	4	4	5
4.4	0.2273	0.2268	0.2262	0.2257	0.2252	0.2247	0.2242	0.2237	0.2232	0.2227	1	1	2	2	3	3	4	4	5
4.5	0.2222	0.2217	0.2212	0.2208	0.2203	0.2198	0.2193	0.2188	0.2183	0.2179	0	1	1	2	2	3	3	4	4
4.6	0.2174	0.2169	0.2165	0.2160	0.2155	0.2151	0.2146	0.2141	0.2137	0.2132	0	1	1	2	2	3	3	4	4
4.7	0.2128	0.2123	0.2119	0.2114	0.2110	0.2105	0.2101	0.2096	0.2092	0.2088	0	1	1	2	2	3	3	4	4
4.8	0.2083	0.2079	0.2075	0.2070	0.2066	0.2062	0.2058	0.2053	0.2049	0.2045	0	1	1	2	2	3	3	3	4
4.9	0.2041	0.2037	0.2033	0.2028	0.2024	0.2020	0.2016	0.2012	0.2008	0.2004	0	1	1	2	2	2	3	3	4
5.0	0.2000	0.1996	0.1992	0.1988	0.1984	0.1980	0.1976	0.1972	0.1969	0.1965	0	1	1	2	2	2	3	3	4
5.1	0.1961	0.1957	0.1953	0.1949	0.1946	0.1942	0.1938	0.1934	0.1931	0.1927	0	1	1	2	2	2	3	3	3
5.2	0.1923	0.1919	0.1916	0.1912	0.1908	0.1905	0.1901	0.1898	0.1894	0.1890	0	1	1	1	2	2	3	3	3
5.3	0.1887	0.1883	0.1880	0.1876	0.1873	0.1869	0.1866	0.1862	0.1859	0.1855	0	1	1	1	2	2	2	3	3
5.4	0.1852	0.1848	0.1845	0.1842	0.1838	0.1835	0.1832	0.1828	0.1825	0.1821	0	1	1	1	2	2	2	3	3

TABLE OF RECIPROCALS OF NUMBERS FROM 1—10 (continued)

	0	1	2	3	4	5	6	7	8	9	1	2	3	4	5	6	7	8	9
5.5	0.1818	0.1815	0.1812	0.1808	0.1805	0.1802	0.1799	0.1795	0.1792	0.1789	0	1	1	1	2	2	2	3	3
5.6	0.1786	0.1783	0.1779	0.1776	0.1773	0.1770	0.1767	0.1764	0.1761	0.1757	0	1	1	1	2	2	2	3	3
5.7	0.1754	0.1751	0.1748	0.1745	0.1742	0.1739	0.1736	0.1733	0.1730	0.1727	0	1	1	1	2	2	2	2	3
5.8	0.1724	0.1721	0.1718	0.1715	0.1712	0.1709	0.1706	0.1704	0.1701	0.1698	0	1	1	1	1	2	2	2	3
5.9	0.1695	0.1692	0.1689	0.1686	0.1684	0.1681	0.1678	0.1675	0.1672	0.1669	0	1	1	1	1	2	2	2	3
6.0	0.1667	0.1664	0.1661	0.1658	0.1656	0.1653	0.1650	0.1647	0.1645	0.1642	0	1	1	1	1	2	2	2	2
6.1	0.1639	0.1637	0.1634	0.1631	0.1629	0.1626	0.1623	0.1621	0.1618	0.1616	0	1	1	1	1	2	2	2	2
6.2	0.1613	0.1610	0.1608	0.1605	0.1603	0.1600	0.1597	0.1595	0.1592	0.1590	0	1	1	1	1	2	2	2	2
6.3	0.1587	0.1585	0.1582	0.1580	0.1577	0.1575	0.1572	0.1570	0.1567	0.1565	0	0	1	1	1	1	2	2	2
6.4	0.1563	0.1560	0.1558	0.1555	0.1553	0.1550	0.1548	0.1546	0.1543	0.1541	0	0	1	1	1	1	2	2	2
6.5	0.1538	0.1536	0.1534	0.1531	0.1529	0.1527	0.1524	0.1522	0.1520	0.1517	0	0	1	1	1	1	2	2	2
6.6	0.1515	0.1513	0.1511	0.1508	0.1506	0.1504	0.1502	0.1499	0.1497	0.1495	0	0	1	1	1	1	2	2	2
6.7	0.1493	0.1490	0.1488	0.1486	0.1484	0.1481	0.1479	0.1477	0.1475	0.1473	0	0	1	1	1	1	2	2	2
6.8	0.1471	0.1468	0.1466	0.1464	0.1462	0.1460	0.1458	0.1456	0.1453	0.1451	0	0	1	1	1	1	1	2	2
6.9	0.1449	0.1447	0.1445	0.1443	0.1441	0.1439	0.1437	0.1435	0.1433	0.1431	0	0	1	1	1	1	1	2	2
7.0	0.1429	0.1427	0.1425	0.1422	0.1420	0.1418	0.1416	0.1414	0.1412	0.1410	0	0	1	1	1	1	1	2	2
7.1	0.1408	0.1406	0.1404	0.1403	0.1401	0.1399	0.1397	0.1395	0.1393	0.1391	0	0	1	1	1	1	1	2	2
7.2	0.1389	0.1387	0.1385	0.1383	0.1381	0.1379	0.1377	0.1376	0.1374	0.1372	0	0	1	1	1	1	1	2	2
7.3	0.1370	0.1368	0.1366	0.1364	0.1362	0.1361	0.1359	0.1357	0.1355	0.1353	0	0	1	1	1	1	1	1	2
7.4	0.1351	0.1350	0.1348	0.1346	0.1344	0.1342	0.1340	0.1339	0.1337	0.1335	0	0	1	1	1	1	1	1	2
7.5	0.1333	0.1332	0.1330	0.1328	0.1326	0.1325	0.1323	0.1321	0.1319	0.1318	0	0	1	1	1	1	1	1	2
7.6	0.1316	0.1314	0.1312	0.1311	0.1309	0.1307	0.1305	0.1304	0.1302	0.1300	0	0	1	1	1	1	1	1	2
7.7	0.1299	0.1297	0.1295	0.1294	0.1292	0.1290	0.1289	0.1287	0.1285	0.1284	0	0	0	1	1	1	1	1	1
7.8	0.1282	0.1280	0.1279	0.1277	0.1276	0.1274	0.1272	0.1271	0.1269	0.1267	0	0	0	1	1	1	1	1	1
7.9	0.1266	0.1264	0.1263	0.1261	0.1259	0.1258	0.1256	0.1255	0.1253	0.1252	0	0	0	1	1	1	1	1	1
8.0	0.1250	0.1248	0.1247	0.1245	0.1244	0.1242	0.1241	0.1239	0.1238	0.1236	0	0	0	1	1	1	1	1	1
8.1	0.1235	0.1233	0.1232	0.1230	0.1229	0.1227	0.1225	0.1224	0.1222	0.1221	0	0	0	1	1	1	1	1	1
8.2	0.1220	0.1218	0.1217	0.1215	0.1214	0.1212	0.1211	0.1209	0.1208	0.1206	0	0	0	1	1	1	1	1	1
8.3	0.1205	0.1203	0.1202	0.1200	0.1199	0.1198	0.1196	0.1195	0.1193	0.1192	0	0	0	1	1	1	1	1	1
8.4	0.1190	0.1189	0.1188	0.1186	0.1185	0.1183	0.1182	0.1181	0.1179	0.1178	0	0	0	1	1	1	1	1	1
8.5	0.1176	0.1175	0.1174	0.1172	0.1171	0.1170	0.1168	0.1167	0.1166	0.1164	0	0	0	1	1	1	1	1	1
8.6	0.1163	0.1161	0.1160	0.1159	0.1157	0.1156	0.1155	0.1153	0.1152	0.1151	0	0	0	1	1	1	1	1	1
8.7	0.1149	0.1148	0.1147	0.1145	0.1144	0.1143	0.1142	0.1140	0.1139	0.1138	0	0	0	1	1	1	1	1	1
8.8	0.1136	0.1135	0.1134	0.1133	0.1131	0.1130	0.1129	0.1127	0.1126	0.1125	0	0	0	1	1	1	1	1	1
8.9	0.1124	0.1122	0.1121	0.1120	0.1119	0.1117	0.1116	0.1115	0.1114	0.1112	0	0	0	0	1	1	1	1	1
9.0	0.1111	0.1110	0.1109	0.1107	0.1106	0.1105	0.1104	0.1103	0.1101	0.1100	0	0	0	0	1	1	1	1	1
9.1	0.1099	0.1098	0.1096	0.1095	0.1094	0.1093	0.1092	0.1091	0.1089	0.1088	0	0	0	0	1	1	1	1	1
9.2	0.1087	0.1086	0.1085	0.1083	0.1082	0.1081	0.1080	0.1079	0.1078	0.1076	0	0	0	0	1	1	1	1	1
9.3	0.1075	0.1074	0.1073	0.1072	0.1071	0.1070	0.1068	0.1067	0.1066	0.1065	0	0	0	0	1	1	1	1	1
9.4	0.1064	0.1063	0.1062	0.1060	0.1059	0.1058	0.1057	0.1056	0.1055	0.1054	0	0	0	0	1	1	1	1	1
9.5	0.1053	0.1052	0.1050	0.1049	0.1048	0.1047	0.1046	0.1045	0.1044	0.1043	0	0	0	0	1	1	1	1	1
9.6	0.1042	0.1041	0.1040	0.1038	0.1037	0.1036	0.1035	0.1034	0.1033	0.1032	0	0	0	0	1	1	1	1	1
9.7	0.1031	0.1030	0.1029	0.1028	0.1027	0.1026	0.1025	0.1024	0.1022	0.1021	0	0	0	0	1	1	1	1	1
9.8	0.1020	0.1019	0.1018	0.1017	0.1016	0.1015	0.1014	0.1013	0.1012	0.1011	0	0	0	0	1	1	1	1	1
9.9	0.1010	0.1009	0.1008	0.1007	0.1006	0.1005	0.1004	0.1003	0.1002	0.1001	0	0	0	0	1	1	1	1	1

LOGARITHMS (continued)

No.	0	1	2	3	4	5	6	7	8	9	1	2	3	4	5	6	7	8	9
10	0000	0043	0086	0128	0170	0212	0253	0294	0334	0374	4	8	13	17	21	25	30	34	38
11	0414	0453	0492	0531	0569	0607	0645	0682	0719	0755	4	8	12	16	20	24	28	32	35
12	0792	0828	0864	0899	0934	0969	1004	1038	1072	1106	4	7	11	15	18	22	26	30	33
13	1139	1173	1206	1239	1271	1303	1335	1367	1399	1430	3	7	10	14	17	21	24	28	31
14	1461	1492	1523	1553	1584	1614	1644	1673	1703	1732	3	6	10	13	16	19	23	26	29
15	1761	1790	1818	1847	1875	1903	1931	1959	1987	2014	3	6	9	12	15	18	21	24	28
16	2041	2068	2095	2122	2148	2175	2201	2227	2253	2279	3	5	8	11	14	16	19	22	25
17	2304	2330	2355	2380	2405	2430	2455	2480	2504	2529	2	5	7	10	12	15	17	20	22
18	2553	2577	2601	2625	2648	2672	2695	2718	2742	2765	2	5	7	9	12	14	16	19	21
19	2788	2810	2833	2856	2878	2900	2923	2945	2967	2989	2	4	7	9	11	13	16	18	20
20	3010	3032	3054	3075	3096	3118	3139	3160	3181	3201	2	4	6	8	11	13	15	17	19
21	3222	3243	3263	3284	3304	3324	3345	3365	3385	3404	2	4	6	8	10	12	14	16	18
22	3424	3444	3464	3483	3502	3522	3541	3560	3579	3598	2	4	6	8	10	12	14	15	17
23	3617	3636	3655	3674	3692	3711	3729	3747	3766	3784	2	4	6	7	9	11	13	15	17
24	3802	3820	3838	3856	3874	3892	3909	3927	3945	3962	2	4	5	7	9	11	12	14	16
25	3979	3997	4014	4031	4048	4065	4082	4099	4116	4133	2	3	5	7	9	10	12	14	15
26	4150	4166	4183	4200	4216	4232	4249	4265	4281	4298	2	3	5	7	8	10	11	13	15
27	4314	4330	4346	4362	4378	4393	4409	4425	4440	4456	2	3	5	6	8	9	11	13	14
28	4472	4487	4502	4518	4533	4548	4564	4579	4594	4609	2	3	5	6	8	9	11	12	14
29	4624	4639	4654	4669	4683	4698	4713	4728	4742	4757	1	3	4	6	7	9	10	12	13
30	4771	4786	4800	4814	4829	4843	4857	4871	4886	4900	1	3	4	6	7	9	10	11	13
31	4914	4928	4942	4955	4969	4983	4997	5011	5024	5038	1	3	4	6	7	8	10	11	12
32	5051	5065	5079	5092	5105	5119	5132	5145	5159	5172	1	3	4	5	7	8	9	11	12
33	5185	5198	5211	5224	5237	5250	5263	5276	5289	5302	1	3	4	5	6	8	9	10	12
34	5315	5328	5340	5353	5366	5378	5391	5403	5416	5428	1	3	4	5	6	8	9	10	11
35	5441	5453	5465	5478	5490	5502	5514	5527	5539	5551	1	2	4	5	6	7	9	10	11
36	5563	5575	5587	5599	5611	5623	5635	5647	5658	5670	1	2	4	5	6	7	8	10	11
37	5682	5694	5705	5717	5729	5740	5752	5763	5775	5786	1	2	3	5	6	7	8	9	11
38	5798	5809	5821	5832	5843	5855	5866	5877	5888	5899	1	2	3	5	6	7	8	9	10
39	5911	5922	5933	5944	5955	5966	5977	5988	5999	6010	1	2	3	4	5	7	8	9	10
40	6021	6031	6042	6053	6064	6075	6085	6096	6107	6117	1	2	3	4	5	6	8	9	10
41	6128	6138	6149	6160	6170	6180	6191	6201	6212	6222	1	2	3	4	5	6	7	8	9
42	6232	6243	6253	6263	6274	6284	6294	6304	6314	6325	1	2	3	4	5	6	7	8	9
43	6335	6345	6355	6365	6375	6385	6395	6405	6415	6425	1	2	3	4	5	6	7	8	9
44	6435	6444	6454	6464	6474	6484	6493	6503	6513	6522	1	2	3	4	5	6	7	8	9
45	6532	6542	6551	6561	6571	6580	6590	6599	6609	6618	1	2	3	4	5	6	7	8	9
46	6628	6637	6646	6656	6665	6675	6684	6693	6702	6712	1	2	3	4	5	6	7	7	8
47	6721	6730	6739	6749	6758	6767	6776	6785	6794	6803	1	2	3	4	5	5	6	7	8
48	6812	6821	6830	6839	6848	6857	6866	6875	6884	6893	1	2	3	4	4	5	6	7	8
49	6902	6911	6920	6928	6937	6946	6955	6964	6972	6981	1	2	3	4	4	5	6	7	8

No.	0	1	2	3	4	5	6	7	8	9	1	2	3	4	5	6	7	8	9
50	6990	6998	7007	7016	7024	7033	7042	7050	7059	7067	1	2	3	3	4	5	6	7	8
51	7076	7084	7093	7101	7110	7118	7126	7135	7143	7152	1	2	3	3	4	5	6	7	8
52	7160	7168	7177	7185	7193	7202	7210	7218	7226	7235	1	2	2	3	4	5	6	7	7
53	7243	7251	7259	7267	7275	7284	7292	7300	7308	7316	1	2	2	3	4	5	6	6	7
54	7324	7332	7340	7348	7356	7364	7372	7380	7388	7396	1	2	2	3	4	5	6	6	7
55	7404	7412	7419	7427	7435	7443	7451	7459	7466	7474	1	2	2	3	4	5	5	6	7
56	7482	7490	7497	7505	7513	7520	7528	7536	7543	7551	1	2	2	3	4	5	5	6	7
57	7559	7566	7574	7582	7589	7597	7604	7612	7619	7627	1	2	2	3	4	5	5	6	7
58	7634	7642	7649	7657	7664	7672	7679	7686	7694	7701	1	1	2	3	4	5	5	6	7
59	7709	7716	7723	7731	7738	7745	7752	7760	7767	7774	1	1	2	3	4	4	5	6	7
60	7782	7789	7796	7803	7810	7818	7825	7832	7839	7846	1	1	2	3	4	4	5	6	6
61	7853	7860	7868	7875	7882	7889	7896	7903	7910	7917	1	1	2	3	4	4	5	6	6
62	7924	7931	7938	7945	7952	7959	7966	7973	7980	7987	1	1	2	3	3	4	5	6	6
63	7993	8000	8007	8014	8021	8028	8035	8041	8048	8055	1	1	2	3	3	4	5	5	6
64	8062	8069	8075	8082	8089	8096	8102	8109	8116	8122	1	1	2	3	3	4	5	5	6
65	8129	8136	8142	8149	8156	8162	8169	8176	8182	8189	1	1	2	3	3	4	5	5	6
66	8195	8202	8209	8215	8222	8228	8235	8241	8248	8254	1	1	2	3	3	4	5	5	6
67	8261	8267	8274	8280	8287	8293	8299	8306	8312	8319	1	1	2	2	3	4	4	5	6
68	8325	8331	8338	8344	8351	8357	8363	8370	8376	8382	1	1	2	2	3	4	4	5	6
69	8388	8395	8401	8407	8414	8420	8426	8432	8439	8445	1	1	2	2	3	4	4	5	6
70	8451	8457	8463	8470	8476	8482	8488	8494	8500	8506	1	1	2	2	3	4	4	5	5
71	8513	8519	8525	8531	8537	8543	8549	8555	8561	8567	1	1	2	2	3	4	4	5	5
72	8573	8579	8585	8591	8597	8603	8609	8615	8621	8627	1	1	2	2	3	4	4	5	5
73	8633	8639	8645	8651	8657	8663	8669	8675	8681	8686	1	1	2	2	3	4	4	5	5
74	8692	8698	8704	8710	8716	8722	8727	8733	8739	8745	1	1	2	2	3	4	4	5	5
75	8751	8756	8762	8768	8774	8779	8785	8791	8797	8802	1	1	2	2	3	3	4	5	5
76	8808	8814	8820	8825	8831	8837	8842	8848	8854	8859	1	1	2	2	3	3	4	5	5
77	8865	8871	8876	8882	8887	8893	8899	8904	8910	8915	1	1	2	2	3	3	4	4	5
78	8921	8927	8932	8938	8943	8949	8954	8960	8965	8971	1	1	2	2	3	3	4	4	5
79	8976	8982	8987	8993	8998	9004	9009	9015	9020	9025	1	1	2	2	3	3	4	4	5
80	9031	9036	9042	9047	9053	9058	9063	9069	9074	9079	1	1	2	2	3	3	4	4	5
81	9085	9090	9096	9101	9106	9112	9117	9122	9128	9133	1	1	2	2	3	3	4	4	5
82	9138	9143	9149	9154	9159	9165	9170	9175	9180	9186	1	1	2	2	3	3	4	4	5
83	9191	9196	9201	9206	9212	9217	9222	9227	9232	9238	1	1	2	2	3	3	4	4	5
84	9243	9248	9253	9258	9263	9269	9274	9279	9284	9289	1	1	2	2	3	3	4	4	5
85	9294	9299	9304	9309	9315	9320	9325	9330	9335	9340	1	1	2	2	3	3	4	4	5
86	9345	9350	9355	9360	9365	9370	9375	9380	9385	9390	1	1	2	2	3	3	4	4	5
87	9395	9400	9405	9410	9415	9420	9425	9430	9435	9440	0	1	1	2	2	3	3	4	4
88	9445	9450	9455	9460	9465	9469	9474	9479	9484	9489	0	1	1	2	2	3	3	4	4
89	9494	9499	9504	9509	9513	9518	9523	9528	9533	9538	0	1	1	2	2	3	3	4	4
90	9542	9547	9552	9557	9562	9566	9571	9576	9581	9586	0	1	1	2	2	3	3	4	4
91	9590	9595	9600	9605	9609	9614	9619	9624	9628	9633	0	1	1	2	2	3	3	4	4
92	9638	9643	9647	9652	9657	9661	9666	9671	9675	9680	0	1	1	2	2	3	3	4	4
93	9685	9689	9694	9699	9703	9708	9713	9717	9722	9727	0	1	1	2	2	3	3	4	4
94	9731	9736	9741	9745	9750	9754	9759	9763	9768	9773	0	1	1	2	2	3	3	4	4
95	9777	9782	9786	9791	9795	9800	9805	9809	9814	9818	0	1	1	2	2	3	3	4	4
96	9823	9827	9832	9836	9841	9845	9850	9854	9859	9863	0	1	1	2	2	3	3	4	4
97	9868	9872	9877	9881	9886	9890	9894	9899	9903	9908	0	1	1	2	2	3	3	3	4
98	9912	9917	9921	9926	9930	9934	9939	9943	9948	9952	0	1	1	2	2	3	3	3	4
99	9956	9961	9965	9969	9974	9978	9983	9987	9991	9996	0	1	1	2	2	3	3	3	4

ANTILOGARITHMS

	0	1	2	3	4	5	6	7	8	9	1	2	3	4	5	6	7	8	9
0.00	1000	1002	1005	1007	1009	1012	1014	1016	1019	1021	0	0	1	1	1	1	2	2	2
0.01	1023	1026	1028	1030	1033	1035	1038	1040	1042	1045	0	0	1	1	1	1	2	2	2
0.02	1047	1050	1052	1054	1057	1059	1062	1064	1067	1069	0	0	1	1	1	1	2	2	2
0.03	1072	1074	1076	1079	1081	1084	1086	1089	1091	1094	0	0	1	1	1	1	2	2	2
0.04	1096	1099	1102	1104	1107	1109	1112	1114	1117	1119	0	1	1	1	1	2	2	2	2
0.05	1122	1125	1127	1130	1132	1135	1138	1140	1143	1146	0	1	1	1	1	2	2	2	3
0.06	1148	1151	1153	1156	1159	1161	1164	1167	1169	1172	0	1	1	1	1	2	2	2	3
0.07	1175	1178	1180	1183	1186	1189	1191	1194	1197	1199	0	1	1	1	1	2	2	2	3
0.08	1202	1205	1208	1211	1213	1216	1219	1222	1225	1227	0	1	1	1	1	2	2	2	3
0.09	1230	1233	1236	1239	1242	1245	1247	1250	1253	1256	0	1	1	1	2	2	2	2	3
0.10	1259	1262	1265	1268	1271	1274	1276	1279	1282	1285	0	1	1	1	2	2	2	2	3
0.11	1288	1291	1294	1297	1300	1303	1306	1309	1312	1315	0	1	1	1	2	2	2	2	3
0.12	1318	1321	1324	1327	1330	1334	1337	1340	1343	1346	0	1	1	1	2	2	2	3	3
0.13	1349	1352	1355	1358	1361	1365	1368	1371	1374	1377	0	1	1	1	2	2	2	3	3
0.14	1380	1384	1387	1390	1393	1396	1400	1403	1406	1409	0	1	1	1	2	2	2	3	3
0.15	1413	1416	1419	1422	1426	1429	1432	1435	1439	1442	0	1	1	1	2	2	2	3	3
0.16	1445	1449	1452	1455	1459	1462	1466	1469	1472	1476	0	1	1	1	2	2	3	3	3
0.17	1479	1483	1486	1489	1493	1496	1500	1503	1507	1510	0	1	1	1	2	2	3	3	3
0.18	1514	1517	1521	1524	1528	1531	1535	1538	1542	1545	0	1	1	1	2	2	3	3	3
0.19	1549	1552	1556	1560	1563	1567	1570	1574	1578	1581	0	1	1	1	2	2	3	3	3
0.20	1585	1589	1592	1596	1600	1603	1607	1611	1614	1618	0	1	1	2	2	2	3	3	3
0.21	1622	1626	1629	1633	1637	1641	1644	1648	1652	1656	0	1	1	2	2	2	3	3	4
0.22	1660	1663	1667	1671	1675	1679	1683	1687	1690	1694	0	1	1	2	2	2	3	3	4
0.23	1698	1702	1706	1710	1714	1718	1722	1726	1730	1734	0	1	1	2	2	2	3	3	4
0.24	1738	1742	1746	1750	1754	1758	1762	1766	1770	1774	0	1	1	2	2	2	3	3	4
0.25	1778	1782	1786	1791	1795	1799	1803	1807	1811	1816	0	1	1	2	2	2	3	3	4
0.26	1820	1824	1828	1832	1837	1841	1845	1849	1854	1858	0	1	1	2	2	3	3	3	4
0.27	1862	1866	1871	1875	1879	1884	1888	1892	1897	1901	0	1	1	2	2	3	3	4	4
0.28	1905	1910	1914	1919	1923	1928	1932	1936	1941	1945	0	1	1	2	2	3	3	4	4
0.29	1950	1954	1959	1963	1968	1972	1977	1982	1986	1991	0	1	1	2	2	3	3	4	4
0.30	1995	2000	2004	2009	2014	2018	2023	2028	2032	2037	0	1	1	2	2	3	3	4	4
0.31	2042	2046	2051	2056	2061	2065	2070	2075	2080	2084	0	1	1	2	2	3	3	4	4
0.32	2089	2094	2099	2104	2109	2113	2118	2123	2128	2133	0	1	1	2	2	3	3	4	4
0.33	2138	2143	2148	2153	2158	2163	2168	2173	2178	2183	1	1	2	2	3	3	4	4	5
0.34	2188	2193	2198	2203	2208	2213	2218	2223	2228	2234	1	1	2	2	3	3	4	4	5
0.35	2239	2244	2249	2254	2259	2265	2270	2275	2280	2286	1	1	2	2	3	3	4	4	5
0.36	2291	2296	2301	2307	2312	2317	2323	2328	2333	2339	1	1	2	2	3	3	4	4	5
0.37	2344	2350	2355	2360	2366	2371	2377	2382	2388	2393	1	1	2	2	3	3	4	5	5
0.38	2399	2404	2410	2415	2421	2427	2432	2438	2443	2449	1	1	2	2	3	3	4	5	5
0.39	2455	2460	2466	2472	2477	2483	2489	2495	2500	2506	1	1	2	2	3	4	4	5	5
0.40	2512	2518	2523	2529	2535	2541	2547	2553	2559	2564	1	1	2	2	3	4	4	5	5
0.41	2570	2576	2582	2588	2594	2600	2606	2612	2618	2624	1	1	2	2	3	4	4	5	5
0.42	2630	2636	2642	2649	2655	2661	2667	2673	2679	2685	1	1	2	3	3	4	4	5	6
0.43	2692	2698	2704	2710	2716	2723	2729	2735	2742	2748	1	1	2	3	3	4	4	5	6
0.44	2754	2761	2767	2773	2780	2786	2793	2799	2805	2812	1	1	2	3	3	4	5	5	6
0.45	2818	2825	2831	2838	2844	2851	2858	2864	2871	2877	1	1	2	3	3	4	5	5	6
0.46	2884	2891	2897	2904	2911	2917	2924	2931	2938	2944	1	1	2	3	3	4	5	5	6
0.47	2951	2958	2965	2972	2979	2985	2992	2999	3006	3013	1	1	2	3	3	4	5	6	6
0.48	3020	3027	3034	3041	3048	3055	3062	3069	3076	3083	1	1	2	3	4	4	5	6	6
0.49	3090	3097	3105	3112	3119	3126	3133	3141	3148	3155	1	1	2	3	4	4	5	6	6

ANTILOGARITHMS (continued)

	0	1	2	3	4	5	6	7	8	9	1	2	3	4	5	6	7	8	9
0.50	3162	3170	3177	3184	3192	3199	3206	3214	3221	3228	1	1	2	3	4	4	5	6	7
0.51	3236	3243	3251	3258	3266	3273	3281	3289	3296	3304	1	2	2	3	4	5	5	6	7
0.52	3311	3319	3327	3334	3342	3350	3357	3365	3373	3381	1	2	2	3	4	5	5	6	7
0.53	3388	3396	3404	3412	3420	3428	3436	3443	3451	3459	1	2	2	3	4	5	6	6	7
0.54	3467	3475	3483	3491	3499	3508	3516	3524	3532	3540	1	2	2	3	4	5	6	6	7
0.55	3548	3556	3565	3573	3581	3589	3597	3606	3614	3622	1	2	2	3	4	5	6	6	7
0.56	3631	3639	3648	3656	3664	3673	3681	3690	3698	3707	1	2	3	3	4	5	6	7	8
0.57	3715	3724	3733	3741	3750	3758	3767	3776	3784	3793	1	2	3	4	4	5	6	7	8
0.58	3802	3811	3819	3828	3837	3846	3855	3864	3873	3882	1	2	3	4	4	5	6	7	8
0.59	3890	3899	3908	3917	3926	3936	3945	3954	3963	3972	1	2	3	4	5	5	6	7	8
0.60	3981	3990	3999	4009	4018	4027	4036	4046	4055	4064	1	2	3	4	5	5	6	7	8
0.61	4074	4083	4093	4102	4111	4121	4130	4140	4150	4159	1	2	3	4	5	6	7	8	9
0.62	4169	4178	4188	4198	4207	4217	4227	4236	4246	4256	1	2	3	4	5	6	7	8	9
0.63	4266	4276	4285	4295	4305	4315	4325	4335	4345	4355	1	2	3	4	5	6	7	8	9
0.64	4365	4375	4385	4395	4406	4416	4426	4436	4446	4457	1	2	3	4	5	6	7	8	9
0.65	4467	4477	4487	4498	4508	4519	4529	4539	4550	4560	1	2	3	4	5	6	7	8	9
0.66	4571	4581	4592	4603	4613	4624	4634	4645	4656	4667	1	2	3	4	5	6	7	9	10
0.67	4677	4688	4699	4710	4721	4732	4742	4753	4764	4775	1	2	3	4	5	7	8	9	10
0.68	4786	4797	4808	4819	4831	4842	4853	4864	4875	4887	1	2	3	4	5	7	8	9	10
0.69	4898	4909	4920	4932	4943	4955	4966	4977	4989	5000	1	2	3	5	6	7	8	9	10
0.70	5012	5023	5035	5047	5058	5070	5082	5093	5105	5117	1	2	4	5	6	7	8	9	11
0.71	5129	5140	5152	5164	5176	5188	5200	5212	5224	5236	1	2	4	5	6	7	8	10	11
0.72	5248	5260	5272	5284	5297	5309	5321	5333	5346	5358	1	2	4	5	6	7	9	10	11
0.73	5370	5383	5395	5408	5420	5433	5445	5458	5470	5483	1	3	4	5	6	8	9	10	11
0.74	5495	5508	5521	5534	5546	5559	5572	5585	5598	5610	1	3	4	5	6	8	9	10	12
0.75	5623	5636	5649	5662	5675	5689	5702	5715	5728	5741	1	3	4	5	7	8	9	10	12
0.76	5754	5768	5781	5794	5808	5821	5834	5848	5861	5875	1	3	4	5	7	8	9	11	12
0.77	5888	5902	5916	5929	5943	5957	5970	5984	5998	6012	1	3	4	5	7	8	10	11	12
0.78	6026	6039	6053	6067	6081	6095	6109	6124	6138	6152	1	3	4	5	7	8	10	11	13
0.79	6166	6180	6194	6209	6223	6237	6252	6266	6281	6295	1	3	4	6	7	8	10	11	13
0.80	6310	6324	6339	6353	6368	6383	6397	6412	6427	6442	1	3	4	6	7	9	10	11	13
0.81	6457	6471	6486	6501	6516	6531	6546	6561	6577	6592	2	3	4	6	7	9	10	12	13
0.82	6607	6622	6637	6653	6668	6683	6699	6714	6730	6745	2	3	5	6	8	9	11	12	14
0.83	6761	6776	6792	6808	6823	6839	6855	6871	6887	6902	2	3	5	6	8	9	11	12	14
0.84	6918	6934	6950	6966	6982	6998	7015	7031	7047	7063	2	3	5	6	8	9	11	13	14
0.85	7079	7096	7112	7129	7145	7161	7178	7194	7211	7228	2	3	5	6	8	10	11	13	15
0.86	7244	7261	7278	7295	7311	7328	7345	7362	7379	7396	2	3	5	7	8	10	12	13	15
0.87	7413	7430	7447	7464	7482	7499	7516	7534	7551	7568	2	3	5	7	9	10	12	14	15
0.88	7586	7603	7621	7638	7656	7674	7691	7709	7727	7745	2	4	5	7	9	11	12	14	16
0.89	7762	7780	7798	7816	7834	7852	7870	7889	7907	7925	2	4	5	7	9	11	13	14	16
0.90	7943	7962	7980	7998	8017	8035	8054	8072	8091	8110	2	4	5	7	9	11	13	15	17
0.91	8128	8147	8166	8185	8204	8222	8241	8260	8279	8299	2	4	6	7	9	11	13	15	17
0.92	8318	8337	8356	8375	8395	8414	8433	8453	8472	8492	2	4	6	8	10	11	13	15	17
0.93	8511	8531	8551	8570	8590	8610	8630	8650	8670	8690	2	4	6	8	10	12	14	16	18
0.94	8710	8730	8750	8770	8790	8810	8831	8851	8872	8892	2	4	6	8	10	12	14	16	18
0.95	8913	8933	8954	8974	8995	9016	9036	9057	9078	9099	2	4	6	8	10	12	14	16	18
0.96	9120	9141	9162	9183	9204	9226	9247	9268	9290	9311	2	4	6	8	11	13	15	17	19
0.97	9333	9354	9376	9397	9419	9441	9462	9484	9506	9528	2	4	7	9	11	13	15	17	20
0.98	9550	9572	9594	9616	9638	9661	9683	9705	9727	9750	2	4	7	9	11	13	15	18	20
0.99	9772	9795	9817	9840	9863	9886	9908	9931	9954	9977	2	5	7	9	11	13	16	18	20

NATURAL SINES

°	0' 0.0°	6' 0.1°	12' 0.2°	18' 0.3°	24' 0.4°	30' 0.5°	36' 0.6°	42' 0.7°	48' 0.8°	54' 0.9°	1'	2'	3'	4'	5'
0	0.0000	0.0017	0.0035	0.0052	0.0070	0.0087	0.0105	0.0122	0.0140	0.0157	3	6	9	12	15
1	0.0175	0.0192	0.0209	0.0227	0.0244	0.0262	0.0279	0.0297	0.0314	0.0332	3	6	9	12	15
2	0.0349	0.0366	0.0384	0.0401	0.0419	0.0436	0.0454	0.0471	0.0488	0.0506	3	6	9	12	15
3	0.0523	0.0541	0.0558	0.0576	0.0593	0.0610	0.0628	0.0645	0.0663	0.0680	3	6	9	12	15
4	0.0698	0.0715	0.0732	0.0750	0.0767	0.0785	0.0802	0.0819	0.0837	0.0854	3	6	9	12	14
5	0.0872	0.0889	0.0906	0.0924	0.0941	0.0958	0.0976	0.0993	0.1011	0.1028	3	6	9	12	14
6	0.1045	0.1063	0.1080	0.1097	0.1115	0.1132	0.1149	0.1167	0.1184	0.1201	3	6	9	12	14
7	0.1219	0.1236	0.1253	0.1271	0.1288	0.1305	0.1323	0.1340	0.1357	0.1374	3	6	9	12	14
8	0.1392	0.1409	0.1426	0.1444	0.1461	0.1478	0.1495	0.1513	0.1530	0.1547	3	6	9	12	14
9	0.1564	0.1582	0.1599	0.1616	0.1633	0.1650	0.1668	0.1685	0.1702	0.1719	3	6	9	12	14
10	0.1736	0.1754	0.1771	0.1788	0.1805	0.1822	0.1840	0.1857	0.1874	0.1891	3	6	9	12	14
11	0.1908	0.1925	0.1942	0.1959	0.1977	0.1994	0.2011	0.2028	0.2045	0.2062	3	6	9	11	14
12	0.2079	0.2096	0.2113	0.2130	0.2147	0.2164	0.2181	0.2198	0.2215	0.2232	3	6	9	11	14
13	0.2250	0.2267	0.2284	0.2300	0.2317	0.2334	0.2351	0.2368	0.2385	0.2402	3	6	8	11	14
14	0.2419	0.2436	0.2453	0.2470	0.2487	0.2504	0.2521	0.2538	0.2554	0.2571	3	6	8	11	14
15	0.2588	0.2605	0.2622	0.2639	0.2656	0.2672	0.2689	0.2706	0.2723	0.2740	3	6	8	11	14
16	0.2756	0.2773	0.2790	0.2807	0.2823	0.2840	0.2857	0.2874	0.2890	0.2907	3	6	8	11	14
17	0.2924	0.2940	0.2957	0.2974	0.2990	0.3007	0.3024	0.3040	0.3057	0.3074	3	6	8	11	14
18	0.3090	0.3107	0.3123	0.3140	0.3156	0.3173	0.3190	0.3206	0.3223	0.3239	3	6	8	11	14
19	0.3256	0.3272	0.3289	0.3305	0.3322	0.3338	0.3355	0.3371	0.3387	0.3404	3	5	8	11	14
20	0.3420	0.3437	0.3453	0.3469	0.3486	0.3502	0.3518	0.3535	0.3551	0.3567	3	5	8	11	14
21	0.3584	0.3600	0.3616	0.3633	0.3649	0.3665	0.3681	0.3697	0.3714	0.3730	3	5	8	11	14
22	0.3746	0.3762	0.3778	0.3795	0.3811	0.3827	0.3843	0.3859	0.3875	0.3891	3	5	8	11	13
23	0.3907	0.3923	0.3939	0.3955	0.3971	0.3987	0.4003	0.4019	0.4035	0.4051	3	5	8	11	13
24	0.4067	0.4083	0.4099	0.4115	0.4131	0.4147	0.4163	0.4179	0.4195	0.4210	3	5	8	11	13
25	0.4226	0.4242	0.4258	0.4274	0.4289	0.4305	0.4321	0.4337	0.4352	0.4368	3	5	8	11	13
26	0.4384	0.4399	0.4415	0.4431	0.4446	0.4462	0.4478	0.4493	0.4509	0.4524	3	5	8	10	13
27	0.4540	0.4555	0.4571	0.4586	0.4602	0.4617	0.4633	0.4648	0.4664	0.4679	3	5	8	10	13
28	0.4695	0.4710	0.4726	0.4741	0.4756	0.4772	0.4787	0.4802	0.4818	0.4833	3	5	8	10	13
29	0.4848	0.4863	0.4879	0.4894	0.4909	0.4924	0.4939	0.4955	0.4970	0.4985	3	5	8	10	13
30	0.5000	0.5015	0.5030	0.5045	0.5060	0.5075	0.5090	0.5105	0.5120	0.5135	3	5	8	10	13
31	0.5150	0.5165	0.5180	0.5195	0.5210	0.5225	0.5240	0.5255	0.5270	0.5284	3	5	8	10	13
32	0.5299	0.5314	0.5329	0.5344	0.5358	0.5373	0.5388	0.5402	0.5417	0.5432	2	5	7	10	12
33	0.5446	0.5461	0.5476	0.5490	0.5505	0.5519	0.5534	0.5548	0.5563	0.5577	2	5	7	10	12
34	0.5592	0.5606	0.5621	0.5635	0.5650	0.5664	0.5678	0.5693	0.5707	0.5721	2	5	7	10	12
35	0.5736	0.5750	0.5764	0.5779	0.5793	0.5807	0.5821	0.5835	0.5850	0.5864	2	5	7	9	12
36	0.5878	0.5892	0.5906	0.5920	0.5934	0.5948	0.5962	0.5976	0.5990	0.6004	2	5	7	9	12
37	0.6018	0.6032	0.6046	0.6060	0.6074	0.6088	0.6101	0.6115	0.6129	0.6143	2	5	7	9	12
38	0.6157	0.6170	0.6184	0.6198	0.6211	0.6225	0.6239	0.6252	0.6266	0.6280	2	5	7	9	11
39	0.6293	0.6307	0.6320	0.6334	0.6347	0.6361	0.6374	0.6388	0.6401	0.6414	2	4	7	9	11
40	0.6428	0.6441	0.6455	0.6468	0.6481	0.6494	0.6508	0.6521	0.6534	0.6547	2	4	7	9	11
41	0.6561	0.6574	0.6587	0.6600	0.6613	0.6626	0.6639	0.6652	0.6665	0.6678	2	4	7	9	11
42	0.6691	0.6704	0.6717	0.6730	0.6743	0.6756	0.6769	0.6782	0.6794	0.6807	2	4	6	9	11
43	0.6820	0.6833	0.6845	0.6858	0.6871	0.6884	0.6896	0.6909	0.6921	0.6934	2	4	6	8	11
44	0.6947	0.6959	0.6972	0.6984	0.6997	0.7009	0.7022	0.7034	0.7046	0.7059	2	4	6	8	10

NATURAL SINES (continued)

°	0' 0.0°	6' 0.1°	12' 0.2°	18' 0.3°	24' 0.4°	30' 0.5°	36' 0.6°	42' 0.7°	48' 0.8°	54' 0.9°	1'	2'	3'	4'	5'
45	0.7071	0.7083	0.7096	0.7108	0.7120	0.7133	0.7145	0.7157	0.7169	0.7181	2	4	6	8	10
46	0.7193	0.7206	0.7218	0.7230	0.7242	0.7254	0.7266	0.7278	0.7290	0.7302	2	4	6	8	10
47	0.7314	0.7325	0.7337	0.7349	0.7361	0.7373	0.7385	0.7396	0.7408	0.7420	2	4	6	8	10
48	0.7431	0.7443	0.7455	0.7466	0.7478	0.7490	0.7501	0.7513	0.7524	0.7536	2	4	6	8	10
49	0.7547	0.7558	0.7570	0.7581	0.7593	0.7604	0.7615	0.7627	0.7638	0.7649	2	4	6	8	9
50	0.7660	0.7672	0.7683	0.7694	0.7705	0.7716	0.7727	0.7738	0.7749	0.7760	2	4	6	7	9
51	0.7771	0.7782	0.7793	0.7804	0.7815	0.7826	0.7837	0.7848	0.7859	0.7869	2	4	5	7	9
52	0.7880	0.7891	0.7902	0.7912	0.7923	0.7934	0.7944	0.7955	0.7965	0.7976	2	4	5	7	9
53	0.7986	0.7997	0.8007	0.8018	0.8028	0.8039	0.8049	0.8059	0.8070	0.8080	2	3	5	7	9
54	0.8090	0.8100	0.8111	0.8121	0.8131	0.8141	0.8151	0.8161	0.8171	0.8181	2	3	5	7	8
55	0.8192	0.8202	0.8211	0.8221	0.8231	0.8241	0.8251	0.8261	0.8271	0.8281	2	3	5	7	8
56	0.8290	0.8300	0.8310	0.8320	0.8329	0.8339	0.8348	0.8358	0.8368	0.8377	2	3	5	6	8
57	0.8387	0.8396	0.8406	0.8415	0.8425	0.8434	0.8443	0.8453	0.8462	0.8471	2	3	5	6	8
58	0.8480	0.8490	0.8499	0.8508	0.8517	0.8526	0.8536	0.8545	0.8554	0.8563	2	3	5	6	8
59	0.8572	0.8581	0.8590	0.8599	0.8607	0.8616	0.8625	0.8634	0.8643	0.8652	1	3	4	6	7
60	0.8660	0.8669	0.8678	0.8686	0.8695	0.8704	0.8712	0.8721	0.8729	0.8738	1	3	4	6	7
61	0.8746	0.8755	0.8763	0.8771	0.8780	0.8788	0.8796	0.8805	0.8813	0.8821	1	3	4	6	7
62	0.8829	0.8838	0.8846	0.8854	0.8862	0.8870	0.8878	0.8886	0.8894	0.8902	1	3	4	5	7
63	0.8910	0.8918	0.8926	0.8934	0.8942	0.8949	0.8957	0.8965	0.8973	0.8980	1	3	4	5	7
64	0.8988	0.8996	0.9003	0.9011	0.9018	0.9026	0.9033	0.9041	0.9048	0.9056	1	3	4	5	6
65	0.9063	0.9070	0.9078	0.9085	0.9092	0.9100	0.9107	0.9114	0.9121	0.9128	1	2	4	5	6
66	0.9135	0.9143	0.9150	0.9157	0.9164	0.9171	0.9178	0.9184	0.9191	0.9198	1	2	3	5	6
67	0.9205	0.9212	0.9219	0.9225	0.9232	0.9239	0.9245	0.9252	0.9259	0.9265	1	2	3	4	6
68	0.9272	0.9278	0.9285	0.9291	0.9298	0.9304	0.9311	0.9317	0.9323	0.9330	1	2	3	4	5
69	0.9336	0.9342	0.9348	0.9354	0.9361	0.9367	0.9373	0.9379	0.9385	0.9391	1	2	3	4	5
70	0.9397	0.9403	0.9409	0.9415	0.9421	0.9426	0.9432	0.9438	0.9444	0.9449	1	2	3	4	5
71	0.9455	0.9461	0.9466	0.9472	0.9478	0.9483	0.9489	0.9494	0.9500	0.9505	1	2	3	4	5
72	0.9511	0.9516	0.9521	0.9527	0.9532	0.9537	0.9542	0.9548	0.9553	0.9558	1	2	3	3	4
73	0.9563	0.9568	0.9573	0.9578	0.9583	0.9588	0.9593	0.9598	0.9603	0.9608	1	2	2	3	4
74	0.9613	0.9617	0.9622	0.9627	0.9632	0.9636	0.9641	0.9646	0.9650	0.9655	1	2	2	3	4
75	0.9659	0.9664	0.9668	0.9673	0.9677	0.9681	0.9686	0.9690	0.9694	0.9699	1	1	2	3	4
76	0.9703	0.9707	0.9711	0.9715	0.9720	0.9724	0.9728	0.9732	0.9736	0.9740	1	1	2	3	3
77	0.9744	0.9748	0.9751	0.9755	0.9759	0.9763	0.9767	0.9770	0.9774	0.9778	1	1	2	3	3
78	0.9781	0.9785	0.9789	0.9792	0.9796	0.9799	0.9803	0.9806	0.9810	0.9813	1	1	2	2	3
79	0.9816	0.9820	0.9823	0.9826	0.9829	0.9833	0.9836	0.9839	0.9842	0.9845	1	1	2	2	3
80	0.9848	0.9851	0.9854	0.9857	0.9860	0.9863	0.9866	0.9869	0.9871	0.9874	0	1	1	2	2
81	0.9877	0.9880	0.9882	0.9885	0.9888	0.9890	0.9893	0.9895	0.9898	0.9900	0	1	1	2	2
82	0.9903	0.9905	0.9907	0.9910	0.9912	0.9914	0.9917	0.9919	0.9921	0.9923	0	1	1	2	2
83	0.9925	0.9928	0.9930	0.9932	0.9934	0.9936	0.9938	0.9940	0.9942	0.9943	0	1	1	1	2
84	0.9945	0.9947	0.9949	0.9951	0.9952	0.9954	0.9956	0.9957	0.9959	0.9960	0	1	1	1	1
85	0.9962	0.9963	0.9965	0.9966	0.9968	0.9969	0.9971	0.9972	0.9973	0.9974	0	0	1	1	1
86	0.9976	0.9977	0.9978	0.9979	0.9980	0.9981	0.9982	0.9983	0.9984	0.9985	0	0	1	1	1
87	0.9986	0.9987	0.9988	0.9989	0.9990	0.9990	0.9991	0.9992	0.9993	0.9993	0	0	0	1	1
88	0.9994	0.9995	0.9995	0.9996	0.9996	0.9997	0.9997	0.9997	0.9998	0.9998	0	0	0	0	0
89	0.9998	0.9999	0.9999	0.9999	0.9999	1.0000	1.0000	1.0000	1.0000	1.0000	0	0	0	0	0
90	1.0000														

NATURAL COSINES

°	0' 0.0°	6' 0.1°	12' 0.2°	18' 0.3°	24' 0.4°	30' 0.5°	36' 0.6°	42' 0.7°	48' 0.8°	54' 0.9°	1'	2'	3'	4'	5'
0	1.0000	1.0000	1.0000	1.0000	1.0000	1.0000	0.9999	0.9999	0.9999	0.9999	0	0	0	0	0
1	0.9998	0.9998	0.9998	0.9997	0.9997	0.9997	0.9996	0.9996	0.9995	0.9995	0	0	0	0	0
2	0.9994	0.9993	0.9993	0.9992	0.9991	0.9990	0.9990	0.9989	0.9988	0.9987	0	0	0	1	1
3	0.9986	0.9985	0.9984	0.9983	0.9982	0.9981	0.9980	0.9979	0.9978	0.9977	0	0	1	1	1
4	0.9976	0.9974	0.9973	0.9972	0.9971	0.9969	0.9968	0.9966	0.9965	0.9963	0	0	1	1	1
5	0.9962	0.9960	0.9959	0.9957	0.9956	0.9954	0.9952	0.9951	0.9949	0.9947	0	1	1	1	1
6	0.9945	0.9943	0.9942	0.9940	0.9938	0.9936	0.9934	0.9932	0.9930	0.9928	0	1	1	1	2
7	0.9925	0.9923	0.9921	0.9919	0.9917	0.9914	0.9912	0.9910	0.9907	0.9905	0	1	1	1	2
8	0.9903	0.9900	0.9898	0.9895	0.9893	0.9890	0.9888	0.9885	0.9882	0.9880	0	1	1	2	2
9	0.9877	0.9874	0.9871	0.9869	0.9866	0.9863	0.9860	0.9857	0.9854	0.9851	0	1	1	2	2
10	0.9848	0.9845	0.9842	0.9839	0.9836	0.9833	0.9829	0.9826	0.9823	0.9820	1	1	2	2	3
11	0.9816	0.9813	0.9810	0.9806	0.9803	0.9799	0.9796	0.9792	0.9789	0.9785	1	1	2	2	3
12	0.9781	0.9778	0.9774	0.9770	0.9767	0.9763	0.9759	0.9755	0.9751	0.9748	1	1	2	2	3
13	0.9744	0.9740	0.9736	0.9732	0.9728	0.9724	0.9720	0.9715	0.9711	0.9707	1	1	2	3	3
14	0.9703	0.9699	0.9694	0.9690	0.9686	0.9681	0.9677	0.9673	0.9668	0.9664	1	1	2	3	4
15	0.9659	0.9655	0.9650	0.9646	0.9641	0.9636	0.9632	0.9627	0.9622	0.9617	1	2	2	3	4
16	0.9613	0.9608	0.9603	0.9598	0.9593	0.9588	0.9583	0.9578	0.9573	0.9568	1	2	3	3	4
17	0.9563	0.9558	0.9553	0.9548	0.9542	0.9537	0.9532	0.9527	0.9521	0.9516	1	2	3	3	4
18	0.9511	0.9505	0.9500	0.9494	0.9489	0.9483	0.9478	0.9472	0.9466	0.9461	1	2	3	4	5
19	0.9455	0.9449	0.9444	0.9438	0.9432	0.9426	0.9421	0.9415	0.9409	0.9403	1	2	3	4	5
20	0.9397	0.9391	0.9385	0.9379	0.9373	0.9367	0.9361	0.9354	0.9348	0.9342	1	2	3	4	5
21	0.9336	0.9330	0.9323	0.9317	0.9311	0.9304	0.9298	0.9291	0.9285	0.9278	1	2	3	4	5
22	0.9272	0.9265	0.9259	0.9252	0.9245	0.9239	0.9232	0.9225	0.9219	0.9212	1	2	3	4	6
23	0.9205	0.9198	0.9191	0.9184	0.9178	0.9171	0.9164	0.9157	0.9150	0.9143	1	2	4	5	6
24	0.9135	0.9128	0.9121	0.9114	0.9107	0.9100	0.9092	0.9085	0.9078	0.9070	1	2	4	5	6
25	0.9063	0.9056	0.9048	0.9041	0.9033	0.9026	0.9018	0.9011	0.9003	0.8996	1	3	4	5	6
26	0.8988	0.8980	0.8973	0.8965	0.8957	0.8949	0.8942	0.8934	0.8926	0.8918	1	3	4	5	7
27	0.8910	0.8902	0.8894	0.8886	0.8878	0.8870	0.8862	0.8854	0.8846	0.8838	1	3	4	5	7
28	0.8829	0.8821	0.8813	0.8805	0.8796	0.8788	0.8780	0.8771	0.8763	0.8755	1	3	4	6	7
29	0.8746	0.8738	0.8729	0.8721	0.8712	0.8704	0.8695	0.8686	0.8678	0.8669	1	3	4	6	7
30	0.8660	0.8652	0.8643	0.8634	0.8625	0.8616	0.8607	0.8599	0.8590	0.8581	1	3	4	6	7
31	0.8572	0.8563	0.8554	0.8545	0.8536	0.8526	0.8517	0.8508	0.8499	0.8490	2	3	5	6	8
32	0.8480	0.8471	0.8462	0.8453	0.8443	0.8434	0.8425	0.8415	0.8406	0.8396	2	3	5	6	8
33	0.8387	0.8377	0.8368	0.8358	0.8348	0.8339	0.8329	0.8320	0.8310	0.8300	2	3	5	6	8
34	0.8290	0.8281	0.8271	0.8261	0.8251	0.8241	0.8231	0.8221	0.8211	0.8202	2	3	5	7	8
35	0.8192	0.8181	0.8171	0.8161	0.8151	0.8141	0.8131	0.8121	0.8111	0.8100	2	3	5	7	9
36	0.8090	0.8080	0.8070	0.8059	0.8049	0.8039	0.8028	0.8018	0.8007	0.7997	2	3	5	7	9
37	0.7986	0.7976	0.7965	0.7955	0.7944	0.7934	0.7923	0.7912	0.7902	0.7891	2	4	5	7	9
38	0.7880	0.7869	0.7859	0.7848	0.7837	0.7826	0.7815	0.7804	0.7793	0.7782	2	4	5	7	9
39	0.7771	0.7760	0.7749	0.7738	0.7727	0.7716	0.7705	0.7694	0.7683	0.7672	2	4	6	7	9
40	0.7660	0.7649	0.7638	0.7627	0.7615	0.7604	0.7593	0.7581	0.7570	0.7559	2	4	6	8	9
41	0.7547	0.7536	0.7524	0.7513	0.7501	0.7490	0.7478	0.7466	0.7455	0.7443	2	4	6	8	10
42	0.7431	0.7420	0.7408	0.7396	0.7385	0.7373	0.7361	0.7349	0.7337	0.7325	2	4	6	8	10
43	0.7314	0.7302	0.7290	0.7278	0.7266	0.7254	0.7242	0.7230	0.7218	0.7206	2	4	6	8	10
44	0.7193	0.7181	0.7169	0.7157	0.7145	0.7133	0.7120	0.7108	0.7096	0.7083	2	4	6	8	10

NATURAL COSINES (continued)

°	0' 0.0°	6' 0.1°	12' 0.2°	18' 0.3°	24' 0.4°	30' 0.5°	36' 0.6°	42' 0.7°	48' 0.8°	54' 0.9°	1'	2'	3'	4'	5'
45	0.7071	0.7059	0.7046	0.7034	0.7022	0.7009	0.6997	0.6984	0.6972	0.6959	2	4	6	8	10
46	0.6947	0.6934	0.6921	0.6909	0.6896	0.6884	0.6871	0.6858	0.6845	0.6833	2	4	6	8	11
47	0.6820	0.6807	0.6794	0.6782	0.6769	0.6756	0.6743	0.6730	0.6717	0.6704	2	4	6	9	11
48	0.6691	0.6678	0.6665	0.6652	0.6639	0.6626	0.6613	0.6600	0.6587	0.6574	2	4	7	9	11
49	0.6561	0.6547	0.6534	0.6521	0.6508	0.6494	0.6481	0.6468	0.6455	0.6441	2	4	7	9	11
50	0.6428	0.6414	0.6401	0.6388	0.6374	0.6361	0.6347	0.6334	0.6320	0.6307	2	5	7	9	11
51	0.6293	0.6280	0.6266	0.6252	0.6239	0.6225	0.6211	0.6198	0.6184	0.6170	2	5	7	9	11
52	0.6157	0.6143	0.6129	0.6115	0.6101	0.6088	0.6074	0.6060	0.6046	0.6032	2	5	7	9	12
53	0.6018	0.6004	0.5990	0.5976	0.5962	0.5948	0.5934	0.5920	0.5906	0.5892	2	5	7	9	12
54	0.5878	0.5864	0.5850	0.5835	0.5821	0.5807	0.5793	0.5779	0.5764	0.5750	2	5	7	9	12
55	0.5736	0.5721	0.5707	0.5693	0.5678	0.5664	0.5650	0.5635	0.5621	0.5606	2	5	7	10	12
56	0.5592	0.5577	0.5563	0.5548	0.5534	0.5519	0.5505	0.5490	0.5476	0.5461	2	5	7	10	12
57	0.5446	0.5432	0.5417	0.5402	0.5388	0.5373	0.5358	0.5344	0.5329	0.5314	2	5	7	10	12
58	0.5299	0.5284	0.5270	0.5255	0.5240	0.5225	0.5210	0.5195	0.5180	0.5165	2	5	7	10	12
59	0.5150	0.5135	0.5120	0.5105	0.5090	0.5075	0.5060	0.5045	0.5030	0.5015	3	5	8	10	13
60	0.5000	0.4985	0.4970	0.4955	0.4939	0.4924	0.4909	0.4894	0.4879	0.4863	3	5	8	10	13
61	0.4848	0.4833	0.4818	0.4802	0.4787	0.4772	0.4756	0.4741	0.4726	0.4710	3	5	8	10	13
62	0.4695	0.4679	0.4664	0.4648	0.4633	0.4617	0.4602	0.4586	0.4571	0.4555	3	5	8	10	13
63	0.4540	0.4524	0.4509	0.4493	0.4478	0.4462	0.4446	0.4431	0.4415	0.4399	3	5	8	10	13
64	0.4384	0.4368	0.4352	0.4337	0.4321	0.4305	0.4289	0.4274	0.4258	0.4242	3	5	8	11	13
65	0.4226	0.4210	0.4195	0.4179	0.4163	0.4147	0.4131	0.4115	0.4099	0.4083	3	5	8	11	13
66	0.4067	0.4051	0.4035	0.4019	0.4003	0.3987	0.3971	0.3955	0.3939	0.3923	3	5	8	11	13
67	0.3907	0.3891	0.3875	0.3859	0.3843	0.3827	0.3811	0.3795	0.3778	0.3762	3	5	8	11	13
68	0.3746	0.3730	0.3714	0.3697	0.3681	0.3665	0.3649	0.3633	0.3616	0.3600	3	5	8	11	14
69	0.3584	0.3567	0.3551	0.3535	0.3518	0.3502	0.3486	0.3469	0.3453	0.3437	3	5	8	11	14
70	0.3420	0.3404	0.3387	0.3371	0.3355	0.3338	0.3322	0.3305	0.3289	0.3272	3	5	8	11	14
71	0.3256	0.3239	0.3223	0.3206	0.3190	0.3173	0.3156	0.3140	0.3123	0.3107	3	6	8	11	14
72	0.3090	0.3074	0.3057	0.3040	0.3024	0.3007	0.2990	0.2974	0.2957	0.2940	3	6	8	11	14
73	0.2924	0.2907	0.2890	0.2874	0.2857	0.2840	0.2823	0.2807	0.2790	0.2773	3	6	8	11	14
74	0.2756	0.2740	0.2723	0.2706	0.2689	0.2672	0.2656	0.2639	0.2622	0.2605	3	6	8	11	14
75	0.2588	0.2571	0.2554	0.2538	0.2521	0.2504	0.2487	0.2470	0.2453	0.2436	3	6	8	11	14
76	0.2419	0.2402	0.2385	0.2368	0.2351	0.2334	0.2317	0.2300	0.2284	0.2267	3	6	8	11	14
77	0.2250	0.2233	0.2215	0.2198	0.2181	0.2164	0.2147	0.2130	0.2113	0.2096	3	6	9	11	14
78	0.2079	0.2062	0.2045	0.2028	0.2011	0.1994	0.1977	0.1959	0.1942	0.1925	3	6	9	11	14
79	0.1908	0.1891	0.1874	0.1857	0.1840	0.1822	0.1805	0.1788	0.1771	0.1754	3	6	9	11	14
80	0.1736	0.1719	0.1702	0.1685	0.1668	0.1650	0.1633	0.1616	0.1599	0.1582	3	6	9	11	14
81	0.1564	0.1547	0.1530	0.1513	0.1495	0.1478	0.1461	0.1444	0.1426	0.1409	3	6	9	11	14
82	0.1392	0.1374	0.1357	0.1340	0.1323	0.1305	0.1288	0.1271	0.1253	0.1236	3	6	9	12	14
83	0.1219	0.1201	0.1184	0.1167	0.1149	0.1132	0.1115	0.1097	0.1080	0.1063	3	6	9	12	15
84	0.1045	0.1028	0.1011	0.0993	0.0976	0.0958	0.0941	0.0924	0.0906	0.0889	3	6	9	12	14
85	0.0872	0.0854	0.0837	0.0819	0.0802	0.0785	0.0767	0.0750	0.0732	0.0715	3	6	9	12	15
86	0.0698	0.0680	0.0663	0.0645	0.0628	0.0610	0.0593	0.0576	0.0558	0.0541	3	6	9	12	15
87	0.0523	0.0506	0.0488	0.0471	0.0454	0.0436	0.0419	0.0401	0.0384	0.0366	3	6	9	12	15
88	0.0349	0.0332	0.0314	0.0297	0.0279	0.0262	0.0244	0.0227	0.0209	0.0192	3	6	9	12	15
89	0.0175	0.0157	0.0140	0.0122	0.0105	0.0087	0.0070	0.0052	0.0035	0.0017	3	6	9	12	15
90	0.0000														

NATURAL TANGENTS

°	0' 0.0°	6' 0.1°	12' 0.2°	18' 0.3°	24' 0.4°	30' 0.5°	36' 0.6°	42' 0.7°	48' 0.8°	54' 0.9°	1'	2'	3'	4'	5'
0	0.0000	0.0017	0.0035	0.0052	0.0070	0.0087	0.0105	0.0122	0.0140	0.0157	3	6	9	12	15
1	0.0175	0.0192	0.0209	0.0227	0.0244	0.0262	0.0279	0.0297	0.0314	0.0332	3	6	9	12	15
2	0.0349	0.0367	0.0384	0.0402	0.0419	0.0437	0.0454	0.0472	0.0489	0.0507	3	6	9	12	15
3	0.0524	0.0542	0.0559	0.0577	0.0594	0.0612	0.0629	0.0647	0.0664	0.0682	3	6	9	12	15
4	0.0699	0.0717	0.0734	0.0752	0.0769	0.0787	0.0805	0.0822	0.0840	0.0857	3	6	9	12	15
5	0.0875	0.0892	0.0910	0.0928	0.0945	0.0963	0.0981	0.0998	0.1016	0.1033	3	6	9	12	15
6	0.1051	0.1069	0.1086	0.1104	0.1122	0.1139	0.1157	0.1175	0.1192	0.1210	3	6	9	12	15
7	0.1228	0.1246	0.1263	0.1281	0.1299	0.1317	0.1334	0.1352	0.1370	0.1388	3	6	9	12	15
8	0.1405	0.1423	0.1441	0.1459	0.1477	0.1495	0.1512	0.1530	0.1548	0.1566	3	6	9	12	15
9	0.1584	0.1602	0.1620	0.1638	0.1655	0.1673	0.1691	0.1709	0.1727	0.1745	3	6	9	12	15
10	0.1763	0.1781	0.1799	0.1817	0.1835	0.1853	0.1871	0.1890	0.1908	0.1926	3	6	9	12	15
11	0.1944	0.1962	0.1980	0.1998	0.2016	0.2035	0.2053	0.2071	0.2089	0.2107	3	6	9	12	15
12	0.2126	0.2144	0.2162	0.2180	0.2199	0.2217	0.2235	0.2254	0.2272	0.2290	3	6	9	12	15
13	0.2309	0.2327	0.2345	0.2364	0.2382	0.2401	0.2419	0.2438	0.2456	0.2475	3	6	9	12	15
14	0.2493	0.2512	0.2530	0.2549	0.2568	0.2586	0.2605	0.2623	0.2642	0.2661	3	6	9	12	16
15	0.2679	0.2698	0.2717	0.2736	0.2754	0.2773	0.2792	0.2811	0.2830	0.2849	3	6	9	12	16
16	0.2867	0.2886	0.2905	0.2924	0.2943	0.2962	0.2981	0.3000	0.3019	0.3038	3	6	9	13	16
17	0.3057	0.3076	0.3096	0.3115	0.3134	0.3153	0.3172	0.3191	0.3211	0.3230	3	6	10	13	16
18	0.3249	0.3269	0.3288	0.3307	0.3327	0.3346	0.3365	0.3385	0.3404	0.3424	3	6	10	13	16
19	0.3443	0.3463	0.3482	0.3502	0.3522	0.3541	0.3561	0.3581	0.3600	0.3620	3	7	10	13	16
20	0.3640	0.3659	0.3679	0.3699	0.3719	0.3739	0.3759	0.3779	0.3799	0.3819	3	7	10	13	17
21	0.3839	0.3859	0.3879	0.3899	0.3919	0.3939	0.3959	0.3979	0.4000	0.4020	3	7	10	13	17
22	0.4040	0.4061	0.4081	0.4101	0.4122	0.4142	0.4163	0.4183	0.4204	0.4224	3	7	10	14	17
23	0.4245	0.4265	0.4286	0.4307	0.4327	0.4348	0.4369	0.4390	0.4411	0.4431	3	7	10	14	17
24	0.4452	0.4473	0.4494	0.4515	0.4536	0.4557	0.4578	0.4599	0.4621	0.4642	4	7	11	14	18
25	0.4663	0.4684	0.4706	0.4727	0.4748	0.4770	0.4791	0.4813	0.4834	0.4856	4	7	11	14	18
26	0.4877	0.4899	0.4921	0.4942	0.4964	0.4986	0.5008	0.5029	0.5051	0.5073	4	7	11	15	18
27	0.5095	0.5117	0.5139	0.5161	0.5184	0.5206	0.5228	0.5250	0.5272	0.5295	4	7	11	15	18
28	0.5317	0.5340	0.5362	0.5384	0.5407	0.5430	0.5452	0.5475	0.5498	0.5520	4	8	11	15	19
29	0.5543	0.5566	0.5589	0.5612	0.5635	0.5658	0.5681	0.5704	0.5727	0.5750	4	8	12	15	19
30	0.5774	0.5797	0.5820	0.5844	0.5867	0.5890	0.5914	0.5938	0.5961	0.5985	4	8	12	16	20
31	0.6009	0.6032	0.6056	0.6080	0.6104	0.6128	0.6152	0.6176	0.6200	0.6224	4	8	12	16	20
32	0.6249	0.6273	0.6297	0.6322	0.6346	0.6371	0.6395	0.6420	0.6445	0.6469	4	8	12	16	20
33	0.6494	0.6519	0.6544	0.6569	0.6594	0.6619	0.6644	0.6669	0.6694	0.6720	4	8	13	17	21
34	0.6745	0.6771	0.6796	0.6822	0.6847	0.6873	0.6899	0.6924	0.6950	0.6976	4	9	13	17	21
35	0.7002	0.7028	0.7054	0.7080	0.7107	0.7133	0.7159	0.7186	0.7212	0.7239	4	9	13	18	22
36	0.7265	0.7292	0.7319	0.7346	0.7373	0.7400	0.7427	0.7454	0.7481	0.7508	5	9	14	18	23
37	0.7536	0.7563	0.7590	0.7618	0.7646	0.7673	0.7701	0.7729	0.7757	0.7785	5	9	14	18	23
38	0.7813	0.7841	0.7869	0.7898	0.7926	0.7954	0.7983	0.8012	0.8040	0.8069	5	9	14	19	24
39	0.8098	0.8127	0.8156	0.8185	0.8214	0.8243	0.8273	0.8302	0.8332	0.8361	5	10	15	19	24
40	0.8391	0.8421	0.8451	0.8481	0.8511	0.8541	0.8571	0.8601	0.8632	0.8662	5	10	15	20	25
41	0.8693	0.8724	0.8754	0.8785	0.8816	0.8847	0.8878	0.8910	0.8941	0.8972	5	10	16	21	26
42	0.9004	0.9036	0.9067	0.9099	0.9131	0.9163	0.9195	0.9228	0.9260	0.9293	5	11	16	21	27
43	0.9325	0.9358	0.9391	0.9424	0.9457	0.9490	0.9523	0.9556	0.9590	0.9623	6	11	17	22	28
44	0.9657	0.9691	0.9725	0.9759	0.9793	0.9827	0.9861	0.9896	0.9930	0.9965	6	11	17	23	28

NATURAL TANGENTS (continued)

°	0' 0.0°	6' 0.1°	12' 0.2°	18' 0.3°	24' 0.4°	30' 0.5°	36' 0.6°	42' 0.7°	48' 0.8°	54' 0.9°	1'	2'	3'	4'	5'
45	1.0000	1.0035	1.0070	1.0105	1.0141	1.0176	1.0212	1.0247	1.0283	1.0319	6	12	18	24	30
46	1.0355	1.0392	1.0428	1.0464	1.0501	1.0538	1.0575	1.0612	1.0649	1.0686	6	12	18	25	31
47	1.0724	1.0761	1.0799	1.0837	1.0875	1.0913	1.0951	1.0990	1.1028	1.1067	6	13	19	25	32
48	1.1106	1.1145	1.1184	1.1224	1.1263	1.1303	1.1343	1.1383	1.1423	1.1463	7	13	20	27	33
49	1.1504	1.1544	1.1585	1.1626	1.1667	1.1708	1.1750	1.1792	1.1833	1.1875	7	14	21	28	34
50	1.1918	1.1960	1.2002	1.2045	1.2088	1.2131	1.2174	1.2218	1.2261	1.2305	7	14	22	29	36
51	1.2349	1.2393	1.2437	1.2482	1.2527	1.2572	1.2617	1.2662	1.2708	1.2753	8	15	23	30	38
52	1.2799	1.2846	1.2892	1.2938	1.2985	1.3032	1.3079	1.3127	1.3175	1.3222	8	16	24	31	39
53	1.3270	1.3319	1.3367	1.3416	1.3465	1.3514	1.3564	1.3613	1.3663	1.3713	8	16	25	33	41
54	1.3764	1.3814	1.3865	1.3916	1.3968	1.4019	1.4071	1.4124	1.4176	1.4229	9	17	26	34	43
55	1.4281	1.4335	1.4388	1.4442	1.4496	1.4550	1.4605	1.4659	1.4715	1.4770	9	18	27	36	45
56	1.4826	1.4882	1.4938	1.4994	1.5051	1.5108	1.5166	1.5224	1.5282	1.5340	10	19	29	38	48
57	1.5399	1.5458	1.5517	1.5577	1.5637	1.5697	1.5757	1.5818	1.5880	1.5941	10	20	30	40	50
58	1.6003	1.6066	1.6128	1.6191	1.6255	1.6319	1.6383	1.6447	1.6512	1.6577	11	21	32	43	53
59	1.6643	1.6709	1.6775	1.6842	1.6909	1.6977	1.7045	1.7113	1.7182	1.7251	11	23	34	45	56
60	1.7321	1.7391	1.7461	1.7532	1.7603	1.7675	1.7747	1.7820	1.7893	1.7966	12	24	36	48	60
61	1.8040	1.8115	1.8190	1.8265	1.8341	1.8418	1.8495	1.8572	1.8650	1.8728	13	26	38	51	64
62	1.8807	1.8887	1.8967	1.9047	1.9128	1.9210	1.9292	1.9375	1.9458	1.9542	14	27	41	55	68
63	1.9626	1.9711	1.9797	1.9883	1.9970	2.0057	2.0145	2.0233	2.0323	2.0413	15	29	44	58	73
64	2.0503	2.0594	2.0686	2.0778	2.0872	2.0965	2.1060	2.1155	2.1251	2.1348	16	31	47	63	78
65	2.1445	2.1543	2.1642	2.1742	2.1842	2.1943	2.2045	2.2148	2.2251	2.2355	17	34	51	68	85
66	2.2460	2.2566	2.2673	2.2781	2.2889	2.2998	2.3109	2.3220	2.3332	2.3445	18	37	55	73	92
67	2.3559	2.3673	2.3789	2.3906	2.4023	2.4142	2.4262	2.4383	2.4504	2.4627	20	40	60	79	99
68	2.4751	2.4876	2.5002	2.5129	2.5257	2.5386	2.5517	2.5649	2.5782	2.5916	22	43	65	87	108
69	2.6051	2.6187	2.6325	2.6464	2.6605	2.6746	2.6889	2.7034	2.7179	2.7326	24	47	71	95	119
70	2.7475	2.7625	2.7776	2.7929	2.8083	2.8239	2.8397	2.8556	2.8716	2.8878	26	52	78	104	131
71	2.9042	2.9208	2.9375	2.9544	2.9714	2.9887	3.0061	3.0237	3.0415	3.0595	29	58	87	116	145
72	3.0777	3.0961	3.1146	3.1334	3.1524	3.1716	3.1910	3.2106	3.2305	3.2506	32	64	96	129	161
73	3.2709	3.2914	3.3122	3.3332	3.3544	3.3759	3.3977	3.4197	3.4420	3.4646	36	72	108	144	180
74	3.4874	3.5105	3.5339	3.5576	3.5816	3.6059	3.6305	3.6554	3.6806	3.7062	41	81	122	163	204
75	3.7321	3.7583	3.7848	3.8118	3.8391	3.8667	3.8947	3.9232	3.9520	3.9812	46	93	139	186	232
76	4.0108	4.0408	4.0713	4.1022	4.1335	4.1653	4.1976	4.2303	4.2635	4.2972	53	107	160	213	267
77	4.3315	4.3662	4.4015	4.4374	4.4737	4.5107	4.5483	4.5864	4.6252	4.6646					
78	4.7046	4.7453	4.7867	4.8288	4.8716	4.9152	4.9594	5.0045	5.0504	5.0970					
79	5.1446	5.1929	5.2422	5.2924	5.3435	5.3955	5.4486	5.5026	5.5578	5.6140			Differences		
80	5.6713	5.7297	5.7894	5.8502	5.9124	5.9758	6.0405	6.1066	6.1742	6.2432			untrustworthy		
81	6.3138	6.3859	6.4596	6.5350	6.6122	6.6912	6.7720	6.8548	6.9395	7.0264			here		
82	7.1154	7.2066	7.3002	7.3962	7.4947	7.5958	7.6996	7.8062	7.9158	8.0285					
83	8.1443	8.2636	8.3863	8.5126	8.6427	8.7769	8.9152	9.0579	9.2052	9.3572					
84	9.514	9.677	9.845	10.02	10.20	10.39	10.58	10.78	10.99	11.20					
85	11.43	11.66	11.91	12.16	12.43	12.71	13.00	13.30	13.62	13.95					
86	14.30	14.67	15.06	15.46	15.89	16.35	16.83	17.34	17.89	18.46					
87	19.08	19.74	20.45	21.20	22.02	22.90	23.86	24.90	26.03	27.27					
88	28.64	30.14	31.82	33.69	35.80	38.19	40.92	44.07	47.74	52.08					
89	57.29	63.66	71.62	81.85	95.49	114.6	143.2	191.0	286.5	573.0					
90	∞														

185

°	0' 0.0°	6' 0.1°	12' 0.2°	18' 0.3°	24' 0.4°	30' 0.5°	36' 0.6°	42' 0.7°	48' 0.8°	54' 0.9°	5'	4'	3'	2'	1'
45	T.8495	T.8502	T.8510	T.8517	T.8525	T.8532	T.8540	T.8547	T.8555	T.8562	6	5	4	2	1
46	T.8569	T.8577	T.8584	T.8591	T.8598	T.8606	T.8613	T.8620	T.8627	T.8634	6	5	4	2	1
47	T.8641	T.8648	T.8655	T.8662	T.8669	T.8676	T.8683	T.8690	T.8697	T.8704	6	5	4	2	1
48	T.8711	T.8718	T.8724	T.8731	T.8738	T.8745	T.8751	T.8758	T.8765	T.8771	6	5	4	2	1
49	T.8778	T.8784	T.8791	T.8797	T.8804	T.8810	T.8817	T.8823	T.8830	T.8836	5	4	3	2	1
50	T.8843	T.8849	T.8855	T.8862	T.8868	T.8874	T.8880	T.8887	T.8893	T.8899	5	4	3	2	1
51	T.8905	T.8911	T.8917	T.8923	T.8929	T.8935	T.8941	T.8947	T.8953	T.8959	5	4	3	2	1
52	T.8965	T.8971	T.8977	T.8983	T.8989	T.8995	T.9000	T.9006	T.9012	T.9018	5	4	3	2	1
53	T.9023	T.9029	T.9035	T.9041	T.9046	T.9052	T.9057	T.9063	T.9069	T.9074	5	4	3	2	1
54	T.9080	T.9085	T.9091	T.9096	T.9101	T.9107	T.9112	T.9118	T.9123	T.9128	5	4	3	2	1
55	T.9134	T.9139	T.9144	T.9149	T.9155	T.9160	T.9165	T.9170	T.9175	T.9181	4	4	3	2	1
56	T.9186	T.9191	T.9196	T.9201	T.9206	T.9211	T.9216	T.9221	T.9226	T.9231	4	3	3	2	1
57	T.9236	T.9241	T.9246	T.9251	T.9255	T.9260	T.9265	T.9270	T.9275	T.9279	4	3	3	2	1
58	T.9284	T.9289	T.9294	T.9298	T.9303	T.9308	T.9312	T.9317	T.9322	T.9326	4	3	2	2	1
59	T.9331	T.9335	T.9340	T.9344	T.9349	T.9353	T.9358	T.9362	T.9367	T.9371	4	3	2	2	1
60	T.9375	T.9380	T.9384	T.9388	T.9393	T.9397	T.9401	T.9406	T.9410	T.9414	4	3	2	2	1
61	T.9418	T.9422	T.9427	T.9431	T.9435	T.9439	T.9443	T.9447	T.9451	T.9455	3	3	2	2	1
62	T.9459	T.9463	T.9467	T.9471	T.9475	T.9479	T.9483	T.9487	T.9491	T.9495	3	3	2	1	1
63	T.9499	T.9503	T.9506	T.9510	T.9514	T.9518	T.9522	T.9525	T.9529	T.9533	3	3	2	1	1
64	T.9537	T.9540	T.9544	T.9548	T.9551	T.9555	T.9558	T.9562	T.9566	T.9569	3	2	2	1	1
65	T.9573	T.9576	T.9580	T.9583	T.9587	T.9590	T.9594	T.9597	T.9601	T.9604	3	2	2	1	1
66	T.9607	T.9611	T.9614	T.9617	T.9621	T.9624	T.9627	T.9631	T.9634	T.9637	3	2	2	1	1
67	T.9640	T.9643	T.9647	T.9650	T.9653	T.9656	T.9659	T.9662	T.9666	T.9669	3	2	2	1	1
68	T.9672	T.9675	T.9678	T.9681	T.9684	T.9687	T.9690	T.9693	T.9696	T.9699	2	2	1	1	1
69	T.9702	T.9704	T.9707	T.9710	T.9713	T.9716	T.9719	T.9722	T.9724	T.9727	2	2	1	1	0
70	T.9730	T.9733	T.9735	T.9738	T.9741	T.9743	T.9746	T.9748	T.9751	T.9754	2	2	1	1	0
71	T.9757	T.9759	T.9762	T.9764	T.9767	T.9770	T.9772	T.9775	T.9777	T.9780	2	2	1	1	0
72	T.9782	T.9785	T.9787	T.9789	T.9792	T.9794	T.9797	T.9799	T.9801	T.9804	2	2	1	1	0
73	T.9806	T.9808	T.9811	T.9813	T.9815	T.9817	T.9820	T.9822	T.9824	T.9826	2	1	1	1	0
74	T.9828	T.9831	T.9833	T.9835	T.9837	T.9839	T.9841	T.9843	T.9845	T.9847	2	1	1	1	0
75	T.9849	T.9851	T.9853	T.9855	T.9857	T.9859	T.9861	T.9863	T.9865	T.9867	2	1	1	1	0
76	T.9869	T.9871	T.9873	T.9875	T.9876	T.9878	T.9880	T.9882	T.9884	T.9885	2	1	1	1	0
77	T.9887	T.9889	T.9891	T.9892	T.9894	T.9896	T.9897	T.9899	T.9901	T.9902	2	1	1	1	0
78	T.9904	T.9906	T.9907	T.9909	T.9910	T.9912	T.9913	T.9915	T.9916	T.9918	1	1	1	1	0
79	T.9919	T.9921	T.9922	T.9924	T.9925	T.9927	T.9928	T.9929	T.9931	T.9932	1	1	1	0	0
80	T.9934	T.9935	T.9936	T.9937	T.9939	T.9940	T.9941	T.9943	T.9944	T.9945	1	1	1	0	0
81	T.9946	T.9947	T.9949	T.9950	T.9951	T.9952	T.9953	T.9954	T.9955	T.9956	1	1	1	0	0
82	T.9958	T.9958	T.9960	T.9961	T.9962	T.9963	T.9964	T.9965	T.9966	T.9966	1	1	0	0	0
83	T.9968	T.9968	T.9969	T.9970	T.9971	T.9972	T.9973	T.9974	T.9975	T.9975	1	1	0	0	0
84	T.9976	T.9977	T.9978	T.9978	T.9979	T.9980	T.9981	T.9981	T.9982	T.9983	1	0	0	0	0
85	T.9983	T.9984	T.9985	T.9985	T.9986	T.9987	T.9987	T.9988	T.9988	T.9989	0	0	0	0	0
86	T.9989	T.9990	T.9990	T.9991	T.9991	T.9992	T.9992	T.9993	T.9993	T.9994	0	0	0	0	0
87	T.9994	T.9994	T.9995	T.9995	T.9996	T.9996	T.9996	T.9997	T.9997	T.9998	0	0	0	0	0
88	T.9997	T.9998	T.9998	T.9998	T.9998	T.9999	T.9999	T.9999	T.9999	T.9999	0	0	0	0	0
89	T.9999	T.9999	0.0000	0.0000	0.0000	0.0000	0.0000	0.0000	0.0000	0.0000	0	0	0	0	0
90	0.0000										0	0	0	0	0

°	0' 0.0°	6' 0.1°	12' 0.2°	18' 0.3°	24' 0.4°	30' 0.5°	36' 0.6°	42' 0.7°	48' 0.8°	54' 0.9°	1'	2'	3'	4'	5'
0	$-\infty$	3.2419	3.5429	3.7190	3.8439	3.9408	2.0200	2.0870	2.1450	2.1961			Differences untrustworthy here		
1	2.2419	2.2832	2.3210	2.3558	2.3880	2.4179	2.4459	2.4723	2.4971	2.5206					
2	2.5428	2.5640	2.5842	2.6035	2.6220	2.6397	2.6567	2.6731	2.6889	2.7041					
3	2.7188	2.7330	2.7468	2.7602	2.7731	2.7857	2.7979	2.8098	2.8213	2.8326					
4	2.8436	2.8543	2.8647	2.8749	2.8849	2.8946	2.9042	2.9135	2.9226	2.9315					
5	2.9403	2.9489	2.9573	2.9655	2.9736	2.9816	2.9894	2.9970	1.0046	1.0120	16	32	48	64	80
6	1.0192	1.0264	1.0334	1.0403	1.0472	1.0539	1.0605	1.0670	1.0734	1.0797	13	26	39	52	65
7	1.0859	1.0920	1.0981	1.1040	1.1099	1.1157	1.1214	1.1271	1.1326	1.1381	11	22	33	44	55
8	1.1436	1.1489	1.1542	1.1594	1.1646	1.1697	1.1747	1.1797	1.1847	1.1895	10	19	29	38	48
9	1.1943	1.1991	1.2038	1.2085	1.2131	1.2176	1.2221	1.2266	1.2310	1.2353	8	15	23	30	38
10	1.2397	1.2439	1.2482	1.2524	1.2565	1.2606	1.2647	1.2687	1.2727	1.2767	7	14	20	27	34
11	1.2806	1.2845	1.2883	1.2921	1.2959	1.2997	1.3034	1.3070	1.3107	1.3143	6	12	19	25	31
12	1.3179	1.3214	1.3250	1.3284	1.3319	1.3353	1.3387	1.3421	1.3455	1.3488	6	11	17	23	28
13	1.3521	1.3554	1.3586	1.3618	1.3650	1.3682	1.3713	1.3745	1.3775	1.3806	5	11	16	21	26
14	1.3837	1.3867	1.3897	1.3927	1.3957	1.3986	1.4015	1.4044	1.4073	1.4102	5	10	15	20	24
15	1.4130	1.4158	1.4186	1.4214	1.4242	1.4269	1.4296	1.4323	1.4350	1.4377	5	9	14	18	23
16	1.4403	1.4430	1.4456	1.4482	1.4508	1.4533	1.4559	1.4584	1.4609	1.4634	4	9	13	17	21
17	1.4659	1.4684	1.4709	1.4733	1.4757	1.4781	1.4805	1.4829	1.4853	1.4876	4	8	12	16	20
18	1.4900	1.4923	1.4946	1.4969	1.4992	1.5015	1.5037	1.5060	1.5082	1.5104	4	8	11	15	19
19	1.5126	1.5148	1.5170	1.5192	1.5213	1.5235	1.5256	1.5278	1.5299	1.5320	4	7	11	14	18
20	1.5341	1.5361	1.5382	1.5402	1.5423	1.5443	1.5463	1.5484	1.5504	1.5523	3	7	10	14	17
21	1.5543	1.5563	1.5583	1.5602	1.5621	1.5641	1.5660	1.5679	1.5698	1.5717	3	6	10	13	16
22	1.5736	1.5754	1.5773	1.5792	1.5810	1.5828	1.5847	1.5865	1.5883	1.5901	3	6	9	12	15
23	1.5919	1.5937	1.5954	1.5972	1.5990	1.6007	1.6024	1.6042	1.6059	1.6076	3	6	9	12	15
24	1.6093	1.6110	1.6127	1.6144	1.6161	1.6177	1.6194	1.6210	1.6227	1.6243	3	6	8	11	14
25	1.6259	1.6276	1.6292	1.6308	1.6324	1.6340	1.6356	1.6371	1.6387	1.6403	3	5	8	11	13
26	1.6418	1.6434	1.6449	1.6465	1.6480	1.6495	1.6510	1.6526	1.6541	1.6556	3	5	8	10	13
27	1.6570	1.6585	1.6600	1.6615	1.6629	1.6644	1.6659	1.6673	1.6687	1.6702	2	5	7	10	12
28	1.6716	1.6730	1.6744	1.6759	1.6773	1.6787	1.6801	1.6814	1.6828	1.6842	2	5	7	9	12
29	1.6856	1.6869	1.6883	1.6896	1.6910	1.6923	1.6937	1.6950	1.6963	1.6977	2	4	7	9	11
30	1.6990	1.7003	1.7016	1.7029	1.7042	1.7055	1.7068	1.7080	1.7093	1.7106	2	4	6	9	11
31	1.7118	1.7131	1.7144	1.7156	1.7168	1.7181	1.7193	1.7205	1.7218	1.7230	2	4	6	8	10
32	1.7242	1.7254	1.7266	1.7278	1.7290	1.7302	1.7314	1.7326	1.7338	1.7349	2	4	6	8	10
33	1.7361	1.7373	1.7384	1.7396	1.7407	1.7419	1.7430	1.7442	1.7453	1.7464	2	4	6	8	9
34	1.7476	1.7487	1.7498	1.7509	1.7520	1.7531	1.7542	1.7553	1.7564	1.7575	2	4	6	7	9
35	1.7586	1.7597	1.7607	1.7618	1.7629	1.7640	1.7650	1.7661	1.7671	1.7682	2	3	5	7	9
36	1.7692	1.7703	1.7713	1.7723	1.7734	1.7744	1.7754	1.7764	1.7774	1.7785	2	3	5	7	8
37	1.7795	1.7805	1.7815	1.7825	1.7835	1.7844	1.7854	1.7864	1.7874	1.7884	2	3	5	6	8
38	1.7893	1.7903	1.7913	1.7922	1.7932	1.7941	1.7951	1.7960	1.7970	1.7979	2	3	5	6	8
39	1.7989	1.7998	1.8007	1.8017	1.8026	1.8035	1.8044	1.8053	1.8063	1.8072	2	3	5	6	8
40	1.8081	1.8090	1.8099	1.8108	1.8117	1.8125	1.8134	1.8143	1.8152	1.8161	1	3	4	6	7
41	1.8169	1.8178	1.8187	1.8195	1.8204	1.8213	1.8221	1.8230	1.8238	1.8247	1	3	4	6	7
42	1.8255	1.8264	1.8272	1.8280	1.8289	1.8297	1.8305	1.8313	1.8322	1.8330	1	3	4	5	7
43	1.8338	1.8346	1.8354	1.8362	1.8370	1.8378	1.8386	1.8394	1.8402	1.8410	1	3	4	5	7
44	1.8418	1.8426	1.8433	1.8441	1.8449	1.8457	1.8464	1.8472	1.8480	1.8487	1	3	4	5	6

LOGARITHMS OF COSINES

°	0′ 0.0°	6′ 0.1°	12′ 0.2°	18′ 0.3°	24′ 0.4°	30′ 0.5°	36′ 0.6°	42′ 0.7°	48′ 0.8°	54′ 0.9°	Subtract 1′	2′	3′	4′	5′
0	0.0000	0.0000	0.0000	0.0000	0.0000	0.0000	0.0000	0.0000	0.0000	$\bar{1}$.9999	0	0	0	0	0
1	$\bar{1}$.9999	$\bar{1}$.9999	$\bar{1}$.9999	$\bar{1}$.9999	$\bar{1}$.9999	$\bar{1}$.9999	$\bar{1}$.9998	$\bar{1}$.9998	$\bar{1}$.9998	$\bar{1}$.9998	0	0	0	0	0
2	$\bar{1}$.9997	$\bar{1}$.9997	$\bar{1}$.9997	$\bar{1}$.9996	$\bar{1}$.9996	$\bar{1}$.9996	$\bar{1}$.9996	$\bar{1}$.9995	$\bar{1}$.9995	$\bar{1}$.9994	0	0	0	0	0
3	$\bar{1}$.9994	$\bar{1}$.9994	$\bar{1}$.9993	$\bar{1}$.9993	$\bar{1}$.9992	$\bar{1}$.9992	$\bar{1}$.9991	$\bar{1}$.9991	$\bar{1}$.9990	$\bar{1}$.9990	0	0	0	0	0
4	$\bar{1}$.9989	$\bar{1}$.9989	$\bar{1}$.9988	$\bar{1}$.9988	$\bar{1}$.9987	$\bar{1}$.9987	$\bar{1}$.9986	$\bar{1}$.9985	$\bar{1}$.9985	$\bar{1}$.9984	0	0	0	0	0
5	$\bar{1}$.9983	$\bar{1}$.9983	$\bar{1}$.9982	$\bar{1}$.9981	$\bar{1}$.9981	$\bar{1}$.9980	$\bar{1}$.9979	$\bar{1}$.9978	$\bar{1}$.9978	$\bar{1}$.9977	0	0	0	0	1
6	$\bar{1}$.9976	$\bar{1}$.9975	$\bar{1}$.9975	$\bar{1}$.9974	$\bar{1}$.9973	$\bar{1}$.9972	$\bar{1}$.9971	$\bar{1}$.9970	$\bar{1}$.9969	$\bar{1}$.9968	0	0	0	1	1
7	$\bar{1}$.9968	$\bar{1}$.9967	$\bar{1}$.9966	$\bar{1}$.9965	$\bar{1}$.9964	$\bar{1}$.9963	$\bar{1}$.9962	$\bar{1}$.9961	$\bar{1}$.9960	$\bar{1}$.9959	0	0	0	1	1
8	$\bar{1}$.9958	$\bar{1}$.9956	$\bar{1}$.9955	$\bar{1}$.9954	$\bar{1}$.9953	$\bar{1}$.9952	$\bar{1}$.9951	$\bar{1}$.9950	$\bar{1}$.9949	$\bar{1}$.9947	0	0	1	1	1
9	$\bar{1}$.9946	$\bar{1}$.9945	$\bar{1}$.9944	$\bar{1}$.9943	$\bar{1}$.9941	$\bar{1}$.9940	$\bar{1}$.9939	$\bar{1}$.9937	$\bar{1}$.9936	$\bar{1}$.9935	0	0	1	1	1
10	$\bar{1}$.9934	$\bar{1}$.9932	$\bar{1}$.9931	$\bar{1}$.9929	$\bar{1}$.9928	$\bar{1}$.9927	$\bar{1}$.9925	$\bar{1}$.9924	$\bar{1}$.9922	$\bar{1}$.9921	0	0	1	1	1
11	$\bar{1}$.9919	$\bar{1}$.9918	$\bar{1}$.9916	$\bar{1}$.9915	$\bar{1}$.9913	$\bar{1}$.9912	$\bar{1}$.9910	$\bar{1}$.9909	$\bar{1}$.9907	$\bar{1}$.9906	0	1	1	1	1
12	$\bar{1}$.9904	$\bar{1}$.9902	$\bar{1}$.9901	$\bar{1}$.9899	$\bar{1}$.9897	$\bar{1}$.9896	$\bar{1}$.9894	$\bar{1}$.9892	$\bar{1}$.9891	$\bar{1}$.9889	0	1	1	1	1
13	$\bar{1}$.9887	$\bar{1}$.9885	$\bar{1}$.9884	$\bar{1}$.9882	$\bar{1}$.9880	$\bar{1}$.9878	$\bar{1}$.9876	$\bar{1}$.9875	$\bar{1}$.9873	$\bar{1}$.9871	0	1	1	1	2
14	$\bar{1}$.9869	$\bar{1}$.9867	$\bar{1}$.9865	$\bar{1}$.9863	$\bar{1}$.9861	$\bar{1}$.9859	$\bar{1}$.9857	$\bar{1}$.9855	$\bar{1}$.9853	$\bar{1}$.9851	0	1	1	1	2
15	$\bar{1}$.9849	$\bar{1}$.9847	$\bar{1}$.9845	$\bar{1}$.9843	$\bar{1}$.9841	$\bar{1}$.9839	$\bar{1}$.9837	$\bar{1}$.9835	$\bar{1}$.9833	$\bar{1}$.9831	0	1	1	1	2
16	$\bar{1}$.9828	$\bar{1}$.9826	$\bar{1}$.9824	$\bar{1}$.9822	$\bar{1}$.9820	$\bar{1}$.9817	$\bar{1}$.9815	$\bar{1}$.9813	$\bar{1}$.9811	$\bar{1}$.9808	0	1	1	1	2
17	$\bar{1}$.9806	$\bar{1}$.9804	$\bar{1}$.9801	$\bar{1}$.9799	$\bar{1}$.9797	$\bar{1}$.9794	$\bar{1}$.9792	$\bar{1}$.9789	$\bar{1}$.9787	$\bar{1}$.9785	0	1	1	2	2
18	$\bar{1}$.9782	$\bar{1}$.9780	$\bar{1}$.9777	$\bar{1}$.9775	$\bar{1}$.9772	$\bar{1}$.9770	$\bar{1}$.9767	$\bar{1}$.9764	$\bar{1}$.9762	$\bar{1}$.9759	0	1	1	2	2
19	$\bar{1}$.9757	$\bar{1}$.9754	$\bar{1}$.9751	$\bar{1}$.9749	$\bar{1}$.9746	$\bar{1}$.9743	$\bar{1}$.9741	$\bar{1}$.9738	$\bar{1}$.9735	$\bar{1}$.9733	0	1	1	2	2
20	$\bar{1}$.9730	$\bar{1}$.9727	$\bar{1}$.9724	$\bar{1}$.9722	$\bar{1}$.9719	$\bar{1}$.9716	$\bar{1}$.9713	$\bar{1}$.9710	$\bar{1}$.9707	$\bar{1}$.9704	0	1	1	2	2
21	$\bar{1}$.9702	$\bar{1}$.9699	$\bar{1}$.9696	$\bar{1}$.9693	$\bar{1}$.9690	$\bar{1}$.9687	$\bar{1}$.9684	$\bar{1}$.9681	$\bar{1}$.9678	$\bar{1}$.9675	1	1	2	2	2
22	$\bar{1}$.9672	$\bar{1}$.9669	$\bar{1}$.9666	$\bar{1}$.9662	$\bar{1}$.9659	$\bar{1}$.9656	$\bar{1}$.9653	$\bar{1}$.9650	$\bar{1}$.9647	$\bar{1}$.9643	1	1	2	2	3
23	$\bar{1}$.9640	$\bar{1}$.9637	$\bar{1}$.9634	$\bar{1}$.9631	$\bar{1}$.9627	$\bar{1}$.9624	$\bar{1}$.9621	$\bar{1}$.9617	$\bar{1}$.9614	$\bar{1}$.9611	1	1	2	2	3
24	$\bar{1}$.9607	$\bar{1}$.9604	$\bar{1}$.9601	$\bar{1}$.9597	$\bar{1}$.9594	$\bar{1}$.9590	$\bar{1}$.9587	$\bar{1}$.9583	$\bar{1}$.9580	$\bar{1}$.9576	1	1	2	2	3
25	$\bar{1}$.9573	$\bar{1}$.9569	$\bar{1}$.9566	$\bar{1}$.9562	$\bar{1}$.9558	$\bar{1}$.9555	$\bar{1}$.9551	$\bar{1}$.9548	$\bar{1}$.9544	$\bar{1}$.9540	1	1	2	2	3
26	$\bar{1}$.9537	$\bar{1}$.9533	$\bar{1}$.9529	$\bar{1}$.9525	$\bar{1}$.9522	$\bar{1}$.9518	$\bar{1}$.9514	$\bar{1}$.9510	$\bar{1}$.9506	$\bar{1}$.9503	1	1	2	3	3
27	$\bar{1}$.9499	$\bar{1}$.9495	$\bar{1}$.9491	$\bar{1}$.9487	$\bar{1}$.9483	$\bar{1}$.9479	$\bar{1}$.9475	$\bar{1}$.9471	$\bar{1}$.9467	$\bar{1}$.9463	1	1	2	3	3
28	$\bar{1}$.9459	$\bar{1}$.9455	$\bar{1}$.9451	$\bar{1}$.9447	$\bar{1}$.9443	$\bar{1}$.9439	$\bar{1}$.9435	$\bar{1}$.9431	$\bar{1}$.9427	$\bar{1}$.9422	1	1	2	3	3
29	$\bar{1}$.9418	$\bar{1}$.9414	$\bar{1}$.9410	$\bar{1}$.9406	$\bar{1}$.9401	$\bar{1}$.9397	$\bar{1}$.9393	$\bar{1}$.9388	$\bar{1}$.9384	$\bar{1}$.9380	1	1	2	3	4
30	$\bar{1}$.9375	$\bar{1}$.9371	$\bar{1}$.9367	$\bar{1}$.9362	$\bar{1}$.9358	$\bar{1}$.9353	$\bar{1}$.9349	$\bar{1}$.9344	$\bar{1}$.9340	$\bar{1}$.9335	1	1	2	3	4
31	$\bar{1}$.9331	$\bar{1}$.9326	$\bar{1}$.9322	$\bar{1}$.9317	$\bar{1}$.9312	$\bar{1}$.9308	$\bar{1}$.9303	$\bar{1}$.9298	$\bar{1}$.9294	$\bar{1}$.9289	1	2	2	3	4
32	$\bar{1}$.9284	$\bar{1}$.9279	$\bar{1}$.9275	$\bar{1}$.9270	$\bar{1}$.9265	$\bar{1}$.9260	$\bar{1}$.9255	$\bar{1}$.9251	$\bar{1}$.9246	$\bar{1}$.9241	1	2	2	3	4
33	$\bar{1}$.9236	$\bar{1}$.9231	$\bar{1}$.9226	$\bar{1}$.9221	$\bar{1}$.9216	$\bar{1}$.9211	$\bar{1}$.9206	$\bar{1}$.9201	$\bar{1}$.9196	$\bar{1}$.9191	1	2	3	3	4
34	$\bar{1}$.9186	$\bar{1}$.9181	$\bar{1}$.9175	$\bar{1}$.9170	$\bar{1}$.9165	$\bar{1}$.9160	$\bar{1}$.9155	$\bar{1}$.9149	$\bar{1}$.9144	$\bar{1}$.9139	1	2	3	3	4
35	$\bar{1}$.9134	$\bar{1}$.9128	$\bar{1}$.9123	$\bar{1}$.9118	$\bar{1}$.9112	$\bar{1}$.9107	$\bar{1}$.9101	$\bar{1}$.9096	$\bar{1}$.9091	$\bar{1}$.9085	1	2	3	4	5
36	$\bar{1}$.9080	$\bar{1}$.9074	$\bar{1}$.9069	$\bar{1}$.9063	$\bar{1}$.9057	$\bar{1}$.9052	$\bar{1}$.9046	$\bar{1}$.9041	$\bar{1}$.9035	$\bar{1}$.9029	1	2	3	4	5
37	$\bar{1}$.9023	$\bar{1}$.9018	$\bar{1}$.9012	$\bar{1}$.9006	$\bar{1}$.9000	$\bar{1}$.8995	$\bar{1}$.8989	$\bar{1}$.8983	$\bar{1}$.8977	$\bar{1}$.8971	1	2	3	4	5
38	$\bar{1}$.8965	$\bar{1}$.8959	$\bar{1}$.8953	$\bar{1}$.8947	$\bar{1}$.8941	$\bar{1}$.8935	$\bar{1}$.8929	$\bar{1}$.8923	$\bar{1}$.8917	$\bar{1}$.8911	1	2	3	4	5
39	$\bar{1}$.8905	$\bar{1}$.8899	$\bar{1}$.8893	$\bar{1}$.8887	$\bar{1}$.8880	$\bar{1}$.8874	$\bar{1}$.8868	$\bar{1}$.8862	$\bar{1}$.8855	$\bar{1}$.8849	1	2	3	4	5
40	$\bar{1}$.8843	$\bar{1}$.8836	$\bar{1}$.8830	$\bar{1}$.8823	$\bar{1}$.8817	$\bar{1}$.8810	$\bar{1}$.8804	$\bar{1}$.8797	$\bar{1}$.8791	$\bar{1}$.8784	1	2	3	4	5
41	$\bar{1}$.8778	$\bar{1}$.8771	$\bar{1}$.8765	$\bar{1}$.8758	$\bar{1}$.8751	$\bar{1}$.8745	$\bar{1}$.8738	$\bar{1}$.8731	$\bar{1}$.8724	$\bar{1}$.8718	1	2	3	4	6
42	$\bar{1}$.8711	$\bar{1}$.8704	$\bar{1}$.8697	$\bar{1}$.8690	$\bar{1}$.8683	$\bar{1}$.8676	$\bar{1}$.8669	$\bar{1}$.8662	$\bar{1}$.8655	$\bar{1}$.8648	1	2	4	5	6
43	$\bar{1}$.8641	$\bar{1}$.8634	$\bar{1}$.8627	$\bar{1}$.8620	$\bar{1}$.8613	$\bar{1}$.8606	$\bar{1}$.8598	$\bar{1}$.8591	$\bar{1}$.8584	$\bar{1}$.8577	1	2	4	5	6
44	$\bar{1}$.8569	$\bar{1}$.8562	$\bar{1}$.8555	$\bar{1}$.8547	$\bar{1}$.8540	$\bar{1}$.8532	$\bar{1}$.8525	$\bar{1}$.8517	$\bar{1}$.8510	$\bar{1}$.8502	1	2	4	5	6

LOGARITHMS OF COSINES (continued)

°	0′ 0.0°	6′ 0.1°	12′ 0.2°	18′ 0.3°	24′ 0.4°	30′ 0.5°	36′ 0.6°	42′ 0.7°	48′ 0.8°	54′ 0.9°	Subtract 1′	2′	3′	4′	5′
45	$\bar{1}$.8495	$\bar{1}$.8487	$\bar{1}$.8480	$\bar{1}$.8472	$\bar{1}$.8464	$\bar{1}$.8457	$\bar{1}$.8449	$\bar{1}$.8441	$\bar{1}$.8433	$\bar{1}$.8426	1	3	4	5	6
46	$\bar{1}$.8418	$\bar{1}$.8410	$\bar{1}$.8402	$\bar{1}$.8394	$\bar{1}$.8386	$\bar{1}$.8378	$\bar{1}$.8370	$\bar{1}$.8362	$\bar{1}$.8354	$\bar{1}$.8346	1	3	4	5	7
47	$\bar{1}$.8338	$\bar{1}$.8330	$\bar{1}$.8322	$\bar{1}$.8313	$\bar{1}$.8305	$\bar{1}$.8297	$\bar{1}$.8289	$\bar{1}$.8280	$\bar{1}$.8272	$\bar{1}$.8264	1	3	4	6	7
48	$\bar{1}$.8255	$\bar{1}$.8247	$\bar{1}$.8238	$\bar{1}$.8230	$\bar{1}$.8221	$\bar{1}$.8213	$\bar{1}$.8204	$\bar{1}$.8195	$\bar{1}$.8187	$\bar{1}$.8178	1	3	4	6	7
49	$\bar{1}$.8169	$\bar{1}$.8161	$\bar{1}$.8152	$\bar{1}$.8143	$\bar{1}$.8134	$\bar{1}$.8125	$\bar{1}$.8117	$\bar{1}$.8108	$\bar{1}$.8099	$\bar{1}$.8090	1	3	4	6	7
50	$\bar{1}$.8081	$\bar{1}$.8072	$\bar{1}$.8063	$\bar{1}$.8053	$\bar{1}$.8044	$\bar{1}$.8035	$\bar{1}$.8026	$\bar{1}$.8017	$\bar{1}$.8007	$\bar{1}$.7998	2	3	5	6	8
51	$\bar{1}$.7989	$\bar{1}$.7979	$\bar{1}$.7970	$\bar{1}$.7960	$\bar{1}$.7951	$\bar{1}$.7941	$\bar{1}$.7932	$\bar{1}$.7922	$\bar{1}$.7913	$\bar{1}$.7903	2	3	5	6	8
52	$\bar{1}$.7893	$\bar{1}$.7884	$\bar{1}$.7874	$\bar{1}$.7864	$\bar{1}$.7854	$\bar{1}$.7844	$\bar{1}$.7835	$\bar{1}$.7825	$\bar{1}$.7815	$\bar{1}$.7805	2	3	5	7	8
53	$\bar{1}$.7795	$\bar{1}$.7785	$\bar{1}$.7774	$\bar{1}$.7764	$\bar{1}$.7754	$\bar{1}$.7744	$\bar{1}$.7734	$\bar{1}$.7723	$\bar{1}$.7713	$\bar{1}$.7703	2	3	5	7	9
54	$\bar{1}$.7692	$\bar{1}$.7682	$\bar{1}$.7671	$\bar{1}$.7661	$\bar{1}$.7650	$\bar{1}$.7640	$\bar{1}$.7629	$\bar{1}$.7618	$\bar{1}$.7607	$\bar{1}$.7597	2	4	5	7	9
55	$\bar{1}$.7586	$\bar{1}$.7575	$\bar{1}$.7564	$\bar{1}$.7553	$\bar{1}$.7542	$\bar{1}$.7531	$\bar{1}$.7520	$\bar{1}$.7509	$\bar{1}$.7498	$\bar{1}$.7487	2	4	6	7	9
56	$\bar{1}$.7476	$\bar{1}$.7464	$\bar{1}$.7453	$\bar{1}$.7442	$\bar{1}$.7430	$\bar{1}$.7419	$\bar{1}$.7407	$\bar{1}$.7396	$\bar{1}$.7384	$\bar{1}$.7373	2	4	6	8	10
57	$\bar{1}$.7361	$\bar{1}$.7349	$\bar{1}$.7338	$\bar{1}$.7326	$\bar{1}$.7314	$\bar{1}$.7302	$\bar{1}$.7290	$\bar{1}$.7278	$\bar{1}$.7266	$\bar{1}$.7254	2	4	6	8	10
58	$\bar{1}$.7242	$\bar{1}$.7230	$\bar{1}$.7218	$\bar{1}$.7205	$\bar{1}$.7193	$\bar{1}$.7181	$\bar{1}$.7168	$\bar{1}$.7156	$\bar{1}$.7144	$\bar{1}$.7131	2	4	6	8	10
59	$\bar{1}$.7118	$\bar{1}$.7106	$\bar{1}$.7093	$\bar{1}$.7080	$\bar{1}$.7068	$\bar{1}$.7055	$\bar{1}$.7042	$\bar{1}$.7029	$\bar{1}$.7016	$\bar{1}$.7003	2	4	6	9	11
60	$\bar{1}$.6990	$\bar{1}$.6977	$\bar{1}$.6963	$\bar{1}$.6950	$\bar{1}$.6937	$\bar{1}$.6923	$\bar{1}$.6910	$\bar{1}$.6896	$\bar{1}$.6883	$\bar{1}$.6869	2	4	7	9	11
61	$\bar{1}$.6856	$\bar{1}$.6842	$\bar{1}$.6828	$\bar{1}$.6814	$\bar{1}$.6801	$\bar{1}$.6787	$\bar{1}$.6773	$\bar{1}$.6759	$\bar{1}$.6744	$\bar{1}$.6730	2	5	7	9	12
62	$\bar{1}$.6716	$\bar{1}$.6702	$\bar{1}$.6687	$\bar{1}$.6673	$\bar{1}$.6659	$\bar{1}$.6644	$\bar{1}$.6629	$\bar{1}$.6615	$\bar{1}$.6600	$\bar{1}$.6585	2	5	7	10	12
63	$\bar{1}$.6570	$\bar{1}$.6556	$\bar{1}$.6541	$\bar{1}$.6526	$\bar{1}$.6510	$\bar{1}$.6495	$\bar{1}$.6480	$\bar{1}$.6465	$\bar{1}$.6449	$\bar{1}$.6434	3	5	8	10	13
64	$\bar{1}$.6418	$\bar{1}$.6403	$\bar{1}$.6387	$\bar{1}$.6371	$\bar{1}$.6356	$\bar{1}$.6340	$\bar{1}$.6324	$\bar{1}$.6308	$\bar{1}$.6292	$\bar{1}$.6276	3	5	8	11	13
65	$\bar{1}$.6259	$\bar{1}$.6243	$\bar{1}$.6227	$\bar{1}$.6210	$\bar{1}$.6194	$\bar{1}$.6177	$\bar{1}$.6161	$\bar{1}$.6144	$\bar{1}$.6127	$\bar{1}$.6110	3	6	8	11	14
66	$\bar{1}$.6093	$\bar{1}$.6076	$\bar{1}$.6059	$\bar{1}$.6042	$\bar{1}$.6024	$\bar{1}$.6007	$\bar{1}$.5990	$\bar{1}$.5972	$\bar{1}$.5954	$\bar{1}$.5937	3	6	9	12	14
67	$\bar{1}$.5919	$\bar{1}$.5901	$\bar{1}$.5883	$\bar{1}$.5865	$\bar{1}$.5847	$\bar{1}$.5828	$\bar{1}$.5810	$\bar{1}$.5792	$\bar{1}$.5773	$\bar{1}$.5754	3	6	9	12	15
68	$\bar{1}$.5736	$\bar{1}$.5717	$\bar{1}$.5698	$\bar{1}$.5679	$\bar{1}$.5660	$\bar{1}$.5641	$\bar{1}$.5621	$\bar{1}$.5602	$\bar{1}$.5583	$\bar{1}$.5563	3	6	10	13	16
69	$\bar{1}$.5543	$\bar{1}$.5523	$\bar{1}$.5504	$\bar{1}$.5484	$\bar{1}$.5463	$\bar{1}$.5443	$\bar{1}$.5423	$\bar{1}$.5402	$\bar{1}$.5382	$\bar{1}$.5361	3	7	10	13	17
70	$\bar{1}$.5341	$\bar{1}$.5320	$\bar{1}$.5299	$\bar{1}$.5278	$\bar{1}$.5256	$\bar{1}$.5235	$\bar{1}$.5213	$\bar{1}$.5192	$\bar{1}$.5170	$\bar{1}$.5148	4	7	11	14	18
71	$\bar{1}$.5126	$\bar{1}$.5104	$\bar{1}$.5082	$\bar{1}$.5060	$\bar{1}$.5037	$\bar{1}$.5015	$\bar{1}$.4992	$\bar{1}$.4969	$\bar{1}$.4946	$\bar{1}$.4923	4	8	11	15	19
72	$\bar{1}$.4900	$\bar{1}$.4876	$\bar{1}$.4853	$\bar{1}$.4829	$\bar{1}$.4805	$\bar{1}$.4781	$\bar{1}$.4757	$\bar{1}$.4733	$\bar{1}$.4709	$\bar{1}$.4684	4	8	12	16	20
73	$\bar{1}$.4659	$\bar{1}$.4634	$\bar{1}$.4609	$\bar{1}$.4584	$\bar{1}$.4559	$\bar{1}$.4533	$\bar{1}$.4508	$\bar{1}$.4482	$\bar{1}$.4456	$\bar{1}$.4430	4	9	13	17	21
74	$\bar{1}$.4403	$\bar{1}$.4377	$\bar{1}$.4350	$\bar{1}$.4323	$\bar{1}$.4296	$\bar{1}$.4269	$\bar{1}$.4242	$\bar{1}$.4214	$\bar{1}$.4186	$\bar{1}$.4158	5	9	14	18	23
75	$\bar{1}$.4130	$\bar{1}$.4102	$\bar{1}$.4073	$\bar{1}$.4044	$\bar{1}$.4015	$\bar{1}$.3986	$\bar{1}$.3957	$\bar{1}$.3927	$\bar{1}$.3897	$\bar{1}$.3867	5	10	15	20	24
76	$\bar{1}$.3837	$\bar{1}$.3806	$\bar{1}$.3775	$\bar{1}$.3745	$\bar{1}$.3713	$\bar{1}$.3682	$\bar{1}$.3650	$\bar{1}$.3618	$\bar{1}$.3586	$\bar{1}$.3554	5	11	16	21	26
77	$\bar{1}$.3521	$\bar{1}$.3488	$\bar{1}$.3455	$\bar{1}$.3421	$\bar{1}$.3387	$\bar{1}$.3353	$\bar{1}$.3319	$\bar{1}$.3284	$\bar{1}$.3250	$\bar{1}$.3214	6	11	17	23	28
78	$\bar{1}$.3179	$\bar{1}$.3143	$\bar{1}$.3107	$\bar{1}$.3070	$\bar{1}$.3034	$\bar{1}$.2997	$\bar{1}$.2959	$\bar{1}$.2921	$\bar{1}$.2883	$\bar{1}$.2845	6	12	19	25	31
79	$\bar{1}$.2806	$\bar{1}$.2767	$\bar{1}$.2727	$\bar{1}$.2687	$\bar{1}$.2647	$\bar{1}$.2606	$\bar{1}$.2565	$\bar{1}$.2524	$\bar{1}$.2482	$\bar{1}$.2439	7	14	20	27	34
80	$\bar{1}$.2397	$\bar{1}$.2353	$\bar{1}$.2310	$\bar{1}$.2266	$\bar{1}$.2221	$\bar{1}$.2176	$\bar{1}$.2131	$\bar{1}$.2085	$\bar{1}$.2038	$\bar{1}$.1991	8	15	23	30	38
81	$\bar{1}$.1943	$\bar{1}$.1895	$\bar{1}$.1847	$\bar{1}$.1797	$\bar{1}$.1747	$\bar{1}$.1697	$\bar{1}$.1646	$\bar{1}$.1594	$\bar{1}$.1542	$\bar{1}$.1489	8	17	25	34	42
82	$\bar{1}$.1436	$\bar{1}$.1381	$\bar{1}$.1326	$\bar{1}$.1271	$\bar{1}$.1214	$\bar{1}$.1157	$\bar{1}$.1099	$\bar{1}$.1040	$\bar{1}$.0981	$\bar{1}$.0920	10	19	29	38	48
83	$\bar{1}$.0859	$\bar{1}$.0797	$\bar{1}$.0734	$\bar{1}$.0670	$\bar{1}$.0605	$\bar{1}$.0539	$\bar{1}$.0472	$\bar{1}$.0403	$\bar{1}$.0334	$\bar{1}$.0264	11	22	33	44	55
84	$\bar{1}$.0192	$\bar{1}$.0120	$\bar{1}$.0046	$\bar{2}$.9970	$\bar{2}$.9894	$\bar{2}$.9816	$\bar{2}$.9736	$\bar{2}$.9655	$\bar{2}$.9573	$\bar{2}$.9489	13	26	39	52	65
85	$\bar{2}$.9403	$\bar{2}$.9315	$\bar{2}$.9226	$\bar{2}$.9135	$\bar{2}$.9042	$\bar{2}$.8946	$\bar{2}$.8849	$\bar{2}$.8749	$\bar{2}$.8647	$\bar{2}$.8543	16	32	48	64	80
86	$\bar{2}$.8436	$\bar{2}$.8326	$\bar{2}$.8213	$\bar{2}$.8098	$\bar{2}$.7979	$\bar{2}$.7857	$\bar{2}$.7731	$\bar{2}$.7602	$\bar{2}$.7468	$\bar{2}$.7330	Differences untrustworthy here				
87	$\bar{2}$.7188	$\bar{2}$.7041	$\bar{2}$.6889	$\bar{2}$.6731	$\bar{2}$.6567	$\bar{2}$.6397	$\bar{2}$.6220	$\bar{2}$.6035	$\bar{2}$.5842	$\bar{2}$.5640					
88	$\bar{2}$.5428	$\bar{2}$.5206	$\bar{2}$.4971	$\bar{2}$.4723	$\bar{2}$.4459	$\bar{2}$.4179	$\bar{2}$.3880	$\bar{2}$.3558	$\bar{2}$.3210	$\bar{2}$.2832					
89	$\bar{2}$.2419	$\bar{2}$.1961	$\bar{2}$.1450	$\bar{2}$.0870	$\bar{2}$.0200	$\bar{3}$.9408	$\bar{3}$.8439	$\bar{3}$.7190	$\bar{3}$.5429	$\bar{3}$.2419					
90	$-\infty$														

LOGARITHMS OF TANGENTS (continued)

°	0' 0.0°	6' 0.1°	12' 0.2°	18' 0.3°	24' 0.4°	30' 0.5°	36' 0.6°	42' 0.7°	48' 0.8°	54' 0.9°	1'	2'	3'	4'	5'
45	0.0000	0.0015	0.0030	0.0045	0.0061	0.0076	0.0091	0.0106	0.0121	0.0136	3	5	8	10	13
46	0.0152	0.0167	0.0182	0.0197	0.0212	0.0228	0.0243	0.0258	0.0273	0.0288	3	5	8	10	13
47	0.0303	0.0319	0.0334	0.0349	0.0364	0.0379	0.0395	0.0410	0.0425	0.0440	3	5	8	10	13
48	0.0456	0.0471	0.0486	0.0501	0.0517	0.0532	0.0547	0.0562	0.0578	0.0593	3	5	8	10	13
49	0.0608	0.0624	0.0639	0.0654	0.0670	0.0685	0.0700	0.0716	0.0731	0.0746	3	5	8	10	13
50	0.0762	0.0777	0.0793	0.0808	0.0824	0.0839	0.0854	0.0870	0.0885	0.0901	3	5	8	10	13
51	0.0916	0.0932	0.0947	0.0963	0.0978	0.0994	0.1010	0.1025	0.1041	0.1056	3	5	8	10	13
52	0.1072	0.1088	0.1103	0.1119	0.1135	0.1150	0.1166	0.1182	0.1197	0.1213	3	5	8	10	13
53	0.1229	0.1245	0.1260	0.1276	0.1292	0.1308	0.1324	0.1340	0.1356	0.1371	3	5	8	11	13
54	0.1387	0.1403	0.1419	0.1435	0.1451	0.1467	0.1483	0.1499	0.1516	0.1532	3	5	8	11	13
55	0.1548	0.1564	0.1580	0.1596	0.1612	0.1629	0.1645	0.1661	0.1677	0.1694	3	5	8	11	14
56	0.1710	0.1726	0.1743	0.1759	0.1776	0.1792	0.1809	0.1825	0.1842	0.1858	3	5	8	11	14
57	0.1875	0.1891	0.1908	0.1925	0.1941	0.1958	0.1975	0.1992	0.2008	0.2025	3	6	8	11	14
58	0.2042	0.2059	0.2076	0.2093	0.2110	0.2127	0.2144	0.2161	0.2178	0.2195	3	6	8	11	14
59	0.2212	0.2229	0.2247	0.2264	0.2281	0.2299	0.2316	0.2333	0.2351	0.2368	3	6	9	12	15
60	0.2386	0.2403	0.2421	0.2438	0.2456	0.2474	0.2491	0.2509	0.2527	0.2545	3	6	9	12	15
61	0.2562	0.2580	0.2598	0.2616	0.2634	0.2652	0.2670	0.2689	0.2707	0.2725	3	6	9	12	15
62	0.2743	0.2762	0.2780	0.2798	0.2817	0.2835	0.2854	0.2872	0.2891	0.2910	3	6	9	12	15
63	0.2928	0.2947	0.2966	0.2985	0.3004	0.3023	0.3042	0.3061	0.3080	0.3099	3	6	9	13	16
64	0.3118	0.3137	0.3157	0.3176	0.3195	0.3215	0.3235	0.3254	0.3274	0.3294	3	6	10	13	16
65	0.3313	0.3333	0.3353	0.3373	0.3393	0.3413	0.3433	0.3453	0.3473	0.3494	3	7	10	13	17
66	0.3514	0.3535	0.3555	0.3576	0.3596	0.3617	0.3638	0.3659	0.3679	0.3700	3	7	10	14	17
67	0.3721	0.3743	0.3764	0.3785	0.3806	0.3828	0.3849	0.3871	0.3892	0.3914	4	7	11	14	18
68	0.3936	0.3958	0.3980	0.4002	0.4024	0.4046	0.4068	0.4091	0.4113	0.4136	4	7	11	15	18
69	0.4158	0.4181	0.4204	0.4227	0.4250	0.4273	0.4296	0.4319	0.4342	0.4366	4	8	12	15	19
70	0.4389	0.4413	0.4437	0.4461	0.4484	0.4509	0.4533	0.4557	0.4581	0.4606	4	8	12	16	20
71	0.4630	0.4655	0.4680	0.4705	0.4730	0.4755	0.4780	0.4805	0.4831	0.4857	4	8	13	17	21
72	0.4882	0.4908	0.4934	0.4960	0.4986	0.5013	0.5039	0.5066	0.5093	0.5120	4	9	13	18	22
73	0.5147	0.5174	0.5201	0.5229	0.5256	0.5284	0.5312	0.5340	0.5368	0.5397	5	9	14	18	23
74	0.5425	0.5454	0.5483	0.5512	0.5541	0.5570	0.5600	0.5629	0.5659	0.5689	5	10	15	20	24
75	0.5719	0.5750	0.5780	0.5811	0.5842	0.5873	0.5905	0.5936	0.5968	0.6000	5	10	16	21	26
76	0.6032	0.6065	0.6097	0.6130	0.6163	0.6196	0.6230	0.6264	0.6298	0.6332	6	11	17	22	28
77	0.6366	0.6401	0.6436	0.6471	0.6507	0.6542	0.6578	0.6615	0.6651	0.6688	6	12	18	24	30
78	0.6725	0.6763	0.6800	0.6838	0.6877	0.6915	0.6954	0.6994	0.7033	0.7073	6	13	19	26	32
79	0.7113	0.7154	0.7195	0.7236	0.7278	0.7320	0.7363	0.7406	0.7449	0.7493	7	14	21	28	35
80	0.7537	0.7581	0.7626	0.7672	0.7718	0.7764	0.7811	0.7858	0.7906	0.7954	8	16	23	31	39
81	0.8003	0.8052	0.8102	0.8152	0.8203	0.8255	0.8307	0.8360	0.8413	0.8467	9	17	26	35	43
82	0.8522	0.8577	0.8633	0.8690	0.8748	0.8806	0.8865	0.8924	0.8985	0.9046	10	19	29	39	49
83	0.9109	0.9172	0.9236	0.9301	0.9367	0.9433	0.9501	0.9570	0.9640	0.9711	11	22	34	45	56
84	0.9784	0.9857	0.9932	1.0008	1.0085	1.0164	1.0244	1.0326	1.0409	1.0494	13	26	40	53	66
85	1.0580	1.0669	1.0759	1.0850	1.0944	1.1040	1.1138	1.1238	1.1341	1.1446	16	32	48	64	81
86	1.1554	1.1664	1.1777	1.1893	1.2012	1.2135	1.2261	1.2391	1.2525	1.2663	Differences untrustworthy here				
87	1.2806	1.2964	1.3106	1.3264	1.3429	1.3599	1.3777	1.3962	1.4155	1.4357					
88	1.4569	1.4792	1.5027	1.5275	1.5539	1.5819	1.6119	1.6441	1.6789	1.7167					
89	1.7581	1.8038	1.8550	1.9130	1.9800	2.0591	2.1561	2.2810	2.4571	2.7581					

LOGARITHMS OF TANGENTS

°	0' 0.0°	6' 0.1°	12' 0.2°	18' 0.3°	24' 0.4°	30' 0.5°	36' 0.6°	42' 0.7°	48' 0.8°	54' 0.9°	1'	2'	3'	4'	5'
0	−∞	3̄.2419	3̄.5429	3̄.7190	3̄.8439	3̄.9409	2̄.0200	2̄.0870	2̄.1450	2̄.1962	Differences untrustworthy here				
1	2̄.2419	2̄.2833	2̄.3211	2̄.3559	2̄.3881	2̄.4181	2̄.4461	2̄.4725	2̄.4973	2̄.5208					
2	2̄.5431	2̄.5643	2̄.5845	2̄.6038	2̄.6223	2̄.6401	2̄.6571	2̄.6736	2̄.6894	2̄.7046					
3	2̄.7194	2̄.7337	2̄.7475	2̄.7609	2̄.7739	2̄.7865	2̄.7988	2̄.8107	2̄.8223	2̄.8336					
4	2̄.8446	2̄.8554	2̄.8659	2̄.8762	2̄.8862	2̄.8960	2̄.9056	2̄.9150	2̄.9241	2̄.9331					
5	2̄.9420	2̄.9506	2̄.9591	2̄.9674	2̄.9756	2̄.9836	2̄.9915	2̄.9992	1̄.0068	1̄.0143					
6	1̄.0216	1̄.0289	1̄.0360	1̄.0430	1̄.0499	1̄.0567	1̄.0633	1̄.0699	1̄.0764	1̄.0828					
7	1̄.0891	1̄.0954	1̄.1015	1̄.1076	1̄.1135	1̄.1194	1̄.1252	1̄.1310	1̄.1367	1̄.1423					
8	1̄.1478	1̄.1533	1̄.1587	1̄.1640	1̄.1693	1̄.1745	1̄.1797	1̄.1848	1̄.1898	1̄.1948					
9	1̄.1997	1̄.2046	1̄.2094	1̄.2142	1̄.2189	1̄.2236	1̄.2282	1̄.2328	1̄.2374	1̄.2419					
10	1̄.2463	1̄.2507	1̄.2551	1̄.2594	1̄.2637	1̄.2680	1̄.2722	1̄.2765	1̄.2805	1̄.2846					
11	1̄.2887	1̄.2927	1̄.2967	1̄.3006	1̄.3046	1̄.3085	1̄.3123	1̄.3162	1̄.3200	1̄.3237					
12	1̄.3275	1̄.3312	1̄.3349	1̄.3385	1̄.3422	1̄.3458	1̄.3493	1̄.3529	1̄.3564	1̄.3599					
13	1̄.3634	1̄.3668	1̄.3702	1̄.3736	1̄.3770	1̄.3804	1̄.3837	1̄.3870	1̄.3903	1̄.3935					
14	1̄.3968	1̄.4000	1̄.4032	1̄.4064	1̄.4095	1̄.4127	1̄.4158	1̄.4189	1̄.4220	1̄.4250					
15	1̄.4281	1̄.4311	1̄.4341	1̄.4371	1̄.4400	1̄.4430	1̄.4459	1̄.4488	1̄.4517	1̄.4546	5	10	16	21	26
16	1̄.4575	1̄.4603	1̄.4632	1̄.4660	1̄.4688	1̄.4716	1̄.4744	1̄.4771	1̄.4799	1̄.4826	5	10	15	20	24
17	1̄.4853	1̄.4880	1̄.4907	1̄.4934	1̄.4961	1̄.4987	1̄.5014	1̄.5040	1̄.5066	1̄.5092	5	9	14	18	23
18	1̄.5118	1̄.5143	1̄.5169	1̄.5195	1̄.5220	1̄.5245	1̄.5270	1̄.5295	1̄.5320	1̄.5345	4	9	13	18	22
19	1̄.5370	1̄.5394	1̄.5419	1̄.5443	1̄.5467	1̄.5491	1̄.5516	1̄.5539	1̄.5563	1̄.5587	4	8	13	17	21
20	1̄.5611	1̄.5634	1̄.5658	1̄.5681	1̄.5704	1̄.5727	1̄.5750	1̄.5773	1̄.5796	1̄.5819	4	8	12	16	20
21	1̄.5842	1̄.5864	1̄.5887	1̄.5909	1̄.5932	1̄.5954	1̄.5976	1̄.5998	1̄.6020	1̄.6042	4	8	12	15	19
22	1̄.6064	1̄.6086	1̄.6108	1̄.6129	1̄.6151	1̄.6172	1̄.6194	1̄.6215	1̄.6236	1̄.6257	4	7	11	15	18
23	1̄.6279	1̄.6300	1̄.6321	1̄.6341	1̄.6362	1̄.6383	1̄.6404	1̄.6424	1̄.6445	1̄.6465	4	7	11	14	18
24	1̄.6486	1̄.6506	1̄.6527	1̄.6547	1̄.6567	1̄.6587	1̄.6607	1̄.6627	1̄.6647	1̄.6667	3	7	10	14	17
25	1̄.6687	1̄.6706	1̄.6726	1̄.6746	1̄.6765	1̄.6785	1̄.6804	1̄.6824	1̄.6843	1̄.6863	3	7	10	13	17
26	1̄.6882	1̄.6901	1̄.6920	1̄.6939	1̄.6958	1̄.6977	1̄.6996	1̄.7015	1̄.7034	1̄.7053	3	6	10	13	16
27	1̄.7072	1̄.7090	1̄.7109	1̄.7128	1̄.7146	1̄.7165	1̄.7183	1̄.7202	1̄.7220	1̄.7238	3	6	9	13	16
28	1̄.7257	1̄.7275	1̄.7293	1̄.7311	1̄.7330	1̄.7348	1̄.7366	1̄.7384	1̄.7402	1̄.7420	3	6	9	12	15
29	1̄.7438	1̄.7455	1̄.7473	1̄.7491	1̄.7509	1̄.7526	1̄.7544	1̄.7562	1̄.7580	1̄.7597	3	6	9	12	15
30	1̄.7614	1̄.7632	1̄.7649	1̄.7667	1̄.7684	1̄.7701	1̄.7719	1̄.7736	1̄.7753	1̄.7771	3	6	9	12	15
31	1̄.7788	1̄.7805	1̄.7822	1̄.7839	1̄.7856	1̄.7873	1̄.7890	1̄.7907	1̄.7924	1̄.7941	3	6	9	12	15
32	1̄.7958	1̄.7975	1̄.7992	1̄.8008	1̄.8025	1̄.8042	1̄.8059	1̄.8075	1̄.8092	1̄.8109	3	6	8	11	14
33	1̄.8125	1̄.8142	1̄.8158	1̄.8175	1̄.8191	1̄.8208	1̄.8224	1̄.8241	1̄.8257	1̄.8274	3	6	8	11	14
34	1̄.8290	1̄.8306	1̄.8323	1̄.8339	1̄.8355	1̄.8371	1̄.8388	1̄.8404	1̄.8420	1̄.8436	3	5	8	11	14
35	1̄.8452	1̄.8468	1̄.8484	1̄.8501	1̄.8517	1̄.8533	1̄.8549	1̄.8565	1̄.8581	1̄.8597	3	5	8	11	14
36	1̄.8613	1̄.8629	1̄.8644	1̄.8660	1̄.8676	1̄.8692	1̄.8708	1̄.8724	1̄.8740	1̄.8755	3	5	8	11	13
37	1̄.8771	1̄.8787	1̄.8803	1̄.8818	1̄.8834	1̄.8850	1̄.8865	1̄.8881	1̄.8897	1̄.8912	3	5	8	11	13
38	1̄.8928	1̄.8944	1̄.8959	1̄.8975	1̄.8990	1̄.9006	1̄.9022	1̄.9037	1̄.9053	1̄.9068	3	5	8	10	13
39	1̄.9084	1̄.9099	1̄.9115	1̄.9130	1̄.9146	1̄.9161	1̄.9176	1̄.9192	1̄.9207	1̄.9223	3	5	8	10	13
40	1̄.9238	1̄.9254	1̄.9269	1̄.9284	1̄.9300	1̄.9315	1̄.9330	1̄.9346	1̄.9361	1̄.9376	3	5	8	10	13
41	1̄.9392	1̄.9407	1̄.9422	1̄.9438	1̄.9453	1̄.9468	1̄.9483	1̄.9499	1̄.9514	1̄.9529	3	5	8	10	13
42	1̄.9544	1̄.9560	1̄.9575	1̄.9590	1̄.9605	1̄.9620	1̄.9635	1̄.9651	1̄.9666	1̄.9681	3	5	8	10	13
43	1̄.9697	1̄.9712	1̄.9727	1̄.9742	1̄.9757	1̄.9772	1̄.9786	1̄.9803	1̄.9818	1̄.9834	3	5	8	10	13
44	1̄.9848	1̄.9864	1̄.9879	1̄.9894	1̄.9909	1̄.9924	1̄.9939	1̄.9955	1̄.9970	1̄.9985	3	5	8	10	13